Roman Conquests:
Britain

Roman Conquests: Britain

Simon Elliott

Pen & Sword
MILITARY

First published in Great Britain in 2021 by
Pen & Sword Military
An imprint of
Pen & Sword Books Ltd
Yorkshire–Philadelphia

ISBN 978 1 52676 5 680

A CIP catalogue record for this book is available from the British Library.

Printed and bound in the UK by CPI Group (UK) Ltd, Croydon, CR0 4YY

FSC www.fsc.org MIX Paper from responsible sources FSC® C013604

Pen & Sword Books Limited incorporates the imprints of Atlas, Archaeology, Aviation, Discovery, Family History, Fiction, History, Maritime, Military, Military Classics, Politics, Select, Transport, True Crime, Air World, Frontline Publishing, Leo Cooper, Remember When, Seaforth Publishing, The Praetorian Press, Wharncliffe Local History, Wharncliffe Transport, Wharncliffe True Crime and White Owl.

For a complete list of Pen & Sword titles please contact

PEN & SWORD BOOKS LIMITED
47 Church Street, Barnsley, South Yorkshire, S70 2AS, England
E-mail: enquiries@pen-and-sword.co.uk
Website: www.pen-and-sword.co.uk

Or
PEN AND SWORD BOOKS
1950 Lawrence Rd, Havertown, PA 19083, USA
E-mail: Uspen-and-sword@casematepublishers.com
Website: www.penandswordbooks.com

Contents

List of Tables

By the same author:

Sea Eagles of Empire
Empire State: How the Roman Military Built an Empire
*Septimius Severus in Scotland**
Roman Legionaries
Ragstone to Riches
Julius Caesar: Rome's Greatest Warlord
Old Testament Warriors
*Pertinax: The Son of a Slave Who Became Roman Emperor**
Romans at War
*Roman Britain's Missing Legion: What Really Happened to IX Hispana?**

* Denotes titles in print with Pen & Sword Books/Greenhill Books

Introduction

Of all the conquests made by the Roman Republic and Empire, Britain was the least successful, specifically because of the way the territory was conquered (or not in the case of the far north and Ireland). This meant it required an exceptionally large military presence that, twinned with its distance from Rome, later made it a hotbed for usurping would-be emperors. To the Romans, Britannia truly was the wild west of the Empire. This sense of difference was then firmly cemented in place by the shattering way Britain left the Roman Empire in the early 5th century AD, an event so dramatic that it still resonates in the world we live in today.

Britain provides one of the starkest examples of the legacy of the Roman Empire. Today many believe it is a place of difference in Western Europe when compared to its continental neighbours. However, few realise this perceived sense of variance dates back directly to the period of Roman rule. Before the arrival of Rome in northwestern Europe, many British tribes had strong political, economic and cultural links with continental Gaul, to the extent that some actually shared the same name. Not so once Caesar had conquered Gaul in the 50s BC, cutting Britain's La Tène cultural umbilical with the continent. The later creation of the province of Britannia by Claudius in AD 43 should have rectified this, integrating Britain into the Roman Empire. However, to a large extent it didn't.

The way that Britain was conquered by the Roman Empire also left very specific legacies in the British landscape today. This was again because of the way the campaigns here were fought. Caesar conquered Gaul in a comparatively short eight years, with the territory there quickly incorporated into Republican Roman provincial territory. A key reason regarding the speed of the latter was the sheer scale of slaughter and destruction as Caesar scoured Gaul again and again, often returning to conquered territories to stamp out rebellion.

However, the story of conquest in Britain was very different. It was a difficult place to invade in the first place, a terrifying land of which the

Romans knew little, across fearsome *Oceanus* as the Romans called the northern seas. Caesar himself failed (if his intention was to stay, this is unlikely) in 55 BC and 54 BC, and the great Augustus and mad Caligula both planned but abandoned conquest. Even the Aulus Plautius-led invasion of Claudius was problematic. Here, the troops were again wary of making the crossing until shamed into boarding the invasion fleet by one of the emperor's senior freedmen. Though this invasion was successful, and the new province of Britannia created, from that point progress to expand Imperial territory was often slow, painful and bloody, ultimately taking 60 years before the highpoint of Gnaeus Julius Agricola's campaigns in the far north. This was the only time the Romans could claim to have conquered the whole main island of Britain, and then very briefly if they did so.

Meanwhile, because of the need to physically lock down newly occupied areas with fortifications large and small, the legacy of Roman conquest here is physically written across the landscape. Many of today's leading cities and towns in England and Wales were originally Roman legionary fortresses or *vexillation* forts, and their *canabae* or *vicus* civilian settlements. Meanwhile, to service the campaigns of conquest and then maintain order, the province was threaded with a well-built system of military trunk roads. Today these remain the template for much of Britain's pre-motorway A-road network.

A further legacy in Britain of the Roman campaigns of conquest is the modern political settlement of the islands here. Firstly, the Romans never invaded Ireland, though Agricola briefly considered it. Therefore it never became part of the Roman Imperial project and has remained a separate political entity to this day. Secondly, despite Agricola's best efforts and those of Septimius Severus (see below), the Romans never permanently conquered the far north, it too remaining a separate political entity (or entities), today in the form of modern Scotland. As to why the whole archipelago was never fully conquered, James (2011, 144) makes the case that this was the result of a failure of the '*...open hand alongside sword...*' strategy that had underwritten much of Rome's early Imperial growth. He says this required an elite sophisticated enough in newly conquered territories to buy into the Imperial project once conquest had taken place. He adds such an elite was singularly lacking in what is now Ireland and Scotland until later in the occupation of Britain, by which time the Romans didn't have the political will or means to carry out campaigns of conquest there.

Most people associate the Roman campaigns of conquest in Britain with those of Caesar, Claudius, and the warrior governors of the mid- and later 1st century AD. However, there were many others. For example, for a short time in the mid-2nd century AD the northern border was driven northwards from the line of Hadrian's Wall to a new frontier along the Clyde-Forth line, today called the Antonine Wall. Then, in the early 3rd century AD, Septimius Severus launched his two enormous campaigns to conquer the far north, gathering the largest ever military force to campaign in Britain. Later in the same century Constantius Chlorus mounted the fourth and final Roman maritime invasion of Britain to defeat the North Sea Empire established by the usurper Carausius. Even in the 4th century AD, as we near the end of the Roman occupation, we have intense military campaigning in Britain as the likes of *Comes* Theodosius and Stilicho (even if not in person) strove to defeat multiple threats from Ireland, the far north and modern Germany. All are considered here.

Moving on to sources and data used in this book, these include primary and modern sources, the archaeological record (including epigraphy and inscriptions), analogy and, where appropriate, anecdote. In terms of the former we are lucky to have multiple ancient sources available, though we should acknowledge that for much of the Roman occupation of Britain these are silent about events here, particularly in the mid-3rd century AD. These primary sources always come with the usual health warnings regarding their variable accuracy and reliability, but are nevertheless invaluable.

Britain was known to the Mediterranean world prior to Caesar's engagements here, but not well. The earliest reference to its existence appears in the 6th-century BC *Massaliot Periplus* merchant's handbook, now lost but referenced in the *Ora Maritime* poem by the late 4th century AD Roman poet Avienus. The original 6th-century BC work is also the first to attribute a name for the inhabitants of the islands of Britain, calling the Britons *Albiones* and the Scots Irish the *Iverni*. Herodotus is the next to reference islands in north-western Europe in the 5th century BC, describing the Cassiterides in his *Histories*. These have often been associated with Britain given the name translates as 'tin islands', the metal being a key export from Britain from prehistoric times. More clarity then comes with the 4th-century BC Greek geographer Pytheas. From Marseille, (the Greek colony of *Massalia*, also home of the *Massaliot Periplus* detailed above), his definitive work is similarly lost to us, but key sections have been preserved by ancient authors including Strabo, Pliny the Elder and

Diodorus. Pytheas was the first person to record a circumnavigation of Britain during his maritime exploration of north-western Europe. This also took in a visit to modern Denmark and seemingly an extraordinary visit to Iceland. His reports on the British Isles set a template for most of what followed in classical literature, highlighting their triangular shape and describing Kent, Land's End in Cornwall and the Orkneys. He also notes for the first time the name from which our current 'Britain' is derived, reporting that the natives were called the *pretani*. This translates as painted ones, referencing the native practice (at least where he visited) of painting themselves in woad designs, and wearing tattoos.

Both Strabo and Pliny made extensive use of Pytheas in their much later descriptions of Britain, the latter going into an immense amount of detail, for instance describing the 40 islands of the Orkneys, the seven of the Shetlands, the 30 of the Hebrides, and also describing the Isle of Anglesey. Pytheas' work is also evident in the physical descriptions of Britain by others, for example Caesar himself. His *Conquest of Gaul* gives us our first detailed first-hand insight into Late Iron Age (LIA) Britain through the descriptions of his two campaigns here. Plutarch also references Britain in various of his *Lives*, as does Cornelius Tacitus with his *Annals, Histories* and *Agricola*, Gaius Suetonius with his *Twelve Caesars*, and Appian in his *Roman History*.

Moving on, we then have the work of geographer Claudius Ptolemaus and his mid-2nd century *Geography*. This extensive gazetteer of the peoples and places of the Empire crucially included latitude and longitude, allowing for the first time a representation of the Britain to be created that vaguely appears recognizable to modern eyes. Further insight comes from Cassius Dio with his *Roman History*, Herodian with his *History of the Roman Empire*, and the now anonymous *Historia Augusta*, a collection of biographies of Roman Emperors, junior colleagues, designated heirs and usurpers from the accession of Hadrian in AD 117 through to the accession of Diocletian in AD 284. The latter was written towards the end of the 4th century AD in Latin, with modern scholars believing it was based on a single work dating to the period of Dio and Herodian. The leading 20th century historian and classicist Sir Ronald Syme believed the author to be an individual he dubbed *'Ignotus'*, while others favour a lost work by the Senator and historian Marius Maximus, at least for part of it. The *Historia Augusta* is thought particularly unreliable, and frequently reads as though the author is more interested in entertaining his audience than reporting historical fact.

To the *Historia Augusta* we can then add Ammianus Marcellinus and his *Later Roman History,* this detailing the later Roman Empire. We can also add the works of the later Latin chroniclers Flavius Eutropius, Aurelius Victor, Jerome and Paulus Orosius. The first three (and given their use as sources by the fourth, that too by default) likely used as a major source the so-called 'Kaisergeschichte' hypothetical set of short histories now lost.

Finally in terms of primary sources we have contemporary or later itineraries and lists. These include the *Tabula Peutingeriana, Antonine Itinerary, Ravenna Cosmography* and *Notitia Dignitatum*, the latter a key list of late Roman military offices across the Empire.

For modern sources, I have accessed the widest possible range. In the first instance this has included my own academic research over the last fifteen years through my MA in War Studies from KCL, MA in Archaeology from UCL and PhD in Classics and Archaeology from the University of Kent. Additionally, my recently published works on Roman themes have proved a fertile source of new information on the campaigns of Roman conquest in Britain. These include *Sea Eagles of Empire: The Classis Britannica and the Battles for Britain*, *Empire State: How the Roman Military Built an Empire*, *Septimius Severus in Scotland: the Northern Campaigns of the First Hammer of the Scots*, *Roman Legionaries*, *Pertinax: the Son of a Slave Who Became Roman Emperor*, *Romans at War* and the shortly to be published *Roman Britain's Lost Legion: What Really Happened to legio IX Hispana.*

To these we can add the various works of Anthony R. Birley, particularly his definitive 2005 edition of *The Roman Government of Britain*, while as ever David Mattingly's 2006 *An Imperial Possession: Britain in the Roman Empire* has proved invaluable. Other key modern works include Patricia Southern's 2013 *Roman Britain*, Sam Moorhead and David Stuttard's 2012 *The Romans Who Shaped Britain*, *The Romanization of Britain* by Martin Millett first published in 1990, and the slightly more dated *Roman Britain* by Peter Salway and Sheppard Frere's *Britannia*. Meanwhile, with regard to works with a focus on Roman interests in Scotland, I have found Andrew Tibbs' *Beyond the Empire*, David Breeze's *Roman Scotland*, Lawrence Keppie's *The Legacy of Rome* and Anthony Kamm's *The Last Frontier* most useful.

Moving on, the many works on the Roman military of Adrian Goldsworthy and Ross Cowan have provided much of the vital detail needed when considering the daily lives of Roman legionaries, auxilia and naval *milites*. Regarding the legions based here, one work has proved particularly useful. This is *The Complete Roman Legions* by Nigel Pollard and Joanne

Berry, published in 2012. Further, given the importance of marching camps (detailed in Chapter 1) in the various Roman campaigns in Britain, Rebecca Jones' *Roman Camps in Scotland* and *Roman Camps in Britain* have proved invaluable, as has Paul Bidwell's *Roman Forts in Britain*. Meanwhile, with regard to the provincial and *diocene* capital, Richard Hingley's *2018 Londinium: A Biography* has proved especially useful. Further, Tim Cornell and John Matthews' *'Atlas of the Roman World'* has provided much detail regarding this far-flung province and later *diocese* of the Empire.

In terms of the archaeological record, epigraphy also plays a key role in the story of the Roman campaigns of conquest in Britain. The word epigraphy, derived from the ancient Greek word for inscription, describes the study of the latter as a form of writing. In that regard we are fortunate that the Romans were prolific inscribers in stone, including in Britain. Such inscriptions were used in the widest range of circumstances, ranging from details of the deceased on funerary monuments, through to altars referencing the lives of those who set them up, to the recording on buildings of the individuals who funded them or built them. Roman inscriptions are particularly useful in this work as they not only detail the individual, individuals or units concerned, but almost always name the reigning emperor, including his honorific and other titles at the time. When cross-referenced with other evidence, this provides a fairly precise way of dating when the inscription was made. In the 1920s scholars in Britain devised their own method of recording Roman epigraphy here, this called the Roman Inscriptions in Britain (RIB) project, following the earlier example of their European counterparts. Thus all such inscriptions referenced in this book are given an RIB number.

Moving on to housekeeping in the book, an understanding of Britain as a Roman political entity is important as this changed over time. The territory conquered in the AD 43 Claudian invasion became the province of Britannia shortly after. The word province itself provides interesting insight into the Roman attitude to its Empire, the Latin *provincia* referencing land *'for conquering'*. There were actually two kinds of province in the Principate Roman Empire. These were senatorial provinces left to the Senate to administer, whose governors were officially called proconsuls and remained in post for a year, and Imperial provinces retained under the supervision of the emperor. The emperor personally chose the governors for these, they often being styled *legati Augusti pro praetor* to officially mark them out as deputies of the emperor. Senatorial provinces tended to be those deep within the Empire where less trouble was expected. Clearly that was not the case with Britannia, which was an Imperial province. This was then divided in two by Caracalla in the early 3rd century AD, a delayed response to the usurpation of the British governor Clodius Albinus in AD 196. The two new provinces were called *Britannia Superior* and *Britannia Inferior*, the former the south of the original province with its capital remaining in London, the latter the north with York as its capital.

Later, following Diocletian's reformation when the Empire was divided into 12 *dioceses* with each controlled by a *vicarius*, the *Laterculus Veronensis* (Verona List) of AD 303–AD 314 details that the two Principate provinces became the single *diocese* of Britanniae, this then divided into four smaller provinces. These were Maxima Caesariensis, Flavia Caesariensis, Britannia Prima and Britannia Secunda. The same provinces are listed a century later in the *Notitia Dignitatum*, with the addition of the problematic province of Valentia.

Meanwhile, military installations played a key role in the Roman campaigns of conquest in Britain. In that regard I have used the current size-based hierarchy as a means of describing their size as they occur in the narrative. Starting with the largest, these are 20 ha-plus legionary fortresses for one or more legions, then 12 ha-plus vexillation fortresses holding a mixed force of legionary cohorts and auxiliaries, next one ha-plus forts for outpost garrisons, and finally fortlets for part of an auxiliary unit. Military settlements associated with such fortifications are called a *canaba* when connected with a legionary fortress, and a *vicus* elsewhere.

In terms of the built environment, this again features heavily in the story of the Roman campaigns of conquest in Britain, especially later. Here, larger towns are referenced as one of three types. These are *coloniae* chartered towns for military veterans (in Britain for example Colchester), *municipia* chartered towns of mercantile origin (in Britain for example St Albans) and *civitas capitals*, these last the Roman equivalent of a County town featuring the local government of a region (in Britain for example Canterbury). Settlement below this level is referenced as either a small town (defined as a variety of diverse settlements which often had an association with a specific activity such as religion, administration or religion), villa estates or non-villa estates.

An understanding of the social structure of Roman society is also very useful when considering the campaigns of conquest in Britain, particularly later. In terms of ranking within the aristocracy, at the very top was the Senatorial class, said to be endowed with wealth, high birth and 'moral excellence'. There were around 600 Senators in the mid-2nd century AD. Those of this class were patricians, a social political rank, with all those below including other aristocrats called plebeians. Interestingly, we know of no Senator who originated here, this again setting Britain as a place of difference within the Empire. Next was the equestrian class, having slightly less wealth but usually with a reputable lineage. They numbered some 30,000 across the Empire in the mid-2nd century AD. Finally in terms of aristocracy there was the curial class, with the bar set slightly lower again. The latter were usually merchants and mid-level landowners, making up a large percentage of the town councillors in the Principate Empire. Below this, one then has freemen who were free in the sense that they had never been slaves. They included the majority of smaller-scale merchants, artisans and professionals in Roman society. All of the above classes were also full *cives Romani* – citizens of the Roman Empire – if they came from Italy. They enjoyed the widest range of protections and privileges as defined by the Roman state, and as such could travel the breadth of the Empire pursuing their professional ambitions. Roman women had limited types of citizenships and were not allowed to vote or stand for public or civil office. Freemen born outside of Italy in the Imperial provinces were called *peregrini* (in Latin meaning *'one from abroad'*) until Caracalla's AD 212 *constitutio Antoniniana* edict which made all freemen of the Empire citizens. As such, in the 1st and 2nd centuries AD *peregrini* made up the vast majority of the Empire's inhabitants. Further down the social ladder one then had freedmen, former slaves who had been manumitted by their masters either through earning enough money to buy their freedom or for good service. Once free these former slaves often remained with the wider family of their *Pater Familias* head of family former owner, frequently taking their name in some way. Providing the correct process of manumission was followed, freedmen could become citizens/*peregrini*, though with less civic rights than a freeman, including not being able to stand for the vast majority of public offices. Their children were freemen. Many freedmen became highly successful, and given they were not allowed to stand for public office found other ways to celebrate their lives. A common example was the provision of monumentalized funerary monuments, a well-known example being that of the baker Marcus Vergilius Eurysaces in Rome. Meanwhile, at the bottom of society were slaves.

In terms of chronology, the story of the Roman campaigns of conquest in Britain took place in the late Roman Republic, and then both the Principate and Dominate phases of Empire. The Principate was the early phase of the Roman Empire's existence, this dating from 27 BC when Augustus was first acknowledged as emperor by the Senate. It lasted until AD 284, with the accession of Diocletian and the end of the 'Crisis of the 3rd Century.' The name is derived from the term *princeps* (chief or master), referencing the Emperor as the leading citizen of the Empire. While not an official term, emperors often assumed it on their accession, it clearly being a conceit that allowed the Empire to be explained away as a simple continuance of the preceding Republic. Then, given the major structural changes required to the nature of the Roman Empire as it exited the 'Crisis of the 3rd Century', the period that followed until the end of the western Empire in AD 476 is called the Dominate. This was a new, far more overtly Imperial system, the title based on the word *Dominus* which referenced lord, the emperor now effectively the equivalent of an eastern potentate.

Finally in terms of housekeeping, with regard to the use of classical and modern names I have (usually) used the modern name where a place is first mentioned, referencing its Roman name at the first point of use in the main text if it is known. Meanwhile, where a classical name for a role, position or event is well understood I use that, referencing the modern name or term at the first use. Further, I reference the contemporary inhabitants of Ireland as Scots, the name by which they were then known. Additionally, when Emperors are first detailed in the main narrative I have listed the actual dates of their reign.

In terms of the chapter flow of the book, after this Introduction Chapter 1 then provides a detailed description of the Roman military in the late Republic and Empire. This is essential given the book's central focus on the military's campaigns of conquest in Britain. Chapter 2 then considers Britain in the LIA, setting the scene for Julius Caesar's two incursions, these detailed in full in Chapter 3. Moving on, Chapter 4 picks up the story of the Roman campaigns of conquest in Britain from that point, discussing the planned but cancelled invasions of Augustus and Caligula, before fully detailing the successful Claudian invasion under Aulus Plautius. This chapter concludes with the creation of the new province of Britannia, and Claudius' return to Rome. Chapter 5 then examines the early breakout campaigns, before closing with a detailed examination of the Boudiccan Revolt of AD 60/ 61 which nearly destroyed the new province. Chapter 6 then picks up the later campaigns of conquest as the new province gradually expanded to incorporate more and more native British territory. Highlights here include Agricola's Flavian campaigns in Scotland, the arrival of Hadrian in AD 122, the Antonine campaigns in the Scottish Borders under the governor Quintus Lollius Urbicus, and the campaigns again in Scotland around the time of the accession of the mad and bad Commodus. The latter sets the scene in Chapter 7 for the arrival of Septimius Severus in AD 208 and his enormous conquest campaigns in the far north in AD 209 and AD 210, these deserving an entire chapter given their scale. Chapter 8 then picks up the story of the later Roman campaigns of conquest in Britain. This is both in the context of the mainland province, for example Constantius Chlorus' campaigns against Carausius and Allectus in the late 3rd century AD, and also in the west and far north as the likes of *Comes* Theodosius strove to shore up the faltering frontiers in Britain in the later 4th century AD. Finally, the Conclusion considers the legacy of the Roman campaigns of conquest in Britain, within which I detail the ending of the Roman occupation here. I also include a Timeline of Roman Britain as a guide for the reader.

Lastly, here I would like to thank the many people who have helped make this work on the Roman campaigns of conquest in Britain possible. As always this includes Professor Andrew Lambert of the War Studies Department at KCL, Dr Andrew Gardner at UCL's Institute of Archaeology and Dr Steve Willis at the University of Kent. Next, my publisher Phil Sidnell, and also Graham Sumner for his amazing colour plates (with special thanks to Thomas Kurtz for the use of those images originally used in the Mules-of-Marius exhibition). Also, Professor Sir Barry Cunliffe of the School of Archaeology at Oxford University and Professor Martin Millett at the Faculty of Classics, Cambridge University for their encouragement. Next, my patient proof-reader and lovely wife Sara, and my dad John Elliott and friend Francis Tusa, both companions in my various escapades to research this book. As with all of my literary work, all have contributed greatly and freely, enabling this work on the Roman campaigns of conquest in Britain to reach fruition. Finally, I would like to thank my family, especially my tolerant wife Sara once again, and children Alex (also a student of military history) and Lizzie.

Thank you all.
Simon Elliott
July 2020

Chapter 1

The Roman Military in the Republic and Empire

The Roman military establishment at the time of the Caesarian and Claudian invasions of Britain was pre-eminent in a world where to that date it lacked a true symmetrical threat, that being one whose military tactics and technology matched its own, unless through weight of numbers. It was to remain so through much of the Principate, though this dominance diminished as the Empire transitioned the 'Crisis of the Third Century' into the later Dominate phase of Empire.

Most often in the later Republic and Principate, when on campaign and in battle, the Roman military won. When it did lose to Britons, Germans, Sarmatians or Parthians, it always learned from its mistakes and came back the better for it. This reflected two key broader Roman military traits. These were the ability to assimilate superior opposing tactics and technology, and the true grit to never accept defeat, fighting on against adversity until ultimate victory.

Given the central role the Roman military played in the Empire's campaigns of conquest in Britain, an understanding of this military establishment in all of its phases of existence is essential to appreciate Rome's many engagements here. Therefore, in this chapter I consider the legions of the late Republic and Principate, then the auxiliaries and regional fleets of the Principate, before finally detailing the Roman military establishment of the later Dominate phase of Empire when the distinctions between earlier troop types becomes much more opaque.

The Legions of the Late Republic and Principate

The Roman legionary of the late Republic and Principate was the elite warrior of the ancient world, and the result of nearly 800 years of military evolution. This progression included five distinct phases prior to the time of Septimius Severus in the early 3rd century AD when the transition began towards the military establishment of the later Dominate. These phases were:

- The Tullian system of Servius Tullius, the sixth king of Rome and second Etrusco-Roman king (575 BC to 535 BC). Based on his Servian Constitution, this was built around *equites* wealthy citizen cavalry, an Etruscan-style hoplite phalanx of armoured spearman known as the First Class, and four classes of supporting troops.
- The Camillan System of Marcus Furius Camillus, consular tribune for the first time in 401 BC. He initiated a major reform of the Roman military after the Tullian system was tested to breaking point in its shattering defeat by the Senone Gauls at the Battle of Allia in 390 BC, and the subsequent traumatic sack of Rome. Camillus introduced the manipular legion of 3,000 men (later up to 5,000) with its three classes of legionary, who were called so for the first time from this point. These were *triarii* veterans, *principes* older warriors and *hastati* 'flower of the young men'.
- The Polybian System (Elliott, 2018, 34) introduced after Rome's conflict with Pyrrhus of Epirus in the late 280s and early 270s BC. An evolution of the Camillan manipular system, this retained the three distinct types of legionary but added other troop types including *velite* skirmishing javelinmen.
- The Marian System introduced by the seven-times warrior consul Gaius Marius. Again reflecting the Roman trait for learning from defeat, these widespread reforms were introduced at the height of the Cimbrian Wars in 107 BC at a time when the legions of the manipular system were losing on a regular basis against the Cimbri Germanic invaders of Gaul. Marius introduced the 6,000-man legion, based around centuries rather than maniples. Each legion had 4,800 legionaries all armed in the same way (see below), with the remaining 1,200 men specialists and support staff (though retaining the ability to fight as front line legionaries when needed). The Marian legions of the late Republic set the template for those of the Principate, with each a self-contained fighting force highly mobile when on campaign and in battle.
- The Augustan System, introduced by the first Emperor after his elevation by the Senate in 27 BC. As Gaius Julius Caesar Octavianus (henceforth styled Octavian) he had inherited 60 legions from the

> last, vicious round of Roman civil wars in the late 1st century BC. Augustus' main contribution to the evolution of the legion was rationalising their number down to 28, this falling to 25 after Varus' losses in Germany in AD 9. The total would then remain around 30 for the next 250 years, peaking at 33 under Septimius Severus in the late 2nd century AD.

The numbering and naming of the legions can seem confusing to a modern audience, reflecting their being raised by a variety of different Republican leaders and later Emperors, and at different times. Many legions shared the same number but had different names, for example there being five third legions. Others shared the same name but had different numbering, for example *legio* I, *legio* II, *legio* III and *legio* IV *Italica.*

From the time of the late Republic, as the might of Rome established control not only of the lands around the western and eastern Mediterranean but also territories deep into continental Europe, the legions were stationed on or near the frontiers of Roman controlled territory. This best positioned them to carry out further campaigns of conquest if so ordered, and also acted as a deterrent against any opponent outside Roman controlled territory bold enough to act aggressively.

Caesar's legions in his two expeditions to Britain were Marian in nature. The latter had aimed to turn each individual legion into a self-contained fighting force. To do this Marius standardised his legionaries on the *pilum* and *gladius*-armed *principes* and *hastati*, with the spear-armed *triarii* and javelin-armed *velites* disappearing entirely. From this point, all of the fighting men in the legion were simply called legionaries, whether the 4,800 battle-line troops or 1,200 specialists. Each Marian century comprised 80 legionaries and 20 support staff, these sub-divided into units of 10 (comprising 8 legionaries and two non-combatants). Each century was commanded by a centurion, they having specific titles which reflected their seniority based on the old Camillan and Polybian manipular legions. The titles, with seniority in ascending order, were:

- *hastatus posterior*
- *hastatus prior*
- *princeps posterior*
- *princeps prior*
- *pilus posterior*
- *pilus prior*

The principal missile weapon of Caesar's legionaries was the *pilum* weighted javelin, these originally of Etruscan or Spanish origin. Each legionary carried two, one light and one heavy (Cowan, 2003b, 30). Both featured a barbed head on a long, tapering iron shank whose lead weighted socket attached it to a wooden shaft and provided the punching force to hammer through enemy shields and armour. The lighter *pilum* was thrown at range, the heavy one immediately prior to impact. The long iron shafts on both were specifically designed to bend after impact and so disable the use of the opponent's shield.

However, the main weapon of the Caesarian legionary was the *gladius hispaniensis* sword. Originally a Spanish design as its name suggests, this was first adopted by the Polybian legions after the Romans fought the Iberian mercenaries of Hannibal in the Second Punic War. Rather than being the short stabbing sword of popular legend, the *gladius* was originally a cut-and-thrust weapon of medium length, around 69cm long and 5cm in width and featuring a tapering sharp stabbing point. Those originally used by the legionaries shocked their Hellenistic pike-wielding opponents in the Second Macedonian War, given the gaping wounds inflicted on the pikemen. This was because a key feature of the *gladius* was that it lacked any blood runnels to let in air (Matyszak, 2009, 64). Therefore the sword had to be viciously twisted to release it. This original type of *gladius* was still the most common in Caesar's legions, and was worn on the legionary's right hip, or left if a centurion. Many have questioned how a legionary could draw the weapon smoothly into the en-guard position from the right hand side, especially given the pommel sat just below the armpit. However, in his detailed analysis of the weapon, Bishop explains (2016, 46):

> *In fact, the gladius can be easily drawn by inverting the right hand, thumb downwards, then grasping the handgrip and pulling straight upwards. It is a quite natural progression to continue this movement forwards to bring the sword down to the side, point forward, in the characteristic 'at the ready position depicted on relief sculpture.*

To complete his offensive weaponry, Caesar's legionaries also carried a *pugio* dagger, worn on the opposite hip to the *gladius*.

For defensive equipment late Republican legionaries were still equipped with the *scutum*, first adopted after the early 4th century BC reforms of Camillus. By Caesar's time this large curved rectangular body shield had increased in size and was now up to 120cm in length and 75cm wide. Made from planed wooden strips that were laminated together in three layers, the shield featured an *umbones* iron boss attached to the centre where the shield was slightly thicker. The *scutum* was completed with a calf-skin/felt facing, this often brightly decorated with unit markings. The legionary *scutum* was very heavy and could weigh up to 10kg, being held by a horizontal grip using a straightened arm. It was used by the legionaries in a brutally efficient fencing technique in close conjunction with the *gladius.* Here, the *scutum* took the blow of an enemy weapon while the legionary was in the crouch position. The *gladius* was then driven upwards into an opponent's exposed midriff, or downward into his face or upper chest. The *scutum* could also be used as an offensive weapon in its own right to smash into an adversary and push them off balance, again exposing them to a lethal blow with the *gladius*.

For armour Caesar's legionaries wore the *lorica hamata* long chainmail hauberk, a design adopted from that worn by better-off Gallic warriors. It weighed around 15kg and offered greatly improved protection over the various bronze pectorals worn by earlier legionaries, fully covering the torso from shoulder to hip. They were made from interlinked iron rings 1mm thick and up to 9mm in external diameter, with up to 20,000 needed for each shirt. By Caesar's day a further type of body armour had also emerged, the *lorica squamata* scale mail hauberk, though the chain mail shirt remained the most popular. Arm guards called *manicae*, thigh guards and greaves could also be worn.

The defensive panoply of the Caesarian legionary was completed with a fine quality helmet. By the late Republic two types predominated, these being the Coolus and Port designs. The former featured a round cap of bronze and small neck guard, while the iron Port type carried a much deeper neck guard. A particularly fine example of a Gallic Coolus helmet was excavated in 2008 at North Bersted, West Sussex by Thames Valley Archaeological Services. This featured an enormous crest that would have set the wearer out as a man of great importance, it showing how versatile this helmet design was (see Chapter 2 for a detailed description of Gallic helmet decoration).

Caesar's legionaries lived, fought and ate together, with each legion developing their own identity around the new *aquila* eagle standards introduced by Marius and carried by an *aquilifer*. Training was also regularised, with Marius insisting on regular fitness drills to ensure the legionaries were always physically fit. This was to ensure they could carry their own equipment on campaign, this weighing up to an impressive

30kg and earning the troops the nickname *muli mariani* (Marius' mules). One should perhaps envision the Marian legionary as having the same body shape as a modern Olympic weight lifter, square and all muscle. His training focused particularly on martial skills, based on the methods used to instruct gladiators. For example, sword drill featured a large stake the size of an opponent set up in the training ground. The trooper then practised his *gladius* and *scutum*-based fencing technique as detailed above, using a wooden replica sword and wicker shield, with the stake being 'the enemy'.

The standard deployment in battle for Caesar's legions remained the '*acies triplex*' three lines of the earlier manipular system. The first two were deployed to sequentially engage the enemy (second line units replacing the front line units as the latter tired), while the third acted as a reserve.

Before the reforms of Marius, the Camillan and Polybian manipular legions comprised a compulsory levy of Roman citizens who met a minimum wealth/property qualification. These formations were raised whenever necessary rather than being forces in being. However, a key aspect of Marius' reforms in 107 BC was to realise that, given Rome's by then widespread military responsibilities, this early Republican system was no longer sustainable. He determined standing units were required that could remain in existence for years or even decades, and thus were born the Marian legions. To man these he mainly relied on volunteer recruits usually aged between 17 and 23, though some were as young as 13 or as old as 36. Additionally, in times of crisis, the number of legionaries was bolstered by conscription under a levy called the *dilectus*. Each Marian legionary, whether recruit or conscript, signed up for a minimum term of six years.

As detailed, Marius also abolished the wealth/property requirement for the legionary, and from that point the majority of recruits came from the landless lower classes. This was a shrewd move that increased the sense of identity within each individual legion, given their loyalty to their military leaders. Julius Caesar then set a trend which underpinned the success of his own legions, regularising pay levels for his troops at 225 denarii a year. It is unclear if his opponents immediately copied the move, but this amount became standard legionary pay well into the Principate phase of the Roman Empire. Late Republican military leaders also ensured that their legionaries were well looked after upon retirement, the veterans being given a stipend in the form of land and often being settled in colonies. Caesar provides a good example, with his retirees after the campaign in

Greece against Pompey being settled in the Hellenistic city of Butrint (Roman *Buthrōtum*) in modern Albania.

Like all armies, the Republican legions marched on their stomachs. Later, the 4th century AD writer Vegetius said in his military manual that troops should never be without corn, salt, wine and vinegar, and that would certainly have been the case for Caesar's legions, with beans, bread, porridge, vegetables and eggs forming the core diet. Meat would be added on feast days, with the wider diet supplemented by local produce and hunting. On campaign, the daily staples were whole-wheat biscuits and hard tack, together with bread baked in the marching camp at the end of the day's march.

Such marching camps were also a key feature in the life of the Republican and later Principate legionary when on campaign, they dating from the time of Rome's conflict with Pyrrhus of Epirus. These large-scale temporary fortifications were built by the legionaries at the end of each day's march in enemy territory. They were constructed in a few hours and came in a variety of sizes dependent on the scale of the force that needed protection, with at the larger end those of almost 70 ha found in the Scottish Borders used there during the Severan campaigns in the early 3rd century AD. Almost always playing card in shape, Roman marching camps generally featured a deep ditch between one and two metres wide, with the spoil then being used to create an internal rampart. Atop this ran a palisade created by the stakes the troops carried as part of their specialist engineering equipment, either a continuous wooden barrier or one created by the stakes being lashed together to form large caltrops. Within this barrier the camp would then be set out for the night, effectively recreating the interior layout of a permanent Roman fortification. The next day (or longer if the camp was occupied for more than a night), the camp was struck in swift order. This was in a very specific way, with the first trumpet call from the *cornicen* signalling the legionaries to strike their tents, the second telling them to ready the pack animals and destroy the camp, and the third to fall into marching ranks. Marching camps play a key role in the story of all of the Roman campaigns of conquest in Britain, often providing a dot-to-dot track across the landscape allowing archaeologists and historians to follow actual campaigns.

Meanwhile, religion was a key feature in the daily lives of the Caesarian legionary, playing a major role in his appreciation of belonging and belief. Roman society, within the military and without, was very conservative. In that regard each legionary was obliged to honour the Gods of the Roman pantheon, in particular the Capitoline triad of Jupiter, Juno and Minerva given their association with Rome. We can add to these Mars, given he was the God of war.

For non-military kit all Caesarian legionaries carried their equipment on a T-shaped pole resting on their shoulders when on the march, with the shield held in place across the back. Helmets were usually strung from the neck across the chest. The marching kit also included a *paenula* hooded woollen bad-weather cloak made from thick wool that fastened with a button or toggles on the centre of the chest. The officers wore a shorter rectangular cloak called a *sagum* that fastened on the right shoulder with a brooch. A very important piece of kit for the Caesarian legionary was his hobnailed *caligae* sandals. Typically these featured a leather upper made from a single leather piece which was sewn at the heel. This was then stitched to a multiple-layer hide sole shod with many iron studs, each sandal weighing up to 1kg. From the time of the Marian reforms each legionary was also a skilled engineer in their own right, with building and engineering playing an enormous part of their working life. To enable the warriors to fulfil such a roll they also carried a stake (as used in the marching camp defences detailed above), saw, pickaxe, chain, sickle, basket and leather strap. Finally, these late Republican legionaries also carried a sturdy cross-braced satchel for their personal effects, a water skin in a net bag, a *patera* bronze mess tin, a cooking pot, canvas bags for grain rations, spare clothing, and bespoke engineering equipment.

Moving forward, by the time of Claudius' (AD 41 to AD 54) AD 43 invasion of Britain Augustus had carried out his wide-ranging reforms of the military, including of the legions. These now numbered 5,500 men, though were still organised in ten cohorts. The first of these had five centuries of 160 men, with the rest six centuries of 80 men each. Each normal century was then broken down into ten eight-man sections called *contubernia* whose men shared a tent when on campaign, and two barrack block rooms when in camp. Additionally, each legion now also featured 120 cavalry who acted as dispatch riders and scouts.

Augustus also formalised the command structure of the legions. Each was now led by a Senatorial-level *legatus legionis*. Second-in-command was a *tribunus laticlavius*. This was a younger man, also of Senatorial-level, gaining the experience to command his own legion in the future. Third in command was the *praefectus castrorum* camp prefect. This was a seasoned former centurion responsible for logistics and administration. Below this were five younger equestrian-level tribunes, called the *tribuni angusticlavii*.

These were allocated responsibilities as required. Control of each cohort in the legion remained the responsibility of centurions as in the late Republic, with six to a normal cohort.

As the world of Rome transitioned from Republic to Principate Empire a number of changes also took place with regard to the panoply of the Roman legionary. These were to remain in place throughout the Roman campaigns of conquest in Britain in the 1st and 2nd centuries AD. Firstly, though the *gladius hispaniensis* remained the principal weapon of the legionary, this had evolved into the Mainz type, which was broader and shorter in shape, but with a longer stabbing point. By the later 1st century AD this had developed further into the Pompeii-type, slightly shorter than the Mainz type and with a shorter, triangular stabbing point. Meanwhile the Principate *scutum* had also evolved from earlier types and was now squarer in form and some 102 cm in length and 83cm wide (Cowan, 2003, 26).

However, the most obvious changes were with regard to the legionary's armour and helmet. In terms of the former, the most striking difference was the appearance of *lorica segmentata* banded iron armour, constructed of articulated iron plates and hoops. This became the standard legionary armour through to the mid-3rd century AD. The origins of this armour, which in terms of protection and mobility wouldn't be bettered until the later medieval period, are unclear, though it may have originally been a form of gladiator armour. The first types emerge in the archaeological record at the end of the 1st century BC when it began to replace *lorica hamata* as the main type worn by the legionary, and from that point the armour evolved through three specific versions, these being (all named after the location where examples were found):

- The Dangestetten-Kalkriese-Vindonissa type, those found dating to between 9 BC to AD 43.
- The Corbridge-Carnumtum type, those found dating to between AD 69 to AD 100.
- The Newstead type, those found dating to between AD 164 to AD 180.

Each successive version was less complicated than that which preceded it, for example that found in the *principia* of the vexillation fort at Newstead (Roman *Trimontium*) in the Scottish Borders in 1905 featuring rivets to replace earlier bronze hinges, a single large girdle plate to replace the two previous ones, and hooks to replace earlier and more complicated belt-buckle fastenings. Other types of armour also continued to be worn, including *lorica hamata* and *lorica squamata*, both of which stayed in use throughout the Principate. Certain troop types within the Principate legions were also often differentially equipped with armour, with for example officers frequently shown wearing iron and bronze muscled cuirasses, and centurions and *aquilifer* standard bearers wearing chainmail.

Meanwhile, by the time of the Claudian invasion of Britain a new and far more substantial type of legionary helmet had emerged. This was the 'Imperial' Gallic type, a development of the Port design. This ubiquitous helmet featured an even larger neck guard, prominent cheek guards and a reinforcing strip on the front of the cap to deflect downward sword cuts, with ear guards added from the AD 50s.

Legionaries of the Principate could be volunteers or conscripted, as with their Republican predecessors. By this time a 1.8m height requirement had been instated as mandatory for new recruits, though this was often overlooked in times of crisis. In his reforms of the legions Augustus also greatly increased the term of service for the legionaries from the six years of the late Republic to 20 years, this designed to maintain a stable base of highly experienced troops in the legions. The last four years were served as a veteran excused fatigues and guard duty, such troops called *vexillum veteranorum*. This length of service was then later extended by Augustus to 25 years, with five as a veteran, a term which lasted well into the Dominate phase of Empire. The increase was due to a shortage of recruits (Augustus being too successful when slimming the number of legions down), and because of the strain placed on the Imperial *fiscus* to pay the *praemia* retirement gratuity for retiring legionaries, given the very large number of troops Augustus inherited.

By the early 1st century AD these retirement gratuities had been formalised into two types. The first was a payment of 3,000 *denarii* in cash, and the second land as in the later Republic. In the latter case this was now in the form of *centuriated* land parcels designed to set the retiree up as a farmer, or in *colonia* settlements as previously. Such retired legionaries often settled near to their former legionary bases, these settlements then developing into *coloniae* towns as happened with Gloucester (Roman *Glevum*), Lincoln (Roman *Lindum Colonia*) and York (Roman *Eboracum*) in Britain. In terms of the legionaries' basic pay, this remained at 225 *denarii* per year until the time of the third Flavian emperor Domitian (AD 81–AD 96) who, at the height of the warrior governor Gnaeus Julius Agricola's campaigns to conquer the far north of Britain in the early AD 80s, increased legionary pay to 300 *denarii*.

Meanwhile, religion continued to play a major role in the daily life of the Principate legionary, with the obligation to worship the Gods of the Roman pantheon now joined by the even more important requirement to worship the Imperial cult of the sitting emperor. Additionally, the worship of certain Gods that had a specific association with the Roman military now also appeared. These were often eastern in origin and included Mithras, Bacchus and Isis. The worship of all of these Gods, and also the dates of the traditional festivals of Rome (together with the accession days and birthdays of Emperors), structured the religious year for the Principate legionary.

The final series of changes to the Principate legions were initiated by Septimius Severus after he emerged victorious following the 'Year of the Five Emperors' in AD 193, and the subsequent civil wars against the Syrian governor Pescennius Niger and British governor Clodius Albinus. From this time the beginning of a change in the panoply of the legionary becomes evident. This was largely a response to the changing nature of their opponents. Previously, the legions had most often faced a similar infantry-heavy foe, excepting the Parthians in the east. However, by the late 2nd century AD they were tackling a multitude of new threats, many of a differing nature that required a more flexible response. In particular, the heavily armoured charging lancers of the Sarmatian tribes faced by the Romans in the Marcomannic Wars made a strong impression.

This change is shown in real time on four monuments set up in Rome by four great warrior Emperors, these being Trajan's Column, the Column of Marcus Aurelius and the Arches of Septimius Severus and Constantine I (AD 306 to AD 337). The latter is particularly important given it is in effect a time machine, built in AD 315 in the Dominate phase of Empire to celebrate Constantine I's victory over Maxentius at the Battle of Milvian Bridge in AD 312. At the time the Imperial *fiscus* was running low, as it had been used by Maxentius to fund his failed defence of Rome. Therefore, the architects of the new arch sourced panels from existing monuments to complement its new and contemporary depictions of Constantine I's martial success. These included four panels called the Great Trajanic Frieze that comprised slabs from a monument to celebrate Trajan's (AD 98 to AD 117) victories in his two Dacian campaigns, and similar panels from a lost Arch of Marcus Aurelius to celebrate the latter's successes in the Marcomannic Wars.

The change in the equipment of the later Principate legionary was first evident in his weaponry. For example, from the reign of Septimius Severus the longer cavalry-style *spatha* sword began to replace the shorter *gladius* for all Roman foot soldiers. This weapon was up to 80cm in length, although some of one metre-length have been identified. The new sword was suspended from a baldric on a Sarmatian-type scabbard slide, and came to dominate Roman military equipment in the west until the Empire's end there, continuing in use in the east long afterwards. It seems likely the adoption of this weapon had its origins in the need for more reach to tackle armoured mounted opponents.

A similar change is also evident in the use of the *pila*, they being gradually replaced by a thrusting spear of between 2m and 2.7m in length in the same time period. This change is visible actually taking place on the four monuments detailed above. Thus on Trajan's Column, the Column of Marcus Aurelius and the reused panels on the Arch of Constantine, legionaries in classic *lorica segmentata* armour are shown armed with *pila*, while on the Arch of Septimius Severus and on the contemporary panels on the Arch of Constantine, these have been replaced by spears. This was again a response to experiences fighting armoured mounted opponents more frequently.

Moving onto the defensive panoply of the later Principate legionary, change is also evident with the shield. In the later 2nd century AD the traditional *scutum* began to be replaced by a large round or oval body shield, confusingly still called a *scutum*. This new design was of simple plank construction, with a stitched-on rawhide facing, and was strengthened with iron bars across the back. The two types of *scutum* appear to have been used side by side for some time, with examples of both found at the fortified frontier-trading town of Dura-Europos in Syria dating to AD 256. This transition is also very evident on the four monuments detailed above, with many of the large round shields featuring on the Severan arch, and even more on the contemporary panels of the Arch of Constantine. Once again this change seems to have been associated with the type of opponent more commonly faced by the Romans, the round shield perhaps more suited to dealing with a mounted threat. It certainly gave greater freedom of movement for the new swords and spears coming into use with their greater reach, and would also have been cheaper to produce.

Not surprisingly, a change is also evident in the body armour of the legionary as the Principate approached its end. Thus on Trajan's Column and the Column of Marcus Aurelius most are wearing *lorica segmentata* still, as they are on the reused panels on the Arch of Constantine. However, on the Arch of Septimius Severus there is a much higher proportion wearing *lorica hamata* and *lorica squamata*, this proportion increasing yet again on the contemporary panels of the Arch of Constantine.

Meanwhile, as the Principate progressed, legionary helmets also became increasingly substantial, with the Gallic 'Imperial' type increasingly supplemented by heavier, single bowl designs reinforced by cross-pieces and fitted with deep napes, leaving only a minimal T-shaped face opening. These helmets provided exceptional levels of protection.

A final change in this time period was the appearance of a new type of legionary. This was the *lanciarii* light trooper armed with a quiver of javelins and lighter armour than their front rank line-of-battle equivalents. Such troops, who operated like the *velites* of the Polybian legions, skirmished forward to deter mounted bowmen and other lightly armed missile troops. They are first attested in gravestone epigraphy serving in the ranks of *legio* II *Parthica* in the context of Caracalla and Macrinus' AD 215–AD 218 Parthian War.

Septimius Severus also made another, very important change in the late Principate legionary's daily life. Before this time, legionaries were officially unable to marry until they retired, though they often contracted technically illegal marriages. Severus changed this, granting the soldiers their right to marry while serving for the first time, and at the same time giving their formerly illegal spouses and offspring legal rights. Ever mindful that he had won the Imperial throne in AD 193 with the support of the military, Severus also drastically increased the basic pay of the legionary to 450 *denarii*. His son Caracalla increased this even further once sole emperor, by a further 50 per cent, following his father's advice to keep the soldiery happy above all else. Additionally, Severus also increased the legionary retirement gratuity to 5,000 *denarii*, up from the earlier 3,000.

Finally, Roman legionaries also provided the battlefield and siege artillery component of Roman armies when on campaign. Such weapons included light *scorpio* dart-throwers and the larger *ballista*, the latter firing large bolts and shaped stones. When at full strength, each cohort fielded one of the latter and each century one of the former. This gave an impressive total of ten *ballistae* and 59 *scorpiones* per legion. A final development with regard to Principate legionary artillery was a move to replace the *ballista* with *onager* catapults, the latter larger and better-suited to siege warfare, from around AD 250.

Finally, regarding the Principate legions of Rome, the below table details all known such formations for reference:

Table 1: The Legions of the Roman Principate

Legion	When Founded	Destroyed/disbanded
legio 1 Germanica	Later republic	Disbanded AD 70 after Civilis Revolt
legio 1 Adiutrix pia fidelis	Provisionally recruited by Nero, then made a regular legion by Galba.	
legio 1 Italica	Under Nero	
legio 1 Macriana	Under Nero	Civil war legion, disbanded AD 69/70
legio 1 Flavia Minervia pia fidelis	Under Domitian	
legio 1 Parthica	Under Septimius Severus	
legio II Augusta	Later Republic/ under Augustus	
legio II Adiutrix pia fidelis	Under Nero	
legio II Italica	Under Marcus Aurelius	
legio II Parthica	Under Septimius Severus	
legio II Traiana fortis	Under Trajan	
legio III Augusta	Later Republic/under Augustus	
legio III Cyrenaica	Later Republic	
legio III Gallica	Under Caesar	
legio III Italica concors	Under Marcus Aurelius	
legio III Parthica	Under Septimius Severus	
legio IIII Flavia felix	Under Vespasian	
legio IIII Macedonica	Under Caesar	Disbanded AD 70
legio IIII Scythica	Under Mark Antony	
legio V Alaudae	Under Caesar	Destroyed under Domitian
legio V Macedonica	Later Republic	

legio VI Ferrata fidelis constans	Under Caesar	
legio VI Victrix	Later Republic	
legio VII Claudia pia fidelis	Under Caesar	
legio VII Gemina	Under Galba	
legio VIII Augusta	Later Republic	
legio IX Hispana	Later Republic	Disappears in the early 2nd century AD
legio X Fretensis	Later Republic	
legio X Gemina	Under Caesar	
legio XI Claudia pia fidelis	Later Republic	
legio XII Fulminata	Under Caesar	
legio XIII Gemina pia fidelis	Later Republic	
legio XIV Gemina Martia Victrix	Later Republic	
legio XV Apollinaris	Under Augustus	
legio XV Primigenia	Under Caligula	Disbanded AD 70
legio XVI Flavia Firma	Under Vespasian	
legio XVI Gallica	Under Augustus	Disbanded AD 70
legio XVII	Under Augustus	Destroyed in AD 9 in Germany
legio XVIII	Under Augustus	Destroyed in AD 9 in Germany
legio XIX	Under Augustus	Destroyed in AD 9 in Germany
legio XX Valeria Victrix	Under Augustus	
legio XXI Rapax	Under Augustus	Possibly destroyed under Domitian
legio XXII Deiotariana	Under Augustus	Possibly destroyed under Hadrian
legio XXII Primigenia pia fidelis	Under Caligula	
legio XXX Ulpia Victrix	Under Trajan	

After Goldsworthy, A. 2003.

The Auxilia

Legionaries were not the only soldiers in the military establishment of the Roman Empire. Before the latter's advent, Republican Roman armies had always used allied auxiliary troops to support the legions, for example Caesar's headhunting Gallic cavalry (Perring, 2017, 46). These troops fought in their own formations, and under their own commanders.

However, one of the most radical changes to the Roman military initiated by Augustus was to professionalize these troops into a regular component of the Roman armed forces. From this point they become known as auxilia. These troops were mostly recruited from the *peregrini* non-Italian freemen through to the time of Caracalla's *constitutio Antoniniana* in AD 212. Even after this, the majority of auxilia were still recruited from the regions, often *en masse* giving each auxiliary unit a distinctly regional feel. They became a key component of the Roman military, with Tacitus (Tacitus, Annals, IV.5) saying that by AD 25 there were as many auxilia in the Roman army as legionaries, the latter numbering at that time around 175,000.

The auxilia provided most of the cavalry and much of the foot complement of Principate Roman armies and they played a key role in the Roman campaigns of conquest in Britain from the Claudian invasion in AD 43 all the way through to the end of the Roman occupation of Britain in the early 5th century AD. Auxiliary cavalry were organised into *quingenary alae* of 512 men or *milliary alae* of 768. Each was commanded by a *Praefectus Alae*. The basic cavalryman was called an *equites*, with each equipped with a *hasta* spear that could be thrown or used as a short lance, and a *spatha* long sword. Their defensive panoply included flat hexagonal or oval shields, short *lorica hamata* chainmail hauberks and a variety of types of iron and bronze helmets, often with neck and cheek guards. Principate *equites* were supported by a variety of different types of light cavalry fighting in the style of their native region, for example Moorish *symmachiarii* javelin-armed skirmishers. As this phase of Empire progressed such specialist light horse were fully integrated into the Roman military establishment, with new types emerging including javelin-armed *equites illyriciani* and bow-armed *equites sagittarii*. Specialist shock cavalry had also begun to appear by the mid-2nd century AD, initially in the form of *numeri* temporary units of indigenous troops recruited in the east, often called *contarii* referencing their long *contos* lances (D'Amato, 2018, 7). These were quickly formalized into full auxiliary *ala*, for example *equites contariorum* and heavily armoured cataphracts called *equites cataphractarii*. The latter, again armed with the *contos*, wore a suit of scale armour called *lorica plumata* which covered the entire body, with a substantial helmet with gilded face plate. Their horses were often similarly fully armoured.

In terms of auxilia foot troops, although these were the junior partners to their legionary counterparts, they were still among the best soldiers of the ancient world. There were many occasions when the fighting was done by the auxilia alone, for example in Britain at the Battle of Mons Graupius in AD 83 when Agricola finally managed to bring the Caledonians to battle south of the Moray Firth in the Grampians (Tacitus, 36.1-2).

Auxilia infantry formations in the Principate were based on a single *quingenary* cohort of 480 troops, or a double-sized *milliary* cohort of 800 troops. These cohorts (both the small and large) were divided into centuries of between 80 and 100 men, these under the command of a centurion, replicating the similar structure in a legionary formation. However the centurions, unlike the auxiliary troopers, were sometimes Roman citizens appointed from the legions. Others were drawn direct from the rank and file of the auxiliary unit. Above this level the cohort was commanded by an equestrian, this being a *praefectus* for a *quingenary* unit and a tribune for a *milliary* unit.

Auxilia foot fought in both close and loose formation, the latter making them especially useful in difficult terrain. As with the cavalry they often retained the skills associated with their place of origin, for example the Batavian auxilia used by Aulus Plautius in the famous river crossing battle described by Dio (60.19–60.23) in Kent during the AD 43 Claudian invasion of Britain (see Chapter 4 for full detail).

The majority of auxiliary foot were line of battle troops who, whether in close or loose formation, fought in a similar manner to the legionaries. They were armed with short, throwable spears called *lancea* rather than *pila* and a sword similar to the legionary *gladius*, this later replaced by the longer cavalry-style *spatha*. The Principate auxiliary infantry shield was usually an elongated oval plank design which covered the torso, with a central iron or bronze boss. Auxilia are most frequently shown wearing *lorica hamata* chainmail or *lorica squamata* scalemail hauberks, these shorter and less sophisticated than those worn by their legionary counterparts. Auxilia helmets were also less sophisticated, often cheaper bronze versions of those worn by the legionaries. The auxilia also provided the majority of the specialist warriors in Roman military formations, for example archers, slingers, staff slingers and javelinmen.

Table 2: Known Auxiliary Cohorts and Alae of the mid-late 2nd century AD

Unit	Location	Date
Brittones Aurelianensis	Upper Germany	AD 200
Cohors Sagittariorum	Hispania Baetica	Later 2nd century AD
Cohors I Aelia Brittonum milliaria	Noricum	Later 2nd century AD
Cohors I Aelia Dacorum millaria	Britannia and Noricum	Later 2nd century AD
Cohors I Dardanorum Aurelia	Dalmatia	Later 2nd century AD
Cohors I Delmatorum	Dalmatia	Later 2nd century AD
Cohors I Frisavonum	Britannia	Later 2nd century AD
Cohors I Hemesenorum eq. mil. Sagittaria CR	Pannonia Inferior	Later 2nd century AD
Cohors I Pasinatum Aurelia Nova	Dalmatia	Later 2nd century AD
Cohors I Sacorum Aurelia Nova	Dalmatia	Later 2nd century AD
Cohors I Septima Belgarum	Upper Germany	AD 200
Cohors I Tungrorum mil.	Britannia	2nd century AD
Cohors I Ulpia Tiaiana Cugernorum CR	Britannia	2nd century AD
Cohors I Ulpia Traiana Campestris Voluntariorum	Dalmatia	2nd century AD
Cohors II Aforum Flavia	Mauretania	Late 2nd century AD
Cohors II Astorum Equitata	Britannia	2nd century AD
Cohors II Dacorum Aurelia	Pannonia Inferior	Late 2nd century AD
Cohors II Gallorum Equitata	Britannia	2nd century AD
Cohors II Tungrorum mil.	Britannia	2nd century AD
Cohors III Aquitanorum equitata CR	Upper Germany	Late 2nd century AD
Cohors III Gallorum	Hispania Baetica	Late 2nd century AD
Cohors III Nerviorum CR	Britannia, Hispania Baetica	Late 2nd century AD

Cohors III Breucorum	Britannia	2nd century AD
Cohors III Tungrorum mil.	Mauretania	Late 2nd century AD
Cohors IV Gallorum	Gallia Lugdunensis	Late 2nd century AD
Cohors IV Tungorum mil.	Lower Germany	2nd century AD
Cohors V Baetica	Hispania Baetica	Late 2nd century AD
Cohors VI Raetorum	Britannia	Late 2nd century AD
Cohors VII Delmatorum eq.	Mauretania	Late 2nd century AD
Ara Colonia Ulpia Traiana	Lower Germany	Late 2nd century AD
Ala Astorum	Gallia Lugdunensis	2nd century AD
Ala (Gallorum) Placentia	Britannia	Late 2nd century AD
Ala (Hispanorum) Vettonum CR	Britannia	2nd century AD
Ala Noricorum	Lower Germany	Late 2nd century AD
Ala (Gallorum) Sebosiana	Britannia	2nd century AD
Ala I (Hispanorum) Aravacorum	Pannonia	Late 2nd century AD
Ala I Astorum	Britannia	2nd century AD
Ala I Britannica	Mauretania	Late 2nd century AD
Ala I Caninafatium	Pannonia	Late 2nd century AD
Ala I Contaforium	Pannonia	Late 2nd century AD
Ala I Ituraeorum	Pannonia	Late 2nd century AD
Ala I (Pannoniourum) Sebosiana	Britannia	2nd century AD
Ala I (Pannoniorum) Tampiana	Britannia	Later 2nd century AD
Ala II Astorum	Britannia	2nd century AD
Ala II Pannoniorum	Pannonia	2nd century AD

After D'Amato, 2016, 14.

Principate auxilia were paid 100 *denarii* per year if infantry and 200 *denarii* if cavalry, with elite cavalry based on the wing of a battle formation paid 333 *denarii*. Terms of service were 25 years from the time of Augustus, as with the legionaries. Prior to Caracalla's *constitutio Antoniniana*, on retirement the trooper was given a citizenship diploma that granted full Roman citizenship to himself and his heirs. It also gave them the legal right to marry a non-citizen woman. This was later replaced with a donative as with the legionaries.

Auxilia units could also be fielded in combined formations that featured both infantry and mounted troops, their organization being less well understood. Such infantry cohorts, cavalry *alae* and combined units were very flexible and could easily be moved around the Empire as needed in the same manner as vexillations of legionaries.

The above table gives an indication of the widespread recruitment and deployment of auxiliary units during the Principate phase of Empire.

The Regional Fleets

The regional navies of the Principate Roman Empire were also the result of the military reforms of Augustus. Before this date the fleets of the Republic were *ad hoc* in nature, often designed to fight symmetrical engagements against opponents including Carthage, the Hellenistic kingdoms and Roman civil war rivals in the Mediterranean. It was just such a fleet that Caesar utilized for his 55 BC invasion of Britain, though he did modify this for the later 54 BC campaign (this fully detailed in Chapter 3). Augustus rationalised this system, consolidating the various fleets he inherited into regional navies that reflected the Empire's expanding geographical reach. By the end of the 1st century AD there were 10 such fleets, each with a specific area of territorial responsibility. These are detailed in the below table which also shows the annual stipend of each fleet's *praefectus classis* admiral, reflecting their status.

The *Classis Britannica* in Britain provides a good example of one of the larger Principate regional fleets, and is particularly relevant given the critical role it played in all of the Roman campaigns of conquest in Britain through to the mid-3rd century AD. This navy featured 900 ships and 7,000 crew, including sailors, marines and support personnel (Elliott, 2016, 63). Each regional fleet had an origin specific to its region of operations, with the core of that in Britain dating to the original vessels built by Caligula

Table 3: Regional Fleets of the Roman Principate.

Fleet	Annual Stipend
Classis Ravenna	300,000 sesterces
Classis Misenensis	200,000 sesterces
Classis Britannica	100,000 sesterces
Classis Germanica	100,000 sesterces
Classis Flavia Pannonica	60,000 sesterces
Classis Flavia Moesica	60,000 sesterces
Classis Pontica	60,000 sesterces
Classis Syriaca	60,000 sesterces
Classis Nova Lybica	60,000 sesterces
Classis Alexandrina	60,000 sesterces

After Ellis Jones, 2012, 61.

for his abortive AD 40 invasion. These were later used by Claudius for his AD 43 invasion. Although this fleet took part in every aspect of the campaigns of conquest in Britain from that point, it was actually first called the *Classis Britannica* by Tacitus in the context of the Batavian uprising in Germania Inferior in AD 70 (Histories, 4.79.3).

All Roman regional fleets performed both military and civilian roles. In the former context the *Classis Britannica* had responsibility for the North Sea, English Channel, Atlantic approaches, Bristol Channel and Irish Sea, the east and west coasts of the main island of Britain, the river systems of Britain and the continental coast up to the Rhine Delta. The latter reflected the way the Romans viewed *Oceanus* separating Britain from the continent, not as a barrier as we do today in the context of recent military history, but as a point of connectivity linking Britannia physically with the rest of the Empire. This is reflected in the fact that the *Classis Britannica*'s headquarters were in Boulogne-sur-mer in north-western Gaul (Roman *Gessoriacum*), with additional bases in Britain including Dover (Roman *Dubris*), Richborough (Roman *Rutupiae*), Lympne (Roman *Portus Lemanis*) and Pevensey (Roman *Anderida*).

Meanwhile, in its civilian activities the *Classis Britannica* was used in a variety of roles. This included administration, engineering and construction, and running industry and agriculture. A prime example of the fleet performing a building task comes from Benwell Fort on Hadrian's

Wall where epigraphy references the fleet constructing the granaries there. As Parfitt (2013, 45) explains:

> *The Classis Britannica seems to have (often) functioned…as some kind of army service corps, supporting the Government and provincial army, rather than (just) as a Navy in the modern sense.*

The principal warship of the *Classis Britannica* was the small and mobile ram and ballista-equipped *liburnian* bireme galley. These had replaced the large polyreme galleys of the Republican civil wars by the end of the 1st century BC. The fleet also used a variety of *myoparo* cutters and *scapha* skiffs, and transport vessels based on Romano-Celtic designs with high freeboards and shallow drafts designed for operation in northern waters, as earlier utilized by Caesar in his 54 BC incursion to Britain.

An equestrian-level *praefectus classis* appointed directly by the Emperor commanded each regional fleet. He reported to a province's procurator rather than governor given each fleet's civilian activities, though clearly he fell under the latter's command when on military duty. Individuals we know of in Britain holding this role include Q. Baienus Blassianus, named in the role in an inscription from Ostia, Lucius Aufidius Pantera who is named on an altar found at Lympne, and Marcus Maenius Agrippa who appears on an inscription from Camerinum in Umbria. As part of his headquarters operation the *praefectus classis* had a specialist staff. This included a *subpraefectus* executive officer and aide-de-camp, *cornicularius* chief of staff, *actuarii* clerks, *scribae* scribes and seconded *dupliarii* ratings attached from the fleet.

Below the headquarters staff the fleets relied heavily on Hellenistic nomenclature in terms of command structure. The commander of a squadron of ships was called a *navarchus* (the most senior the *navarchus principes*), and the captain of an individual vessel a *trierarchus*. The latter post is particularly important in the story of the *Classis Britannica* given the last ever reference to the fleet dates to between AD 244 and AD 249 in the form of a funerary inscription found in Arles, southern France, to one Saturninus, a North African-born former captain in the *Classis Britannica*.

Aboard ship the *trierarchus'* executive team including a *gubernator* senior officer responsible for the steering oars, a *proretus* second lieutenant and the *pausarius* rowing master. Other junior officers included the *secutor* master-at-arms, *nauphylax* officers of the watch and specialists including the *velarii* with responsibility for the sails and *fabri* ships' carpenters.

Below this level the ship's company was based on the military organization of their land-based counterparts, with the basic unit called a century. This was commanded by a centurion. He was assisted by an *optio* second-in-command, a *suboptio* junior assistant, a *bucinator* bugler or *cornicen* horn player, and finally an *armorum custos* armourer. The rest of the ship's complement comprised marines (*ballistarii* artillery crew, *sagittarii* archers and *propugnatores* deck soldiers), *velarius* sailors, and plenty of *remiges* oarsmen. The latter were always professional rather than the slaves often depicted in popular culture, the whole company being styled *milites* (soldiers, the singular being *miles*) as opposed to *nautae* sailors, again indicating the link to their land-based counterparts.

In the Principate, service as a naval *milite* was regarded in a similar way to being an auxiliary. Those in the *Classis Britannica* were often recruited from the former tribes of the coastal regions in north-western Gaul. Terms of service for all ranks was 26 years, a year longer than with the auxilia, the reward on completion being Roman citizenship. We have unique insight into this in the form of a recent archaeological discovery. This was the finding of the copper alloy military diploma of one Tigernos, a sailor of the *Classis Germanica*, granting his citizenship after completing his service. Interestingly, he may prove to be Britain's first known sailor as, despite his service on the Rhine, the diploma was found broken into eight pieces at the Roman fort in Lanchester (Roman *Longuvicium*), County Durham.

Each naval *miles* received three gold pieces or 75 *denarii* upon enlistment. Their basic annual pay at the beginning of the Principate for the lower ranks was 100 *denarii*, with those given greater responsibilities paid an additional bonus on top. In that context, those paid 1.5 times the basic salary were called *sesquiplicarii* and those paid double called *duplicarii*.

Clothing for the naval *milites* differed between the regional fleets. This reflected differing climatic and operational conditions. Again using the *Classis Britannica* as an example, an essential item of clothing in the northern waters would have been the *birrus* rain-proofed hooded cloak for which the province was famous. Other key items of clothing for the *milites* of this regional fleet would have been the *pilos* conical felt hat, belted tunic with trousers, and sandals or felt stockings with low-cut leather boots rather than *caligae*. The short *sagum* cloak was worn when on formal duty.

For weaponry the marines of the regional navies were armed in a similar manner to the land-based auxilia. Principal missile weapons, in addition to ship-based artillery, included bows, slings, javelins and darts.

For hand-to-hand work the marines also carried boarding pikes, the *hasta navalis* naval spear, various types of sword and the *dolabra* boarding axe.

The Roman Military of the Dominate Empire

As detailed earlier, the Roman Empire that emerged from the disastrous 'Crisis of the Third Century' was very different to that of the earlier Principate, it now being styled the Dominate. The same was true with regard to the Roman military establishment, which continued to evolve following the initial reforms of Septimius Severus. These reforms began slowly but accelerated as time went on. In that regard, the troop types and their organization that campaigned in the early Dominate in Britain with Constantius Chlorus would have been broadly recognisable to an earlier Severan commander. However, those which campaigned in Britain in the 4th and early 5th centuries AD were very different.

The two key factors driving change in the Roman military during the Dominate phase of Empire were the continual ramping up of military threats to the Empire, and the strain countering this placed on the Roman economy. The principal phases of military reform were carried out by Diocletian (AD 284 to AD 305) as part of his reformation of the wider structure of the Empire, and later Constantine I. By the end of the latter's reign these changes were manifest in six broad ways, these being:

- A general levelling of the difference between the legionaries and auxiliaries in terms of their equipment, roles on campaign and in battle, and standing within the Roman military establishment.
- Military units in general being smaller (sometimes much smaller), with an emphasis on creating brigades of differing troop types (and ultimately field armies) appropriate to a given task rather than having a single type of homogenous force.
- From the time of Constantine I, a clear distinction between *comitatenses* field army troops and *limitanei* border troops. This followed the adoption of a defence-in-depth strategy as the Imperial experience transitioned from offence to defence, with the latter acting in a policing and 'trip wire' role on the borders of the Empire, and the former deployed far back to counter any significant incursion into Imperial territory. In the later Empire such field armies were commanded by a *Comes* (the origin of the title count) or a *Dux* (the origin of the title duke).

- A much larger mounted component within the field armies, with a greater range of specialist types.
- The gradual disappearance of the Principate regional fleets, with a reversion to the Republican concept of *ad hoc* fleets created as required.
- Again reflecting earlier Republican practice, the increasingly widespread use of *foederate* irregular troops, initially armed in their own fashion but under Roman officers, and later under their own officers.

Until the reforms of Constantine I the legions of the early Dominate phase of Empire were still recognizably Principate in size and nature. However, that changed dramatically once the founder of the Constantinian dynasty initiated his great changes to the Roman military. His new legions were now only 1,200 men strong as opposed to the 5,500 men legions of the Principate, with the old cohort system totally abandoned. The new legions were now structured on six *ordines* each with two centuries of legionaries containing 10 *contubernia*, with each *ordo* comprising 200 men. An equestrian-class tribune who had usually served as one of the emperor's *protectores* corps of advisors and guards commanded them, assisted by a *primicerius* second in command, the latter title an evolution of the Principate *Primus Pilus* senior legionary centurion. Each *ordo* was then commanded by a *decenarius*. He also directly commanded the first century of each *ordo*, with a *centenarius* (the equivalent of the old centurion) commanding the second. Each century then had a second-in-command called a *biarchus* who effectively replaced the *optio* of the former Principate legions, while each *contubernia* was commanded by a *semissalis* non-commissioned officer.

There has been much speculation as to why Constantine I reduced the size of his legions given they remained much in demand. A key reason would have been administrative given the difficulties in billeting large numbers of men among civilian population centres deep within the Empire. Another was the difficulty the Empire faced in recruiting new troops after the tribulations of the 'Crisis of the 3rd Century', to the extent that Diocletian had earlier made the military profession hereditary (Valentinian I, AD 364 to AD 375, was later forced to reduce the height requirement to join the ranks), with the sons of serving soldiers or veterans required by law to enlist themselves to ensure the complement of troops in legionary and auxiliary units remained stable. However, one key advantage of the new system was that it was now much easier to rapidly brigade the smaller legions into field armies (most late Roman legions were *comitatenses* rather than *limitanei* in nature) to counter the multitude of threats faced by the late Roman Empire.

Despite their reduction in size the new legions were still based on their Principate predecessors, often initially retaining the same numbering and naming system. However, this did change over time, with the numbering in particular disappearing. For example, the *legio* V *Iovia* and *legio* VI *Herculia* founded by Diocletian as his own personal legions to balance the power of the Praetorian Guard later became the *Iovani* and *Herculiani* elite legions that fought with Julian the Apostate at Strasbourg in AD 357.

Turning to the auxilia, these troops provided much of the *comitatenses* manpower in the field armies and nearly all of the *limitanei* troops. One new development in the Dominate phase of Empire was the appearance of a new, elite type of auxiliary formation. These were called *auxilia palatina* and were first raised by Constantine I to help bolster the legions in his field armies. Some of the most senior (and probably oldest) were given names, for example the *Petulantes, Heruli, Cornuti* and *Brachiati* who fought with Julian the Apostate at Strasbourg. Many units of *auxilia palatina* were recruited directly from the individual Germanic tribes, often the origins of their unit names, each having a strong sense of élan that matched or even bettered those of the legions. Auxiliaries in field armies, including *auxilia palatina*, were organised in a similar way to the post-Constantinian reform late Roman legions, though at half the strength, with only three *ordines* with two centuries each. They also featured the same command structure. Auxiliary *limitanei* units continued to be organised as in the Principate, maintaining their cohort-based structure and commanded by a tribune. Meanwhile, *foederates* fighting in their own units rather than those recruited directly into the ranks of the legions and auxilia were organised and fought in their own native style.

In terms of equipment, from the time of Constantine I the *Comitatenses* legionaries and auxilia were armed in much the same way. For their defensive panoply they retained the circular or oval body shield of the later Principate. Meanwhile, for armour most line of battle troops (whether legionaries or auxilia) wore *lorica hamata* chainmail or *lorica squamata* scalemail hauberks, these often much longer than their Principate counterparts and offering even greater protection. *Lorica segmentata* disappears in the later 3rd century AD.

A major change in the *Comitatenses* legionary and auxilia panoply was with regard to their helmets. As the Dominate progressed the 'Imperial' Gallic type and its developments all but disappeared, to be replaced broadly by two new mass-produced types made in the Imperial *fabricae* arms factories. These were ridge helmets and the spangenhelm, both usually made of iron though sometimes bronze. The former were made by creating a bowl of two or four parts, these designs called 'Intercisa' and 'Berkasovo' types, which were then held together by a central longitudinal ridge. The former had ear holes while the latter didn't. Copied from a Sassanid Persian design, the earliest known example dates to around AD 280 and was found in the Saxon Shore fort at Richborough. Given the simplicity of their construction it proved easy for Roman armourers to add levels of protection to ridge helmets as required, including nose guards, brow ridge, cheek guards and deep neck guards.

Meanwhile the *spangenhelm* design originated in the Central Asian steppe, its vector of transfer into the Roman military being the various Sarmatian tribes fighting with and against the Romans from the time of Trajan's campaigns in Dacia in the early 2nd century AD. The basic design featured a framework of metal strips that connected three to six longitudinal plates, giving a more conical appearance than the more rounded ridge helmet. Again given the simplicity of design, it proved easy to add nose guards (sometimes integrally built into spangenhelms), brow ridges, cheek guards and deep neck guards. Two features unique to this design were the frequent addition of eye protectors resembling modern eyeglass frames, and chainmail aventails to provide neck protection.

For offensive weaponry the *comitatenses* legionaries and auxilia were all now armed with the long spear and *spatha,* with many also equipped with javelins and darts. The javelins came in a variety of types, for example the armour-piercing *spiculum*, this a technological innovation combining the features of the earlier Roman *pilum* with German throwing spears and featuring a characteristically large barbed head. Another armour piercing javelin type was the *angon*, a weapon of Frankish origin featuring a barbed head on a long narrow socket or shank made of iron mounted on a wooden haft. Meanwhile *plumbatae* or *martiobarbuli* lead-weighted darts were a specific innovation of the Dominate phase of Empire. These were carried in clips on the back of the legionary and auxiliary large oval body shields and could be thrown over-arm for distance or under-arm to give a steep descending trajectory designed to fall on the heads of an approaching enemy.

The *comitatenses* legionaries and auxilia armoured and armed in the above fashion fought in deep formations, often with integral bowmen forming the rear ranks to fire over the heads of those in front. Their opponents were therefore faced with the same impenetrable spear wall as those fighting the old Tullian First Class hoplite phalanx. However, the Dominate legionaries and auxilia were far better trained, able to rapidly make complex manoeuvres on the battlefield, and could shower their enemies with javelins, darts and their integral bow-fire.

Meanwhile, Dominate *limitanei* infantry were equipped in a similar manner to less well-armed *comitatenses* field army troops. While few wore armour, most had helmets and carried the round or oval body shield. For a weapon the long spear was used, together with the *spatha*. However, as the Dominate progressed, particularly in the west, the quality of the *limitanei* fell, and from the beginning of the 5th century AD they should be regarded more as a local genderarmie, excepting pseudocomitatenses units deployed to serve in the field armies. The latter were *limitanei* units drafted to serve in the field armies in times of peril.

Meanwhile, as detailed, cavalry units in the Dominate formed a far larger component of the Roman military establishment than in the Principate, particularly in the field armies. The basic unit of organization was now the *vexillatio* commanded by a tribune, this broadly tracking the administrative structure of auxiliary units, with three *ordines* of two centuries each, giving a total complement of 600 horsemen.

The basic cavalryman remained the *equite*, with the same panoply as their Principate forebears. They were still supported by the specialist types that had originated in the Principate, for example the *equites contariorum* and *equites cataphractarii* shock cavalry, and *equites illyriciani* and *equites sagittarii* light cavalry. However, in the Dominate phase of Empire other types now proliferated, including *equites clibanarii* fully armoured lancers, *equites dalmatae* who were armed in a similar way to the *equites illyriciani* (their names indicating where they were initially recruited from), *equites mauri* who were based on their Moorish *symmachiarii* predecessors and who were much in demand when fighting the Sassanid Persians, and finally *equites scutarii* who may have been regular bodyguard cavalry. Towards the end of the Dominate phase of Empire many standard *equites* also began to carry the bow, a response to conflict with the Huns, as did some units of *equites clibanarii*.

In terms of their defensive panoply, the biggest change when compared to their Principate predecessors followed the similar trend in the infantry, with the widespread use from this time of ridge helmets and *spangenhelms*.

Finally, one of the results of the economic crash caused by the 'Crisis of the 3rd Century' was the gradual abandonment of the Augustan system of regional fleets across the Empire. This is very evident in Britain when the last reference to the *Classis Britannica* is that regarding Saturninus detailed above which is dated to no later than AD 249. Here, from this point on we see a gradual change from a system of maritime offence controlling the open ocean to one of defence, with the focus now on defending littoral coastal areas and the riparian control of river systems. This is best illustrated by the construction of the Saxon shore forts around the south-eastern coast of Britain. While fleets were occasionally built *ad hoc* for specific tasks, they were by no means the fleets-in-being of the earlier Empire.

Chapter 2

Britain in the Late Iron Age

Prior to their first contact with the world of Rome the indigenous peoples of the British Isles had a rich cultural history, dating back almost 10,000 years to a time when reoccupation began here after the end of the last Ice Age. Throughout this lengthy period they maintained strong links with their continental neighbours, sharing each societal and technological development. This reached its height with the La Tène culture that dominated in much of Britain at the time of Rome's first serious engagement here, this in the form of Julius Caesar's two incursions in 55 BC and 54 BC.

Understanding pre-Roman Britain is important to provide context for Caesar's sorties, and the later campaigns of conquest following the AD 43 Claudian invasion. To that end this chapter will first consider the political, economic and social structure of pre-Roman Late Iron Age (LIA) Britain. It will then discuss the geology and geography of the main islands here to show how these played a key role in all of the phases of Roman conquest in Britain, before similarly considering the prevailing weather systems here from the LIA through to the end of the Roman occupation of Britain.

Britain Before the Romans

The British Isles are the most north-westerly archipelago of the European landmass. Repopulation of what was then a peninsula began around 9,600 BC after the end of the 1,200 year-long Younger Dryas cold spell that interrupted the gradual warming of northern Europe after the end of the last Ice Age. Those arriving back were hunter-gatherers, originally from the Upper Paleolithic Ahrensburgian culture, whose influence stretched from the Atlantic coast to Poland (Cunliffe, 2013, 102). These were later replaced by various Mesolithic cultures.

Then, around 5,500 BC, an event occurred that has defined Britain geographically ever since. This was the final submergence of Doggerland, the North Sea land-bridge linking Britain to the continent (Gaffney, Fitch and Smith, 2009, 31). However, this didn't stop the islands here remaining culturally connected to the continent. Britain continued to fully participate in each new wave of social and technological advancement originating on the continent, with the usual vector of transmission being through the south-eastern region, from where the new ideas and practices gradually spread throughout the rest of the British Isles. A key development in this regard was the arrival of farming at the onset of the Neolithic period around 4,200 BC.

The next cultural development was the advent of the Chalcolithic period, otherwise known as the Copper Age. In Britain this happened from 3,000 BC, to be followed by the Bronze Age from 2,500 BC. The latter coincided with the arrival of the Bell Beaker culture that culturally linked the islands of Britain to every corner of the European landmass, including the Mediterranean. This level of connection is dramatically illustrated by the contemporary Amesbury Archer burial near Stonehenge (Cunliffe, 2013, 212). Oxygen Isotope Analysis on this individual's tooth enamel indicates he had travelled to this key ritual site on the exposed grassy plains of Wiltshire from an Alpine region in central Europe. This, and the fact that Britain itself was the source of much bronze exported back to the continent given the prevalence of tin here, shows that Britain was fully engaged in long-range European trading networks spanning far and wide across the continent. Crossing the English Channel or North Sea was certainly no barrier to this, as evidenced by the Bronze Age boat dating to 2,500 BC that was discovered in Dover in 1992 and is now displayed in the museum there. At this time many argue that Britain was actually part of an integrated Atlantic Coast Bronze Age trading system. This ranged from the Rhine Delta in the north to the southeastern Iberia Peninsula.

The British Iron Age began around 800 BC. This featured five phases:

- The Earliest Iron Age from 800 BC to 600 BC. In this phase much of Britain was part of the Hallstatt culture that predominated in western and central Europe.
- The Early Iron Age from 600 BC to 400 BC. During this period much of Britain continued to be part of the Hallstatt culture, and was later part of its La Tène evolution.
- The Middle Iron Age from 400 BC to 100 BC, where La Tène culture continued to predominate.

- The Late Iron Age (LIA) from 100 BC to 50 BC, once more La Tène in nature.
- The Latest Iron Age from 50 BC to the creation of the Roman Province of Britannia in AD 43. Again La Tène culture featured strongly, with parts of Britain (particularly the south and the east) being its last redoubt in north-western Europe after Caesar's conquest of Gaul from 58 BC.

Up to the latter event, it is clear from all of the preceding cultural developments in Britain that the islands here were intrinsically linked with their continental neighbours through thousands of years of engagement. Immediately prior to Caesar's Gallic campaigns these links were manifest in many ways. For example, key tribes here shared their names with counterparts on the continent, including the Belgae on the south coast, Atrebates in the Thames Valley and Parisi above the Humber. The export of goods from Britain to the continent was also well known to contemporary audiences, for example iron as detailed by the Greek geographer Strabo (*The Geography*, IV.5) and Caesar himself (*The Conquest of Gaul*, V.135). Another cross-channel export was very fine greensand millstones and quern stones manufactured by a thriving industry at East Cliff in Folkestone (Parfitt, 2013, 36). Examples are found throughout north-western France. Other exports at the time included woollen goods, hunting dogs and slaves (Elliott, 2016, 113).

This connectivity was brutally dislocated by Caesar's conquest of Gaul. From that time Britain became a place of refuge for those on the continent fleeing Caesar's sanguineous campaigns there. Plutarch (*Life of Caesar*, 15.5) later calculated that these cost the lives of one million Gauls and the enslavement of another million. To contextualise the scale of this loss, the entire population of LIA Britain at this time was around two million. This level of slaughter might explain the comparative ease with which Gaul was incorporated into the Empire, with the Romans finding it comparatively straightforward to impose their system of administration, economy, art and literary culture. Soon the provincial structure of the region had been firmly established, with four provinces in Gaul itself, two German provinces along the Rhine and three small Alpine provinces bordering Italy. Suddenly, Britain's connections with continental neighbours of like mind and culture had been shut off. The tribes here now had to deal with Romans casting an avaricious eye across the English Channel.

By the first century BC the main island of Britain, in which Rome later carved its province through its campaigns of conquest, featured a dense network of tribes who were often at war with each other. Beginning in modern Kent and heading roughly clockwise, these included the Cantiaci, the Trinovantes to their north in eastern Essex, the Catuvellauni in western Essex through to Oxfordshire, the Atrebates in the Thames Valley and the Regni and Belgae on the south coast. In the South West, one then had the Durotriges and Dumnonii, with the Dubonni and Cornovii to their north reaching into the Welsh Marches. Into Wales proper were the Silures, Demetae, Ordovices and Deceangli ranging south to north, with the Brigantes in the north of modern England, the Carvetii in the North West, the Parisi north of the Humber, Coritani south of the Humber and Iceni in modern north Norfolk.

Heading into modern Scotland, scene of so much campaigning during the Roman occupation of the south, the tribes there included the Votadini in the eastern Scottish Borders, the Selgovae in the central Borders, the Novantae in the western Borders, the Dumnonii around the Clyde, and the Epidii in the Mull of Kintyre. Then above the Clyde on the west coast, going south to north, the Creones, the Carnonacae and (at the far north western tip of Scotland) the Caereni. On the east coast around the River Tay were the Venicones, and above them in Aberdeenshire, the Vacomagi and Taexali. Broadly, throughout the Grampians, were located the Caledonii, then around the Moray Firth, again going south to north, the Decantae, Lugi, Smertae and finally the Cornacii. By the end of the 2nd century AD many of these tribes had coalesced into two huge confederations, the Maeatae either side of the Clyde-Forth line, and above them the Caledonians. Late in the Roman occupation of Britain the Picts then came to dominate the far north of Scotland down into the Midland Valley. Additionally, the Romans also interacted with the various Scots peoples of modern Ireland across the Irish Sea.

The economy of LIA Britain was dominated by agriculture. However industry did exist, for example with the minting of coins (mostly copies of Mediterranean issues), pottery production, mill and quern stone manufacture, and mining and metal production. Technological innovation also occurred, for example with the adoption of the potter's wheel, the rotary quern and the lathe.

Agriculture was at its most advanced in the lowlands of LIA Britain, with all members of society except the upper elite levels of the aristocracy involved. In general, in the lowlands mixed agriculture was practised with both livestock and crops farmed (Jones and Mattingly, 1990, 5). Most of the farming was subsistence in nature, with any agricultural surplus supplied to tribal leaders for storage. This helped mitigate against any harvest shock and also underpinned trade for manufactured goods both regionally and with the continent. Based on the archaeological record, the main animals farmed included pigs, goats, cattle and sheep, the balance depending on where in Britain the farming was taking place. In terms of crops, native Britons used rectangular fields for the most part, and may also have used a field rotation system whereby a given field would be left fallow for a year, with livestock grazing on it. This would help keep weeds in check and also fertilize the land with manure. LIA Britons used an *ard* type plough drawn by oxen, this a simple design which lacked a mud board. Sometimes called a scratch plough, this could only cut a shallow and narrow furrow. However, as the LIA progressed the Britons did make some advances in agricultural practice, for example digging drainage ditches to drain waterlogged land (and thus open it up to agriculture) and to water their fields. The most common arable crops were spelt, emmer and einkhorn wheat, and barley. Oats, rye and millet were also grown.

In terms of settlement there was no stone built urban environment in LIA Britain, with the largest communities gathered in *oppida* proto-towns in the southeast of Britain. These were the central administrative centres for the larger tribes there, and were defined by their well-designed ditch and bank defensive linear earthworks. Jones and Mattingly (1990, 47) say that some of these settlements were huge, with vast areas of land contained within massive systems of dykes. They cite the Catuvellauni capital of Camulodunon, later the early Roman provincial capital *Colonia Claudia Victricensis* and now modern Colchester, as a prime example. These settlements appear to have been an innovation of the early 1st century BC, with Haywood (2009, 78) arguing they had evolved from the hillforts, long a key feature of the British rural landscape. Below this level the majority of the population lived in farming villages of varying sizes and types, or in isolated farmsteads.

The military system of the native Britons fought first by Caesar, and later by the Roman Empire in its various campaigns of conquest in Britain, remained the same for most of the Roman occupation and was rooted in the LIA La Tène traditions of the continent. This featured a chariot riding aristocracy, skirmishing cavalry riding ponies, short spear armed line of battle troops, and sling or javelin armed skirmishing foot.

In terms of army size, given few native British troops were professional warriors (unlike the *Gaesati* in earlier Gallic armies (Allen, 2001, 14)), various sized gatherings are reported in contemporary history. For example, when Cassivellaunus, likely the tribal leader of the Catuvellauni in the mid-1st century BC, fought Caesar he fielded a large force of chariots manned by 4,000 charioteers late in the 54 BC campaign, having sent the rest of his army home. However, given he was the leader of all resistance to Caesar in the South East of Britain, it has been estimated he could have led up to 80,000 men if needed. Meanwhile, as detailed in Chapter 5, Boudicca could have led a force of 230,000 (Dio's figure, *Roman History*, 62.8), including 100,000 warriors, in her incendiary insurrection against the Roman occupation in AD 60/61. However, at the other end of the scale the Caledonians who fought Agricola at Mons Graupius in AD 83 only numbered 30,000, and were easily defeated by the Roman auxilia alone.

The elite troops in native British armies were the chariot-riding nobility, these reported in many engagements through to the 5th century AD (the latter in the context of the Scots and Picts). They were most popular among the tribes in the southeast and east of the main island of Britain at the time of the Caesar's 55 BC and 54 BC incursions, but were used throughout the British Isles given the status they bestowed on the chariot rider. Native British chariots featured two ponies harnessed with a yoke and breast-straps to a draft pole, a wooden fighting platform with wicker sides, and two wheels on a centrally mounted axle (Allen, 2001, 47). They featured two crewmembers, these being an unarmed driver and the noble. The latter carried a large Gallic shield that was either oval, sometimes with the upper and lower ends removed, or round. Both types featured a central boss. All were of plank construction, often covered in a sheet of bronze or with a leather hide. The noble also wore various kinds of Gallic helmet and a chainmail hauberk. He was armed with javelins and the long iron Gallic slashing sword. Gallic nobles tended towards flamboyancy, always wanting to demonstrate their wealth and status, with their defensive equipment often brightly decorated. The 1st century BC Greek historian Diodorus Siculus provides a detailed description of this, saying (V.30.2):

> *Their arms include man-sized shields decorated according to individual taste. Some of these have projecting figures in bronze skilfully made not only for decoration but also for protection. They wear bronze helmets with large figures, which give the wearer the appearance of enormous*

> *size. In some cases horns are attached, in others the foreparts of birds and beasts.*

Caesar, Dio and Tacitus all describe these native chariots in action, with all reporting how manoeuvrable they were and saying the Britons deliberately rode them across the front of an enemy battle line which they showered with javelins and insults. The noble then often jumped down to fight on foot, leading his own war band.

Meanwhile, British cavalry were much lighter than their Gallic counterparts. They acted in a supporting role to the chariots. Specifically, they skirmished with javelins, attacked flanks and pursued routers. When used in conjunction with the chariots they proved a particular nuisance for Caesar in his two incursions to Britain, and later the Aulus Plautius-led Claudian invasion.

By far the biggest component of native British armies was their line of battle spearmen. These were mostly farmers called up in a mass levy when needed who were armed in a similar manner to the warriors faced by Caesar in his conquest of Gaul. The main defensive equipment was the Gallic shield as used by the chariot-riding nobility, or a simpler wicker and hide design. Few wore helmets and fewer any form of armour. The main weapon was a light spear or javelin, with some troops also armed with the long Gallic slashing sword or a dagger. In Britain these warriors formed a spear wall if required, usually in a strong defensive position as with those opposing Plautius in his river crossing battle in Kent in AD 43 (Elliott, 2016, 115), and the Caledonians deploying on the steep slopes of Mons Graupius in AD 83. However, the preferred tactic was the use of natural terrain to ambush their opponents, often as part of a guerrilla campaign. The Maeatae and Caledonian confederations fighting Septimius Severus in AD 209 and AD 210 provide a good example of this (Elliott, 2018a, 159).

In Britain the favoured missile weapon used by skirmishers was the sling, particularly in the South West. The Durotriges and Dumnonii tribes who fought Vespasian (AD 69 to AD 79) are a good example of this. Javelin armed skirmishers are also reported, though no bowmen, at least until the later occupation.

Regional variations to the military establishment detailed above are considered at the appropriate place in the following chapters, for example with the native Britons of the far north fought by Agricola and Severus. However, special note is made here regarding the only major change in the nature of the opponents encountered by the Romans in Britain. This is again in the far north, and comes in the form of the Picts mentioned earlier who appear from the later 3rd century AD, with them gradually taking over the territory in the north of what is now modern Scotland (Haywood, 2009, 77).

The Picts are first mentioned in contemporary history by the writer Eumenius in AD 297, the name referencing their propensity for body tattoos and woad body paint. They were not a single tribe, but rather a large confederation, as with the earlier Maeatae and Caledonians. Their armies continued to use light chariots and skirmishing light cavalry, but many of their infantry were now differentially armed compared to their predecessors. The most obvious change was a switch to a different shield design over time, these made of hide stretched across two crossed sticks held together at the juncture. Many warriors are depicted in Pictish artwork, usually as enigmatic carvings on stone monuments, which depict such shields as small square or round designs rather than the larger shields used earlier in the region. Axes also feature as side arms on these carvings, as do bowmen.

The Attacotti, a people who frequently fought with the Picts against the Romans and others, also deserve a final mention. Of possible Scots Irish descent, these fierce warriors are mentioned by a number of late Roman historians who detail their role in the 'Great Conspiracy' in AD 367 (see Chapter 8 for detail).

Geology and Geography

The Roman campaigns of conquest in Britain, through all of its phases, were heavily influenced by the geology and geography of the main island in the archipelago. Jones and Mattingly (1990, 1) highlight that broadly there are two geological zones here. These are the western and northern region, featuring many older and harder rock formations (both igneous and metamorphic), and the southern and eastern region (including much of the Midlands) where many of the rocks are softer and sedimentary in nature. Though by no means uniform, the former two feature much of the highlands of Britain where military campaigning was difficult, while the latter two feature much of the more fertile lowlands.

Focusing specifically on modern Scotland in the far north given the frequency of Roman campaigning there, its geology and geography is unusually varied even for a largely highland region, with a large number of different geological features often complicated by drift geology. The three main geographical sub-divisions are:

- The Southern Uplands, lying to the south of the Southern Uplands Fault (and largely composed of Silurian deposits).
- The Central Lowlands, a rift valley mainly comprising Paleozoic formations.
- The Highlands and Islands, a diverse area lying to the north and west of the Highland Boundary Fault.

It is this latter Highland Boundary Fault that played the key geological role in the campaigns in Scotland of both Agricola and Septimius Severus given it runs south west to north east from the Isle of Arran to Stonehaven, delineating the Scottish Highlands from the more fertile Midland Valley and Scottish Borders to its south and east.

A further key feature of the geography of the main island of Britain is its extensive system of rivers and waterways. These were widely used in the campaigns of conquest by the Romans, Germanic raiders and settlers towards the end of the Roman occupation of Britain, and later the Vikings. It is no coincidence that nearly all of the Roman fortresses, forts and stone-built settlements in Britain, most of which track the campaigns of conquest, are all sited on navigable rivers. In that regard the most important were:

- On the south coast, the rivers Arun, Avon and Exe.
- Up the west coast, the rivers Wye, Severn (and its Avon tributary penetrating deep into the Midlands), Dee, Mersey, Ribble, Lune and the Solway Firth.
- Down the east coast (starting in the far north) the Moray Firth, then the rivers Tay, the Firth of Forth, Tyne, Tees, Derwent, Ouse, Trent, Witham, Nene, Great Ouse, the now lost Great Estuary in modern Norfolk (today the Yare and Waveney), Stour (in modern Suffolk), Thames, Darent, Medway and the various branches of the Stour in Kent.

Weather

In terms of the specific weather conditions for the whole of the British Isles during the Roman campaigns of conquest in Britain, modern scientific research has provided us with a useful picture. This shows the weather in the region was not too far removed from that which we experience today, excepting that it was perhaps slightly warmer and wetter earlier in the Roman occupation (Grainge, 2005, 37). York provides a good example in that regard, where excavations have revealed the remains of insect species that thrived in a warmer climate than that experienced today, the data suggesting a mean July temperature in northern England 1°C higher in the 1st and 2nd centuries AD (Ottaway, 2013, 16).

The principal type of system dominating weather patterns in the islands of Britain during the occupation were Atlantic lows (as they are today), these leading to prevailing winds originating most often from the westerly quadrant. These winds are created by North Atlantic depressions moving east or north-easterly across the open ocean before meeting the north-western European landmass, usually hitting Ireland and Britain first. Indeed, it is this type of system that Julius Caesar described proving so troublesome to his 55 BC expedition to Britain, while another delayed the sailing of his 54 BC expedition (Elliott, 2016, 43, see Chapter 3). Such weather systems are often modified as they interact with high pressure systems when they approach the continental land mass, and it is this set of interactions that leads to what can at best be described as the cheerfully unpredictable weather conditions which are so much part of the modern British cultural experience, and which the Romans described as wet and cold.

Both Dio and Herodian make the weather in the far north of Britain sound grimmer than in the south, and certainly when Caesar (V.135) himself famously described Britain at the time of the 55 BC sortie as being densely populated and heavily cultivated, it was clearly the south he was describing given the more favourable weather conditions there. In that regard Ottaway (2013, 16) highlights that in 1971–2000 on the south coast of Britain there was an average of 1,750 hours of sunshine per year, compared to 1,149 in Malham Tarn in North Yorkshire. This differential is even more pronounced as one heads into the far north. Meanwhile, again using Yorkshire as an example in the same time period, Ottaway (2013, 16) adds that in terms of rainfall there is a very pronounced difference in the amount experienced in the upland Pennines when compared to the lowlands, 1,518mm per annum at Malham Tarn compared to 600mm in York, this a useful analogy for the rest of Britain. Thus the overall picture is one where the north of the islands of Britain receives less sunlight than the south, to an extent restricting agricultural activity, with more rain on the upland regions (especially on the western side given the prevailing weather systems detailed above). Poor weather proved a key consideration in many of the Roman campaigns of conquest in Britain, particularly those of Septimius Severus when he invaded the far north in AD 209 and AD 210 (see Chapter 7).

Chapter 3

Julius Caesar and Britain

Gaius Julius Caesar was the greatest warlord of the later Roman Republic. A renowned risk taker, he often acted unpredictably, catching opponents off-guard time and again in war and politics. Yet his decision to invade mysterious Britain across terrifying *Oceanus* in 55 BC was his most perilous, fraught with danger and at great personal risk, both to his life and reputation. This was a land that Suetonius (*Julius Caesar*, 1.25) says was a '*...hitherto unknown country...*', an accurate description of Roman knowledge of the British Isles at the time. Failing the first time if he intended to stay, he repeated the same expedition in 54 BC, but with a much bigger army. Even this failed to carve out a foothold large enough to enable him to overwinter in Britain, and he withdrew again to Gaul. He never returned, though his campaigns did establish the first official links between Britain and Rome. This set the scene for the Roman conquest almost a century later under Claudius.

To understand Caesar's decisions to invade Britain, and follow the course of his two campaigns, one first has to understand the man. In that regard, here his early life and career to that point are briefly considered to give insight into his later actions. Next I detail the early part of his sanguineous campaign to conquer Gaul, of which his two British adventures were an integral part. I then set out in full his two perilous incursions to Britain, including a discussion about why he took such a dramatic risk to travel to Britain twice in the first place, before concluding with a short appreciation of their aftermath.

Early Life and Career

Julius Caesar belonged to the Julia clan, one of Rome's oldest patrician *gentes*. They originated in the Latin city of Alba Longa, 19km to the south east of Rome. Later in the Republic, when it was fashionable for clans to associate themselves with a divine origin, the Julii claimed lineage from Iulus, son of Aeneas and founder of the town. Further, in the origin myths of Rome Aeneas himself claimed to be the son of Venus. This was an association later embraced by Caesar himself whenever the mythical connection offered political advantage.

After the Julii moved to Rome in the mid-7th century BC they proved an unremarkable *gentes* before the time of Caesar. One of its first members to rise to prominence was a Julius Caesar who reached the praetorship during the Second Punic War. This man was the first to have the *cognomen* Caesar. It was later claimed this derived from *caesai*, the Punic word for elephant, after he killed one in battle.

The clan later split into two lines, each registered to a different tribe in the Roman voting census. The direct family of Caesar sat within the less successful branch. Little is known of his grandfather, Gaius Julius Caesar, other than his wife's name, Marcia. She was the daughter of Quintus Marcius Rex, praetor in 144 BC, with the couple having at least two children. These were Caesar's father Gaius and a daughter named Julia. Gaius embarked on a public service career following the *cursus honorum* set career path for aristocratic Roman men of Senatorial rank, he entering the Senate at 25. Gaius married Aurelia of the Aurelii Cottae clan, an association that certainly boosted Gaius' career given they were a leading plebian noble *gentes*. However, it was patronage through his sister's marriage that played the greatest role in his career. This was because Julia married Marius, the leader of the *populares* faction in Roman politics and the political and military titan of the age (see Chapter 1). Gaius was soon nominated one of the ten commissioners tasked with overseeing the settlement of Marius' veterans after the Cimbrian War. Elected *praetor* around 92 BC, he was then appointed governor of the western Anatolian province of Asia. This was a post that should have financially set the family up for life given the untold riches streaming into Rome from its recent conquests in the region. However, his bounding career was dramatically cut short when in 85 BC while back in Rome he died unexpectedly while putting his shoes on one morning. At the age of 16, his son Julius Caesar suddenly became the *Pater Familias* head of his family (Elliott, 2019, 66).

Caesar had been born on the 13th of July 100 BC, which in his own time would have been recorded as the third day before the Ides of Quinctilis in the consulship of Marius and Lucius Valerius Flaccus, in the 654th year after the foundation of Rome. He was the youngest of Gaius and Aurelia's three known children, with two elder sisters, both called Julia. The boy was named with the full *tria nomina* of the elite Roman upper classes, this comprising the *praenomen* or first name, *nomen* clan name, and *cognomen* that identified a particular family branch. He received the standard education for aristocratic children, this arduous and repetitive and taught seven days a week. No doubt the young Caesar would have been delighted when his schooling ended with his graduation at the age of 16.

Caesar's coming of age was well timed given the opportunities it presented, especially as he was now the head of his own household. Though Marius had died in January 86 BC aged 71, a year later the *populares* were still ascendant in Rome. Caesar was soon nominated as the new *Flamen Dialis* high priest of Jupiter, an astonishing advancement given his young age. He then quickly married Cornelia, daughter of the leading *populares* politician Cinna.

It is unclear if Caesar was officially appointed the *Flamen Dialis*, but even if he did take up the post he didn't stay there for long as political turmoil soon returned to Rome. This was because in 83 BC Sulla, champion of the *optimates* and the Senate, returned to Italy victorious after the First Mithridatic war. His arrival began Sulla's Second Civil War that concluded with another victory when he successfully stormed Rome in 82 BC. Rapidly seizing political control, he then declared himself dictator before turning on the leading *populares* with a savage vengeance.

Caesar was 18 by this time and though Sulla didn't see the Julii as a threat the young man was quickly targeted given his wife was the daughter of Cinna, and Marius had been his uncle-in-law. In the first instance Sulla ordered Caesar to divorce Cornelia (Goldworthy, 2006, 57). Caesar showed great personal bravery here, a trait evident throughout his life, repeatedly refusing to obey. Sulla then targeted Caesar's finances, stripping away Cornelia's dowry and nominating another to become the *Flamen Dialis*. Finally he confiscated Caesar's family inheritance, and soon afterwards the inevitable order was given for his arrest. This was a sure sign execution was to follow.

Caesar wisely went on the run in the Sabine Hills, talking his way out of trouble when finally arrested. He was eventually saved by his mother who convinced two of her Aurelii Cottae cousins, leading *optimates*, to plead with Sulla for her son's life. The strategy worked better than expected as Sulla not only relented but also allowed Caesar to resume his public career. However, Suetonius provides a sting in the tail, having Sulla say the following (*The Twelve Caesars*, Julius Caesar, 1.1):

> *Very well then, you win! Take him! But never forget that the man you want me to spare will one day prove the ruin of the party*

> *[the optimates] which you want and I have so long defended. There are many Mariuses in this fellow.*

Despite the pardon, Caesar decided caution was the best path to take. Fearful Sulla would change his mind, he left for Anatolia to join the military. Here he learned his trade as a junior officer, observing the *legates,* centurions and legionaries as they performed their various tasks on campaign. Caesar served on the front line with great distinction, particularly when the town of Mitylene on the island of Lesbos was stormed. For his bravery here he was given Rome's highest award for gallantry, the *corona civica* crown of oak leaves (Elliott, 2019, 75).

Caesar then campaigned in Cilicia on the south coast of Anatolia under Publius Servius Vatia Isauricus, fighting against the Cilician pirates endemic there. It was here that dramatic news reached him in 78 BC. Sulla was dead. Caesar now felt secure enough to return home, trying his hand at a legal career. In this he was again successful, though perhaps too much so as word reached him he was making enemies in high places. Once more he decided caution was the best route to take and again left the capital for the east, this time aiming to study in Rhodes.

On his way there the first famous event in Caesar's life occurred. This was his capture by Cilician pirates near the island of Farmakonisi (Roman *Pharmacussa*), off the coast of south-western Anatolia. Once in captivity Caesar sent the companions travelling with him to the nearby cities on the Anatolian mainland to raise loans to pay the ransom of 20 talents of silver being demanded. Then, when free, he went straight to nearby Miletus and raised a crew and small fleet. With this he headed back to Farmakonisi, rounded up his previous captors and sent them in chains to the provincial capital of Pergamum. There he asked for them to be executed. However, the regional governor Marcus Junctus showed no interest, so Caesar promptly had the captive pirates crucified. Here we can see the complex nature of Caesar's personality. Crucifixion was a brutal form of capital punishment usually reserved by the Romans for recalcitrant slaves (Holland, 2019, xiii), indicating Caesar was here making a deliberate point. However, having developed some respect for the pirates when he was their captive, he showed a small degree of mercy in having their throats cut first. He then resumed his journey to Rhodes where he studied as planned.

In 74 BC Caesar received another religious appointment back in Rome, this time to become one of the 15 pontiffs who served the *Pontifex Maximus*, the chief priest of the state religion. Returning home once more, he took up his legal career again, next being elected to his first political post as one of the 24 military tribunes in 72 BC.

Caesar's star was now beginning to rise, with his rhetorical skills and legal expertise widely acknowledged. He was also now a father as Cornelia had given birth to their daughter Julia in the mid-late 70s BC. He began his first term as *quaestor* in early 69 BC, this one of the junior magisterial posts in Rome. Shortly after the appointment, Cornelia died. Caesar was then attached to the staff of the governor of Hispania Ulterior (Further Spain), Antistius Vetus. This was one of two Spanish provinces formed following Rome's victory in the Second Punic War.

When he again returned to Rome Caesar remarried, his second wife being a grand-daughter of Sulla called Pompeia who was distantly related to his later great rival Gnaeus Pompey. Continuing his progression along the *cursus honorum*, Caesar was elected to the post of *curule aedile* in 65 BC. Next, in 63 BC he ran for the post of *Pontifex Maximus*, and was again successful. He was then appointed a *praetor*, obtaining his first governorship in 62 BC and returning to Hispania Ulterior as proconsul.

Caesar excelled in his new position. Ever mindful of the never-ending threats of raiding into his province from unconquered parts of Spain, he raised 10 new cohorts of legionaries. These were formed into his new *legio* X, this elite unit to become his own personal legion and one that later accompanied him to Britain twice. He then destroyed two Lusitanian tribes challenging the authority of Rome. The victories were so total that his troops hailed him *imperator*, allowing Caesar to formally claim a triumph on his return to Rome.

When back in the Republican capital in 61 BC he divorced Pompeia in the context of unfounded accusations of infidelity while the latter had hosted the festival of *Bona Dea* in 62 BC. Despite her protestations of innocence, Plutarch quotes Caesar as saying (*Life of Caesar*, 9–10) *'I thought my wife should be above suspicion.'*

Caesar was next elected consul for 59 BC, and once in power introduced a bill to the Senate that he hoped would make him the leading politician in Rome. This was the controversial Land Bill, aimed at redistributing publicly-owned land to Pompey's veteran troops and the many urban poor in Rome. The move was to be financed by the fabulous wealth Pompey had brought back from his campaigns in the east. The passing of this legislation became a grinding battle of wills between the reactionary and pro-Senate *optimates*, led by Cato, and the more radical *populares* for whom Caesar was increasingly the champion. He was greatly helped here by a new re-alignment in Roman politics, the formation of the First Triumvirate between the three leading men of Rome. These were the enormously wealthy Crassus, Pompey, and the newly arriviste Caesar. Each pledged to support the others in the Senate, with many in Rome unaware of the development until Caesar started to overtly promote Pompey through the proposed resettlement of his veterans. In short order the Land Bill passed after a show of force by Pompey's men in the Senate chamber.

With his humiliation of the *optimates* complete, Caesar was now ascendant. Suetonius says a popular joke in Rome described the consuls for the year 59 BC as Julius and Caesar, rather than Caesar and his fellow consul Bibulus, the *optimates'* candidate who was forced to retire from public life. Next he married again, this time to Calpurnia, the daughter of Lucius Piso who had been elected to replace him as consul the following year.

Caesar now looked to his fortunes beyond his year as consul, knowing once out of office he would be targeted in court by the *optimates* and his many creditors. His solution was again to take an office that would make him immune from prosecution, namely another governorship. While consul he had had himself appointed as the proconsul in Cisalpine Gaul (the former Gallic lands in northern Italy, yet to become part of Italy proper) and Illyricum. He later added Transalpine Gaul (also known to the Romans as *Provincia*, now modern Provence) in southern Gaul to his Gallic responsibilities after the death of its governor. The Gallic territories gave him four legions, including his own founding, *legio* X which had moved north from Hispania Ulterior, together with the VIIth, VIIIth and IXth legions. He set his tenure in post for five years from 58 BC and then quickly left for Cisalpine Gaul to take up his post, leaving his creditors once more out of pocket. This set the scene for the Gallic Wars that were to follow, within which sat his two invasions of far off Britain.

Caesar in Gaul

When Caesar set out from Rome for his new province of Cisalpine Gaul he was 41 and already had his eyes on the Gallic kingdoms north of the Alps and Transalpine Gaul. He knew conquest there would grant the two things he craved the most, namely money and glory. The former would help pay off his debts, while the latter would place him on an equal footing with Crassus and Pompey.

To the north of Caesar in Gaul and beyond were six broad tribal regions (Haywood, 2009, 59), these being:

- Gallia Aquitania in the southwest.
- Armorica in the west.
- Gallia Celtica in central Gaul.
- Gallia Belgica to its north.
- Germania across the River Rhine to the north and east.
- Britain across *Oceanus* to the far off northwest, a comparatively unknown entity.

Once in Cisalpine Gaul Caesar lost no time mobilizing his four legions and recruiting two more, *legios* XI and XII. He then mounted two campaigns in 58 BC, against the Helvetii and the Suebi. The former were a confederation of five inter-related tribes living on the Swiss plateau. They began a huge migration westwards early in the year, almost certainly caused by climate change, with the weather dryer and colder, featuring 368,000 migrants including 92,000 warriors. In a three-month-long campaign that often hung in the balance, Caesar eventually defeated them at the Battle of Bibracte, causing great slaughter. Only 110,000 Helvetii survivors made it back to their homeland. The brutal nature of this victory set the tone for Caesar's ongoing campaign to conquer Gaul, he next targeting the German Suebi. This was an enormous confederation of tribes to the north and east of the Rhine, 120,000 of them now camped across the river in eastern Gaul. Caesar acted with characteristic swiftness and was again victorious, finally securing victory at the Battle of Vosgues. No quarter was given and the German army massacred.

While in Cisalpine Gaul during the winter of 58 and 57 BC Caesar recruited two more new legions, *legio* XIII and *legio* XIV. Next, in 57 BC he set off north again, this time targeting the Belgae tribes in northern Gaul. His specific target was the Nervii, a particularly warlike confederation whipping up resistance to the Romans. Caesar forced an engagement at the Battle of the Sabis and was again victorious, the Gauls butchered as they fled. After the distraction of renewing his triumvirate with Crassus and Pompey at the Conference of Lucca in 56 BC, Caesar again looked back to Gaul for more wealth and glory. This time his targets were the tribes along the Atlantic coastline, defeating the Veneti at the naval Battle of Morbihan Gulf in the late summer of 56 BC. Soon only the Morini tribe around modern Boulogne and the Menapii to their north, the tribes closest to Britain across *Oceanus*, were left refusing to submit to Rome. The region was broadly at peace again.

Once more Caesar wintered in Cisalpine Gaul, hoping his work to the north was now done. However, in the spring of 55 BC word reached him that a new German migration was underway. This comprised the Usipetes and Tencteri tribes from the eastern bank of the River Rhine, with some 430,000 crossing into Gaul to flee the predations of the Suebi. Caesar ordered an all-out attack, catching them by surprise. Another massacre followed, with archaeological finds recently found near the battle site at Kessel in the Netherlands showing as many 200,000 were slaughtered. Even the Senate back in Rome recoiled at brutality on this scale, but Caesar revelled in it. He felt he had prevented another German incursion into Gaul similar to that of the Suebi in 58 BC. Ignoring any criticism, he already had his eye on his next target in this intense campaigning year. This was fantastical Britain, just across today's English Channel, where he knew his ultimate glory might be found.

To this point in his career Caesar had already displayed the traits that were to later define him. Speed of thought and action, personal bravery, being a first class leader of men in battle, military skill at a strategic and tactical level, and grit and determination. Yet his next decision was to test all of these to the absolute limit, in a move that Mattingly (2006, 64) describes as '*...treading a thin line between qualified success and outright disaster*'. It is difficult to explain to a modern audience what an outlandish adventure he planned here. In the first instance his force would have to cross *Oceanus*, a sea frightful to contemporary audiences used to the comparatively benign Mediterranean. Then, once there he would be campaigning in a land of which the Romans knew little. This was truly a leap in the dark.

Caesar and Britain

Why did Caesar choose to invade Britain in the first place when there was still plenty of time in the campaigning season of 55 BC for him to seek out new opponents on the continent, or even travel to his other province of Illyricum in the north-eastern Balkans? To answer that, we can first look at basic geography. To this point, after three years of brutal campaigning and with thousands of Gallic and German warriors dead or taken prisoner, Caesar believed Gaul and Germany pacified. Meanwhile, Illyricum was too far away for the next quick victory he craved. He therefore turned his attention to the nearest suitable target in his on-going quest for wealth and glory, namely nearby Britain.

Next, Caesar himself acknowledged that Britain remained a source of instability in Gaul, saying that (*Conquest of Gaul*, V.1):

> *...in almost all the Gallic campaigns the Gauls had received reinforcements from the Britons.*

To that end, the Cantiaci in Kent were only 33km away across the English Channel, while a number of other British tribes had direct links with their counterparts in Gaul, as detailed in Chapter 2. Caesar himself confirms this, giving a prime example (*Conquest of Gaul*, V.2):

> *The Suessiones (a Belgae tribe)...possessed huge tracts of very fertile territory...ruling not only much of Belgic territory but of Britain as well.*

The tribes in Britain were also increasingly taking in large numbers of refugees from Gaul, particularly tribal elites fleeing the predations of the Romans. These and their descendants continued to be a thorn in the side of Roman Gaul until the Claudian invasion of Britain in AD 43. Additionally, thanks to the few pieces of intelligence provided by the Mediterranean merchants and geographers of prior centuries (as detailed in the Introduction), and also news gathered from those Gallic tribes with maritime contacts in Britain, Caesar knew it was a land rich in raw materials.

Finally, and most importantly, Britain presented Caesar with his ultimate challenge. A chance of unmatchable, divine glory. It is hard to explain to a modern audience what a truly fantastical adventure Caesar planned here. In the first instance his force would have to cross *Oceanus*. Such a voyage was a frightful proposition to sailors and legionaries used to the comparatively benign *mare nostrum*. Then, once in mysterious Britain, he would be campaigning in a land of which the Romans knew little. As seen, he was a man driven by destiny and the need for prestige amongst both peers and the popular classes back in Rome, as well as with his legionaries. Just landing in Britain, let alone its conquest, would set him above all of his Republican warlord rivals and predecessors, including Crassus and Pompey, and the great Marius and unbeaten Sulla. This is important as it sets Caesar's exploits in Britain firmly in the context of the winner-takes-all battle between the *optimat*es and *populares* political factions back in Rome that would eventually see the Republic implode after Caesar's later assassination in 44 BC.

Caesar states his first visit to Britain in 55 BC was more an armed reconnaissance than an attempt at conquest. This was because of the lateness of the campaigning season in 55 BC. Specifically, he says he (*Conquest of Gaul*, V.1):

> *...thought it would be of great advantage to him to merely visit the island, to see what its inhabitants were like, and to make himself acquainted with the lie of the land, the harbours, and the landing places.*

By now a seasoned commander, battle-hardened through his initial conquest campaigns in Gaul, Caesar realised his lack of intelligence about the mysterious island across *Oceanus* presented a serious problem. He quickly set out to remedy this. In the first instance, he says he (*Conquest of Gaul*, V.1):

> *...summoned to his presence traders from a wide area, but he was unable to gain any intelligence whatsoever from them: nothing about the size of the island: nor the nature or numbers of the tribes who inhabited it; nor their customs nor about such harbours as might be suitable for a sizeable fleet of large ships.*

Moorhead and Stuttard (2012, 13) argue this actually amounted to a deliberate policy of disinformation by the Gauls and Britons he interviewed, to deter him from invading. This is understandable given the severity with which Caesar had dealt with the Veneti leadership the previous year after their revolt, executing them after signing a peace agreement.

This lack of intelligence is just one manifestation of what many modern commentators say was Caesar's uncharacteristic lack of detailed planning for his 55 BC expedition. This is surprising given the level of jeopardy involved. Mattingly (2006, 65) says this lack of preparation was the principal shortcoming of what proved a flawed campaign, while Moorhead and Studdard (2012, 14) say the lack of planning was an unusual mistake for the otherwise canny Caesar.

More mistakes followed. First, he sent the wrong man to reconnoitre potential landing beaches on the eastern coast of Kent. This was Gaius

Volusenus Quadratus, the *tribunus militum* of the XIIth legion who had served with distinction in the 57 BC campaign. Caesar thought he was courageous and had good strategic sense, dispatching him with a single galley. However, even though he spent four days scouting the region, in which time he '*…sailed as far as he could without actually disembarking and risking contact with the barbarians…*' (*Conquest of Gaul*, V.1), the most suitable place he could find was the strip of beach beneath the white cliffs of Dover. This was a bizarre choice for such an experienced warrior, given the impossibility of getting off the invasion beaches if the cliff tops were defended. Just to the north were much more appropriate landing places, including the 14km broad expanses of beach ranging from modern Walmer through Deal up to Richborough, and the natural sheltered harbourage of the then navigable Wantsum Channel. Caesar clearly made a bad error selecting Volusenus (Elliott, 2019, 114).

A further miscalculation was the odd decision to send Commius, king of the Gallic branch of the Atrebates and later king of the Atrebates across the Channel, to Britain to win over hearts and minds among the tribal ruling families in Britain ahead of Caesar's arrival. Commius owed his position to Caesar, having been appointed king after the Romans had defeated the Atrebates' tribal confederation during his 57 BC campaign in northern Gaul. Caesar says he was (*Conquest of Gaul*, V.1):

> *…a man whose bravery, good sense and loyalty he had a high opinion (of) and whose authority was well respected in Britain.*

This mission was a spectacular failure, with Commius arrested and tied up as soon as he arrived in Britain. This had major repercussions when Caesar actually landed as he appears to have been relying on the natives to supply his troops with food, he not carrying enough provisions to keep his army in the field.

The campaign proper began when Caesar ordered his '*…whole army…*' (*Conquest of Gaul*, V.1), by now numbering eight legions with up to 48,000 legionaries plus allied troops, to march into the territory of the Morini tribe in north-eastern Gaul, closest to Britain. As detailed, these were one of the few tribes to refuse to submit to Rome in the 56 BC Atlantic coast campaign. However, seeing the scale of Caesar's military might, they now did so, handing the Romans a large number of hostages.

Caesar decided he only needed two of his legions for the first expedition to Britain and chose his own elite *legio* X and *legio* VII. He then selected an embarkation point, unspecified in this campaign, where he gathered a fleet of 80 transports and some war galleys to carry the legionaries. An additional 18 transports were modified to carry horses, though these were prevented from joining the fleet due to a change in wind direction. They therefore waited 13km further along the coast for the allied cavalry to arrive at their location. To protect his rear Caesar then appointed the *legates* Sabinus and Cotta to lead the six remaining legions north into the land of the Menapii, who were still refusing to submit to Roman rule. There they spent the rest of the campaigning year seeking out the elusive Gauls who concealed themselves in dense forest, the Romans eventually resorting to a slash and burn strategy to destroy their crops and villages. Meanwhile, Caesar instructed another *legate* called Publius Sulpicus Rufus to build defences around, and then to protect, his main port of embarkation.

Caesar now waited for favourable weather conditions before setting off across *Oceanus* to Britain, departing just before midnight on the chosen day. His cavalry transports had orders to follow, but were too late in departing and missed the tide, they being carried back to the Gallic coast. A new attempt to transport the cavalry four days later also failed, leaving Caesar to fight the forthcoming campaign in unknown territory without his cavalry. These would have provided his main scouting function, as well as the means to pursue a broken enemy to prevent them regrouping. The lack of both capabilities proved serious shortcomings in the forthcoming campaign.

His main fleet began to arrive off the White Cliffs of Dover around 9am the following morning, with Caesar in one of the lead ships. The flawed choice of landing place by Volusenus was immediately clear, as was the failure of the hearts and minds gamble with Commius, given the cliff and hilltops were swarming with native British warriors. Viewing the arrayed enemy, Caesar immediately decided this first choice of landing place was highly impractical and ordered the arriving fleet to drop anchor just off the coast out of missile range. By 3pm all of the main force transports and warships had arrived. Caesar now gathered his officers to consider his options. After taking counsel he decided to act quickly, setting off northwards to find an uncontested landing place before nightfall. The fleet eventually anchored off Deal where the fine, evenly sloped expanse of beach was undefended (*Conquest of Gaul*, V.1). However, when the Romans tried to run the transports aground to allow the legionaries to disembark they found the size of the vessels made this impractical in the shallow foreshore. To compound his difficulties, by the time Caesar became aware of this the Britons had begun to arrive, first the chariots and cavalry and then the foot troops. Soon the native army was once more arrayed to oppose his landing.

Caesar was now forced to carry out a full amphibious assault. For this he drove his war galleys hard ashore to the north of the landing beaches where he aimed to turn the Britons' right flank. From here the galleys enfiladed the landing area with ballista, bows and slings to try to drive the natives from the shore. He then ordered the transports to get as close to the beach as possible. However, even with the covering fire from his war galleys, the legionaries were reluctant to land. An iconic incident now occurred when the *aquilifer* standard bearer of *legio* X, carrying the legion's *aquila* eagle standard, leapt into the shallows, shouting (*Conquest of Gaul*, V.1):

> *Leap, fellow soldiers, unless you wish to betray your eagle to the enemy. I, for my part, will perform my duty to the Republic and to my general.*

The shamed legionaries now jumped into the shallows and swarmed ashore to protect their eagle, this taking longer than expected given the larger transports continued to struggle to get close to the beach. Once ashore the legionaries rallied to the nearest unit standard rather than their own usual *vexilla* given the confusion, with the Britons trying to isolate small groups as they landed and kill them. Caesar countered by ordering the *myoparo* and *scapha* cutters and skiffs (Elliott, 2016, 43) supporting the fleet to be loaded with troops and used as a maritime mobile reserve, deploying here and there where the fighting was fiercest. The picture painted by Caesar is of a very confusing battle, often the case with contested beach landings, the engagement clearly a close run thing. Caesar himself admits that both sides fought hard (*Conquest of Gaul*, V.1). However, eventually the legionaries' better training and equipment came to the fore and they pushed the Britons back off the beach. Soon the native troops began to flee and the Romans secured the landing zone. As night fell Caesar could claim victory given they had control of the battlefield, though the lack of cavalry prevented the Romans from pursuing the beaten enemy who soon reformed close by.

Having been on the receiving end of the Roman military machine for the first time, the British leaders quickly decided that peace, at least in the short term, was the most desirable outcome and sent envoys to Caesar. These said that they had only attacked the Romans through ignorance, and to show their good intentions handed over Commius, Caesar's failed envoy (Elliott, 2019, 115). The Romans demanded more hostages to secure the agreement, and when these started to arrive an uneasy peace settled in eastern Kent.

The beachhead secure, Caesar now ordered the building of a large marching camp for his two legions. However, the British weather now dramatically intervened. While Caesar's legionaries were well protected in their new camp, the vessels used by the Romans to travel from the continent were not. On the fourth day ashore a violent storm arose, which together with a high tide damaged many of the Roman ships riding at anchor, some being destroyed. It was this event that prevented the cavalry transports arriving on their second attempt to cross to Britain. It also presented Caesar with a conundrum as he had travelled without any significant food stores, hoping to rely on the natives or on his fleet ferrying provisions from the continent. He was now forced to divide his army into two, the Xth legion to repair his ships and the VIIth to forage locally for what he describes as corn (*Conquest of Gaul*, V.1). The former were successful at their task, with all but 12 vessels repaired. However the latter presented the native Britons with too tempting an opportunity. Their leadership, having learned of Caesar's misfortune, now resumed their hostility.

Caesar narrates that as the VIIth legion went about their business gathering food they were ambushed by the Britons and found themselves in danger of being overwhelmed (*Conquest of Gaul*, V.1). The Roman marching camp guards noticed the native advance in the distance as a large dust cloud and Caesar ordered two cohorts of the Xth legion, led by him in person, to march to the relief of the VIIth. This they did, the Romans then withdrawing in good order back to the safety of their camp. For some reason the Britons didn't press their attack and withdrew. The Roman lack of cavalry is again evident here as this would have provided both an earlier warning of the initial attack, and then been in place to pursue the Britons as they departed.

More bad weather followed, allowing the British leadership to send messengers far and wide to gather an army large enough to challenge Caesar's two legions. They impressed on the neighbouring tribes the small size of the Roman force and the chance for booty, egged on no doubt by the Gallic refugees within their midst. Caesar decided to draw them to him rather than risk another ambush and deployed his two legions in front of his marching camp, bolstered by the arrival of 30 horsemen from Gaul (not his actual cavalry contingent, these from his legionary port of embarkation). The Britons took the bait and attacked, though again the Romans were victorious, with the Britons once more fleeing. Caesar pursued as far as possible, before again withdrawing his troops back to the safety of the camp.

The defeated natives now sued for peace again. As before Caesar agreed, but this time asked for twice as many hostages. Soon after this he decided to withdraw back to Gaul, knowing he lacked the provisions to overwinter in Britain, and not wanting to subject his repaired ships to a crossing of *Oceanus* any later in the year. A favourable wind made the return crossing a success, excepting two transports that were blown too far to the north. These landed among Morini still hostile to Rome, and soon 300 legionaries were surrounded by an increasingly large force of natives keen on booty. They held out for four hours until Caesar's rescue force of cavalry arrived, at which point the Morini fled. Caesar then sent the *legate* Labienus with the VIIth and Xth legions, newly back from Britain, to attack the rebellious Morini, who were all killed or captured. Caesar then gathered his scribes, as he had at the end of each earlier year campaigning in Gaul, and sent dispatches back to Rome. As usual these portrayed his campaigns in a positive light and were well received given the Senate decreed 20 days of public thanksgiving. However, looking back across *Oceanus* towards Britain, Caesar knew he still had unfinished business there. Suetonius certainly thought so too, describing Caesar's first incursion to Britain as one of only three serious reverses in his military career, though being careful to say it was in the context of the poor weather (*The Twelve Caesars*, 1.25).

Caesar made his decision to carry out a second expedition to Britain before the end of 55 BC, giving orders to his *legates* to start building a bespoke fleet of ships more appropriate for a large invasion than those used in his first incursion. He then headed back to Cisalpine Gaul to winter in his usual quarters there.

Early in the New Year, after a brief visit to his other province of Illyricum, he returned to the territory of the Morini where he gathered his entire army of eight legions again, together with 4,000 Gallic allied cavalry. This time we learn the name of the chosen port of embarkation for Britain, *Portus Itius*. Grainge (2005, 90) usefully sets out the various candidate sites in the region, all to the south of modern Calais with its short journey across *Oceanus* to Britain. The most northerly is Wissant near Cap Gris Nez, while the most southerly is the later major port site at Boulogne (the future headquarters of the *Classis Britannica* regional fleet). The latter seems the most likely given the fine harbourage there in the estuary of the River Liane.

When Caesar arrived he was pleased with the work of his *legates* and their shipbuilders, with 600 specially built vessels ready for service. These, based on designs of the Veneti, featured lower freeboards than his earlier Mediterranean designs to enable easier disembarkation, banks of oars as well as a large sail to give good manoeuvrability in shallow waters, and wider beams to carry bulkier loads (*The Conquest of Gaul*, V.2). To these he added 200 locally chartered transports, over 80 Roman transport ships that had survived the previous year's incursion, and his 28 remaining war galleys.

Before starting his second British campaign Caesar quickly moved to secure his rear once more, mounting a brief campaign against the Treveri tribe to the north bordering the Rhine. These were famous for their cavalry, and here he helped resolve a leadership dispute. All was now set for his second invasion.

Caesar's force this time was far bigger, taking five entire legions with 30,000 legionaries and 2,000 cavalry. He left the remainder, three legions and 2,000 more cavalry, under the command of the *legate* Labienus with orders to protect the regional ports on the Gallic coast, ensure a regular supply of provisions to Caesar in Britain, and generally keep an eye on Gaul.

The fleet set sail northwards on 6 July at sunset using a light south-westerly breeze. At first progress across *Oceanus* was good, but around midnight the wind dropped and Caesar's fleet began to drift with the tide northwards. At daybreak on 7 July it became evident that the fleet had drifted '*far out of his course by the tidal current….(with) Britain left behind on the port side*' (*The Conquest of Gaul*, V.2). Modern interpretations, based on our knowledge of the then tidal streams and weather, have interpreted Caesar's location at this point as anywhere between Dover and, to north, the treacherous Goodwin Sands off the then Isle of Thanet (Grainge, 2005, 102). Wherever they were as the sun rose, this expedition was far better prepared than that of the previous year and Caesar calmly gave orders for the transports and warships to deploy their oars and row for the British coast. He aimed for the invasion beaches of 54 BC, greatly aided by a far better knowledge of the tidal streams in the Dover Strait than the previous year. The rowers worked in shifts and soon the large fleet made landfall near Deal again.

This time Caesar's far bigger force intimidated the Britons and the landing was unopposed. Later intelligence indicated a native army had gathered on the high ground above the invasion beaches, but when the leaders saw the size of the Roman fleet they withdrew inland. Once ashore the

Romans looked to build a large marching camp, and here new archaeological evidence has enabled us to piece together the strategy followed by Caesar.

As detailed in Chapter 1, Roman marching camps are of great use to the archaeologist and historian when attempting to understand a specific military campaign. This is because even though deliberately slighted they frequently leave very noticeable crop marks outlining their playing card shape, not surprising given their substantial size when in use. Matching these to the known size of the campaigning force allows us to track the routes taken by various campaigning armies, for example in a British context those in Scotland of Agricola in the late 1st century AD or Severus in the early 3rd century AD. In that regard, there should therefore be three such routes visible in Kent, namely those of Caesar in his 55 BC and 54 BC campaigns, and that of the AD 43 Claudian invasion. Surprisingly, until recently none have been found. However, we are fortunate that now one has been located, and identified in the context of Caesar's second 54 BC incursion.

The camp in question is 20ha in size, large enough to accommodate two legions. It was first located in 2010 when archaeologists found a large defensive ditch five metres wide and two metres deep during a rescue archaeology project in advance of the building of a road at Ebbsfleet near Pegwell Bay. The ditch is the standard size for one protecting a Roman marching camp. Later investigations at the site by University of Leicester archaeologists funded by the Leverhulme Project using geophysical surveys in 2015–16 and trial excavations in 2016–17 confirmed it as such. The geophysical survey revealed the plan of the western part of the camp including two standard marching camp entrances. The overall design is very similar to those later used by Caesar in his Alesia campaign in 52 BC. Meanwhile, the excavations found coins and pottery that have been used to date it to the 54 BC campaign. A discarded *pilum* head, and human bones showing signs of combat trauma, were also found there. The latter are likely the remains of British dead hastily buried in the ditch when the camp was abandoned. However, its location is the most interesting factor as it is actually on what was then the Isle of Thanet, separated from the British mainland by the Wantsum Channel. As detailed earlier in the chapter this was then a substantial waterway. This location is some way from the invasion beaches at Deal, and therefore presents a conundrum as at no time does Caesar indicate that he built his landing marching camp away from the native Britons across a substantial waterway.

There are two explanations for this perceived discrepancy. First, Caesar was being deliberately disingenuous in his narrative in *The Conquest of Gaul* and actually started his 54 BC campaign on a defensive footing, mindful of his difficulties the previous year. Or secondly, the camp on Thanet is of a different nature, namely a supply base to ensure Caesar had sufficient provisions in a defendable location to support his second campaign. Analogously this is a common feature of many Roman campaigns where a significant commitment in terms of manpower was made. Good examples include the fortified supply bases at Cramond on the River Forth and Carpow on the River Tay. The former, just over 2ha in size, was first built in the Antonine period as part of the Antonine Wall construction programme for which it played a major supporting role. It was later used as a key node in the east coast supply chain during the attempts by Septimius Severus to conquer Scotland in AD 209 and AD 210. Meanwhile, Carpow was built to support the Agricolan attempts to conquer Scotland in the Flavian period, later again being used during the campaigns of Septimius Severus (Elliott, 2018a, 71). The implication of this latter interpretation is that Caesar may have actually been planning to stay in Britain in 54 BC, his invasion a full attempt at conquest.

If the camp on Thanet was a supply depot, then the marching camp he references would have been opposite on the mainland, to the south nearer the invasion beaches. Here Caesar left a force of 10 cohorts of legionaries and 300 of his allied cavalry under the legate Quintus Atrius to protect his invasion fleet. These vessels had all been anchored in a sheltered location. This was almost certainly in the Wantsum Channel itself, to the north of the invasion beaches. The aim here was to avoid the damage suffered the previous year during bad weather.

Caesar set off at midnight the day after landing, his cavalry quickly locating the gathered Britons 20km inland. The British leaders tried to halt Caesar's advance on a river line, probably one of the branches of the nearby River Stour. Here they deployed their chariots and cavalry forward. These were quickly driven back by Caesar's cavalry and soon the Romans were across the river line and heading for the major Cantiaci *oppida* settlement where Canterbury is located today. There he learned that the British force had withdrawn to the nearby hill fort at Bigbury 3.2km to the west. Here they had blocked up all of the main entrances with felled logs. This 10.7 ha fortification, atop high ground overlooking modern Canterbury, presented Caesar with a significant obstacle. He decided to storm it at once and ordered the VIIth legion into the attack. The veteran legionaries used their *testudo* tortoise formation with interlocked shields around and above them to force the gates under cover of a missile bombardment of ballista bolts and slingshot. The Britons quickly capitulated, those able to do so escaping to nearby woods. Caesar ordered his cavalry to pursue for a short distance. He then reformed his force to build a marching camp for the night.

Next morning Caesar resolved to force a meeting engagement with the Britons, dividing his force into three legionary spearheads. However, as he progressed and with the enemy now in sight, he got word from Atrius that the fleet had yet again been devastated by a violent overnight Channel storm. This had been so severe that the anchors and cables holding them in place, even in the sheltered waters where they were located, had broken or snapped. Many had been driven hard ashore or against each other, with every ship damaged in some way. Some 40 were totally wrecked and unsalvageable. Caesar therefore left a holding force facing the Britons at Bigbury and then sent all of his remaining legionaries back to the ships to begin urgent repairs. He also sent word by swift galley to Labienus in Gaul to send more specialist carpenters and to build more vessels to replace those damaged. When this vessel returned it was with very sad news for Caesar. His daughter Julia, wife of Pompey, had died during childbirth, their baby dying shortly afterwards. Caesar set aside his grief for the moment and focused on the campaign at hand. The ship repairs took 10 days and once complete Caesar had all the vessels hauled on to the nearby beaches. He then extended his coastal marching camp around them to provide protection. This huge undertaking complete, he left the same 10 cohorts and 300 cavalry to guard the site and set off once more inland.

This time Caesar kept his legions together as one large legionary force, and was soon making serious headway into Kent. Here it faced a combined British tribal army commanded by a king called Cassivellaunus. In his *Conquest of Gaul* Caesar doesn't reference his tribe, but does say the River Thames divided the lands he ruled. He adds that in recent inter-tribal conflict Cassivellaunus had beaten the Trinovantes in eastern Essex. This seems to indicate he was the king of the Catuvellauni to their west. The description of the Thames dividing the lands he ruled would indicate the Cantiaci in Kent were his vassals at the time.

The Britons avoided a set piece battle at this stage, relying on hit and run tactics by their chariots and cavalry to engage the Romans on the march. Their infantry also ambushed out of woodland when the Romans were building their marching camps. Caesar says that on every occasion his troops bested the Britons, though it did test the discipline of the Romans who were eager to pursue their defeated opponents. He realized the enemy were trying to lure small parties into ambushes and ensured that the order of march was maintained. Only on one occasion did he feel his forces endangered, when a large British force attacked a part-built marching camp. Caesar responded quickly, sending two cohorts to their rescue. The rescuers themselves then came under pressure, with a military tribune called Quintus Laberius Drurus killed during the fighting. Caesar was forced to send in more cohorts to stabilize the situation, and eventually the Britons were driven off again.

Caesar describes the Britons using complex tactics in these engagements, always trying to lure the Romans away in small numbers and using concealed troops to screen any advances or retreats. He notes particularly that when the enemy were operating in this fluid way the legionaries in their heavy *lorica hamata* mail hauberks were at a disadvantage as they simply couldn't keep up with their elusive foe. He adds that even his allied cavalry was at a disadvantage against the British chariots as his Gauls often pursued the British into terrain unsuitable for mounted troops. At that point the charioteers would dismount and fight on foot where they had the advantage (*The Conquest of Gaul*, V.2).

The following day Caesar got his meeting engagement, though not on his own terms. The combined British force under Cassivellaunus had re-gathered and deployed on high ground some distance from Caesar's overnight marching camp. The Romans felt secure enough to send three legions out to forage, together with all of the cavalry. This force was put under the command of the experienced *legate* Gaius Trebonius. However, as soon as the foraging column had travelled some distance from the camp the Britons attacked in a fluid movement that enveloped the head and both flanks of the column. Caesar (*The Conquest of Gaul*, V.2) describes the fighting as so fierce that the Britons came close to capturing the legionary *aquila* eagle standards. This battle was clearly a close run thing, far too close for comfort for Caesar. However, Roman discipline again won out and eventually a ferocious charge by Caesar's cavalry routed the Britons who fled in panic, thousands being cut down in the ensuing pursuit. Any surviving Britons returned to their respective tribes as quickly as possible, with Cassivellaunus unable to gather a combined army from that point. He fled back north over the Thames, with Caesar in hot pursuit.

At this point Caesar gives the first insight into the likely route taken by his legionaries and allied cavalry, given there is no mention of any other river than the Thames. This is in direct contrast to the AD 43

Claudian invasion. Here, Cassius Dio in his *Roman History* describes the famous river crossing battle where the Roman advance through central Kent was almost halted at a defended river line bisecting the modern county (*Roman History*, 60.19 - 23). This was almost certainly the River Medway, with Aylesford located as the battle site (Elliott, 2016, 115). The lack of any mention of this natural defensive feature by Caesar indicates he was operating north of the North Downs along the northern coast of Kent where the Romans later built Watling Street. Here he would have been able to rely on his fleet to protect his littoral flank and keep him supplied as necessary.

Caesar now decided to force a crossing of the Thames in pursuit of Cassivellaunus. He chose a place he describes as the only one fordable by his army. Again, analogy with the later Claudian invasion is useful here to enable this location to be identified. It has recently been determined that the AD 43 invasion force under the *legate* Aulus Plautius crossed the Thames at a location between Higham on the south bank and Tilbury on the north, the line of the later medieval ferry there and the lowest fordable point during the Roman period when it was marshy and featured many islands, particularly at low tide (Elliott, 2016, 116). This was almost certainly where Caesar chose to cross, which would take him into the lands of the Trinovantes. These were now allies of Cassivellaunus given his recent victory over them when he had killed their king and replaced him with a supporter.

Cassivellaunus had not been idle and had gathered a new army from among his own Catuvellauni tribe, and from his Trinovantian allies. This he arrayed on the north bank of the Thames to oppose any crossing by Caesar. The latter knew momentum was the key to success here, though he checked his advance for a short time to scout the crossing, wary of further British ambushes. This proved a shrewd move as his reconnaissance, together with intelligence from captive Britons, revealed the north side of the crossing was protected with sharpened stakes. These had been placed both along the bank, and below the waterline. Caesar therefore deployed his legionary pioneers and engineering specialists in the vanguard of the assault. He then ordered a general advance, his cavalry following the pioneers as the latter opened routes through the British defences. To cover this operation he deployed his war galleys, where the *ballistae*, archers and slingers kept the heads of the British defenders down. Caesar then ordered his legionaries forward. These were so eager to get to grips with the enemy that, even though up to their necks in the river as they crossed, they soon caught up with the cavalry. Both the mounted troops and foot thus hit the Britons on the north bank at the same time. The defenders were soon overpowered and again fled.

Caesar pursued a short distance, then recalled his troops to build a marching camp for the night, his first north of the Thames. Cassivellaunus, defeated again and again when the Romans could get to grips with his warriors, now disbanded his foot troops and headed westward to his own Catuvellaunian territory. Here he changed his strategy back to the use of hit and run ambushes using only his chariots. Caesar says he retained 4,000 charioteers to man them (*Conquest of Gaul*, V.2). These repeatedly attacked Roman scouting cavalry and foraging parties, using pathways they knew well through local woodland to mask their approach and make their escape.

Given his enemy was now avoiding open battle, Caesar instigated a scorched earth policy as he passed through the territory of the Catuvellauni, burning settlements and crops and totally destroying the local economy. At this point, a delegation arrived in his camp from the Trinovantes to the east. This was led by Mandubracius, a young prince who had fled to seek protection from Caesar on the continent at the beginning of the decade. His father, a king of the Trinovantes possibly called Imanuenteous, had been killed by Cassivellaunus when the latter had earlier asserted his authority over his eastern neighbours. Mandubracius asked that Caesar allow him to return home to rule the Trinovantes as an ally of Rome. Caesar agreed, in return for 40 hostages and grain. When these arrived Mandubracius was duly installed as the new Trinovantian king, with Cassivellaunus' own puppet ruler deposed. When word of this spread elsewhere other tribes now came forward to surrender to Caesar. From these he learned that Cassivellaunus had retreated to his capital. This was a heavily fortified *oppida* featuring substantial surrounding ditches, earthen banks, palisades and defended gateways. Its location has long been contested, with candidate sites including Gatesbury, Redbourn, Baldock, Ravensburgh Castle and Wallbury Camp (Moorhead and Stuttard, 33). However, the most likely location is Wheathampstead in the upper Lea Valley in modern Hertfordshire. Here, the Late Iron Age defences were so impressive that some remain visible today, particularly the 30m wide and 12m deep Devil's Dyke.

Keen to bring the campaign to a conclusion, Caesar headed straight for the *oppida*. Given it was now late in the campaigning season he resolved to immediately assault the fortification rather than risk a lengthy siege. His legionaries attacked on two sides in *testudo* formation, forcing the gateways under covering fire from *ballistae* and slingers. Soon, despite the impressive defences, Caesar was again victorious. Those Britons that could fled through the gateways on a side the Romans had yet to attack.

Cassivellaunus once more sought sanctuary in nearby woodland. He now changed tactics yet again, this time sending word to his Cantiaci vassals back in Kent to attack Caesar's naval camp. This was either the mainland camp that had been extended to protect the beached ships, or the supply base on Thanet detailed earlier. Caesar here names four Cantiaci kings as the recipients of the new orders, these being Cingetorix, Carvilius, Taximagulus and Segovax. They were singularly unsuccessful, the defending 10 cohorts of legionaries and 300 cavalry intercepting the British force and quickly defeating it on open battle. Again many Britons were killed as they fled, including a leading noble called Lugotorix.

This was the last attempt by Cassivellaunus to resist the Romans. Having suffered so many reverses on the battlefield, seen his allies desert him, had his capital captured and his lands ravaged, he now sued for peace. Terms were quickly agreed, including supplying more hostages and agreeing to pay an annual tribute to Rome. The Catuvellauni king also pledged to leave the Trinovantes unmolested. Honour satisfied, Caesar now returned to the landing zone in Kent. Here he determined to return to Gaul for the winter, having received word that some of the Gallic tribes were again considering rebellion. Given his large number of hostages, the captive Britons due to be sold into slavery, and his earlier ship losses, Caesar decided to embark back to the continent in two waves. The first travelled back safely, but these vessels were then prevented from returning by more bad weather. Caesar now decided to risk packing his remaining troops onto the few serviceable vessels left in Britain, these the war galleys that had supported his Thames operation. They arrived back safely in Gaul at the end of September, and thus ended Caesar's adventures in Britain.

Aftermath

Caesar was never to return to the mysterious island of Britain across *Oceanus*. When he arrived back in Gaul he found it was indeed on the verge of rebellion, and the final two years of his conquest of Gaul was spent in an increasingly brutal series of campaigns to stamp out the last embers of Gallic resistance. At first he suffered a number of severe setbacks, including the wiping out of the entire *legio* XIV by the Eburones tribe in Gallia Belgica. However, gradually the Romans asserted their authority in their usual sanguineous fashion and the final Great Revolt led by Vercingetorix was crushed at the Siege of Alesia in 52 BC.

Distractions back in Rome were also to divert Caesar's attention away from any further visit to Britain. Here, his triumvirate with Pompey and Crassus was coming to a dramatic end. First, his ties with Pompey unravelled as soon as his daughter Julia passed away in childbirth, with the champion of the *optimates* declining a subsequent offer of marriage to Caesar's great-niece. Next, his relationship with Crassus and his supporters dramatically ended when the highly-ambitious patrician was killed while leading his legions in a doomed campaign in the east against the Parthians in 53 BC. Further, when he had arrived back in Gaul in 54 BC after his last British campaign, Caesar also learned that his mother Aurelia, whose family had strong ties with the *optimates*, had died. From now on Caesar and Pompey, the leaders of the two political factions in Rome, were increasingly at odds, with matters coming to a head as the decade ended. This set the scene for the subsequent bitter civil wars of the AD 40s and Caesar's ultimate demise at the hands of the pro-Republic *libatores*.

In terms of the specific legacy of Caesar's two incursions to Britain, although they were clearly not the campaigns of conquest that were to follow in the Principate Empire, they did for the first time put Britain on the Roman map. Tacitus (*Agricola*, 13) neatly sums this up, saying Caesar '*...bequeathed Britain to future generations (of Romans)*'. A strong case can be made that Caesar himself certainly thought he was doing this. Before he returned to Gaul in 54 BC he established political links with his defeated opponent Cassivellaunus and other leaders in Britain. This included the all-important tribute, flowing annually to Rome, this reminding the native leaders who had the upper hand in this new relationship. Now an insidious process began whereby Roman influence, particularly economic, began to gradually manifest in Britain, certainly in the southeast. The final conquest of Gaul and its assimilation into the Roman world accelerated this process. As Haywood says (2009, 82):

> *Caesar's...conquest of Gaul opened south-eastern Britain to strong Romanizing influences through trade and diplomacy. Romanizing influences are apparent in an increase in luxury imports, especially wine and a (new) Roman-style coinage with inscriptions in the Latin alphabet. British kings actively sought Roman support and some even travelled to Rome itself.*

One manifestation of this growing Roman influence in once-feared Britain was the arrival in increasing numbers of Roman merchants, there to import Roman material culture to the native elites and export the latter's own agricultural surplus, manufactured goods and slaves back to the continent (Elliott, 2016, 18). This soon led to the setting up of Roman trading posts, one perhaps atop Cornhill on the high ground north of the River Thames where the later provincial capital London (Roman *Londinium*) was established. Roman political and economic influence was here to stay. Military conquest was to follow in short order.

Chapter 4

The Claudian Invasion of Britain

Caesar's assassination in 44 BC initiated a vicious spiral of violence between the leading *optimates* and *populares* warlords across the Roman world. In these circumstances Britain was, for a time, forgotten as a candidate territory for the next phase of Roman territorial expansion. However, trade did continue through Roman mercantile activity, with Strabo indicating just how profitable this was (*Geography*, 5.8):

> *At the moment more revenue is gained from customs duties than tribute could bring in, if you deduct the cost of the forces that would be needed to garrison the country and collect the tribute.*

Interestingly, it is not clear from this statement whether the tribute promised to Caesar by Cassivellaunus and other leaders in Britain was still being paid by the time Strabo began his best-known work in the 20s BC. Even if not though, it seems Britain was for a time still seen as a source of steady revenue for the late Republic, if only from customs alone.

However, foreign adventure was soon back on the agenda. Octavian was by now the last man standing after the last bitter round of Republican civil wars, and from that time onwards the Romans increasingly cast their eyes avariciously across *Oceanus* to the archipelago less than a day's sailing away from Gaul. From that point there were three serious phases of planned invasion of Britain. The first involved a number of initiatives by the now mighty Augustus himself. The next involved the unlikely sounding Caligula, while the last was the successful AD 43 invasion of Claudius. All are considered here, the latter in great detail.

Augustus and Caligula

The Senate's styling of Octavian as Augustus in 27 BC traditionally marks the beginning of the Roman Empire, and end of the Republic. However, his interest in Britain actually began earlier, even before his climactic victory at the naval Battle of Actium in 31 BC against Mark Antony and Cleopatra VII Philopator. We know this through Dio who says that in 34 BC Octavian planned an expedition to Britain, but called it off because of a revolt in Dalmatia, the newly conquered territories to the north and east of Caesar's old province of Illyricum (*Roman History*, 49.38). Augustus next planned to invade Britain in 27 BC, with the political classes in Rome clearly wanting another successful foreign adventure and grand triumph. For example, the late-1st century BC Latin poet Albius Tibullus wrote in anticipation ahead of his departure (III, 7,147f):

> *Where ocean embraces the world with its waters, no kingdom will meet you with hostile intent, only the Briton remains, still undefeated by Rome's might.*

However, once more the new conquest was not to be, with Dio saying (53.22):

> *He set out to make his expedition to Britain, but on coming to the provinces of Gaul lingered there. For the Britons seemed likely to make terms with him, and the affairs of the Gauls were…unsettled.*

Southern (2013, 48) makes the case that the context for this second planned invasion was the cessation of tribute payment to the Romans at some stage by the British. She argues that the tribal elites there would have been far more comfortable dealing with a specific individual, this initially in the form of Caesar himself, than with the comparatively amorphous Roman state. Under this hypothesis, the tribute would have been paid as normal until Caesar's murder in 44 BC, and then may have gradually fallen off. Indeed, this may also have been the reason Augustus had planned to launch his earlier 34 BC expedition to Britain.

Even if the threat of his second invasion was enough to have the tribute from Britain resume, this clearly wasn't for long because in 25 BC Augustus planned a third incursion to Britain, with Dio saying that in that year (53.25):

> *"Augustus was planning an expedition into Britain, since the people there would not come to terms, but he was detained by the revolt of the Salassi and by the hostility of the Cantabri and Astures."*

Here Augustus, already in Gaul with his legions preparing to invade Britain, suddenly found himself fighting on two unexpected fronts. The Salassi were a particularly troublesome Gallic or Celticized Ligurian tribe whose lands were located on the Italian side of the Little St Bernard Pass and the Great St Bernard Pass, over the Pennine Alps. Only recently conquered by Rome, they now rose in revolt, though they were quickly defeated and then disappear from history. Meanwhile, in Spain Augustus' armies were in the midst of his Cantabrian War, the lengthy campaign from 29 BC to 19 BC where he aimed to conquer the far north of the Iberian Peninsula. There, the Cantabri and Astures now went on the offensive, forcing Augustus to redeploy some of his legions south from Gaul to bolster the Roman forces already engaged.

The timing of the Spanish belligerence here is interesting. The lands of the Cantabri and Astures were the only free regions left in the Iberian Peninsula. The peoples there had long engaged in a once expansive long-range maritime trading network with Britain (Cunliffe, 2008, 231). In that context, it is not unreasonable to suggest that the Britons still in contact with Spain encouraged their trading partners to turn Augustus' attention away from Britain. This was clearly successful, with Augustus having to maintain a significant military presence in Spain for another six years. Ultimately he would have to commit eight legions before he was finally victorious, and even afterwards the Romans always maintained a legion at modern León (the Roman legionary fortress of *Castra Legionis*) to maintain order there.

Augustus had two final opportunities to engage directly with Britain. He recorded these himself in his *Res Gestae Divi Augustus* (The Deeds of the Divine Augustus) list of his own accomplishments. This was written down at some stage before his death in AD 14, and then left in his will with instructions for the Senate to set up inscriptions of it across the Empire to celebrate his life. Many copies were made, some of which survive today. The most complete was found in the ruins of a temple to Augustus in Ankara (Roman *Ankrya*, capital of the province of Galatia).

In his *Res Gestae* Augustus details two British kings who came to visit him, either separately or together, to ask for help fighting off their aggressive neighbours. One is named only in part as 'Tin…' on the various surviving sections of the inscription, with the remaining letters missing. This man was initially identified as Tincommius, a son or descendant of the Atrebatian king Commius of Julius Caesar fame (see Chapter 3). However, more recently coins minted in the name of a king called Tincomarus have been found in Atrebatian territory in Hampshire, and it is now thought the latter was most likely the individual named. The two may actually reference the same person. Meanwhile, the other king is named in full as Dubnovellaunus of the Trinovantes (Southern, 2013, 50). The fact that the chiefs were from the Atrebates and Trinovantes tribes seems to point the finger of aggression squarely at the Catuvellauni, with whom they were neighbours to the south and east respectively. By now the latter's territories extended from the Thames Valley to western Essex, and then north as far as Northamptonshire. They were increasingly dominating political and military activity in the south east of Britain, and we are fortunate to have direct evidence of this. Once again this is in the form of minted coins, this time in the name of a king of the Catuvellauni called Tasciovanus, who by 15 BC had succeeded Caesar's protagonist Cassivellaunus (if indeed the latter had been king of the Catuvellauni, see Chapter 3). Some of Tasciovanus' coinage has stamps indicating they were minted in Colchester, the usual capital of the Trinovantes. This indicates that by this time the Catuvellauni had conquered much of the territory of the Trinovantes, including their capital. Indeed, later when Aulus Plautius led the Claudian invasion of Britain, this huge *oppida* had become the actual capital of the Catuvellauni's expanded territory. In a further link to the AD 43 campaign, Tasciovanus was the predecessor of the well-known Catuvellauni king Cunobelinus whose later death set in train the events that led to the successful Claudian invasion of Britain (see below).

Returning to Augustus, sadly the *Res Gestae* doesn't provide a date for the visit, or visits, of the two kings he details. It could be that they were associated with Augustus' three known planned campaigns in Britain, detailed above. However, we have no specific evidence to tie either king to these. If they weren't involved with those, then their visits occurred at some stage between 25 BC and AD 7, by which time the *Res Getae* is thought to have been completed.

We therefore have at least three, and possibly five, occasions when the great Augustus could have campaigned in Britain. The fact he didn't might seem odd given his earlier impeccable campaigning credentials, indicating he was perhaps fighting shy of such an epic undertaking, especially given Caesar's earlier failures to overwinter there. However, the one thing Augustus was above all else by this stage in his career was pragmatic. In that regard, Goldsworthy (2014, 3) notes that although he was at times a gambler, by and large this was a far more common trait earlier when fighting in the last round of Republican civil wars. Later in his career, with regard to Britain, he would certainly have been aware what a mighty undertaking invading there was. I therefore think he simply judged that when each opportunity presented itself, it was ultimately not worth the effort, especially given the known distractions at the time of the three detailed opportunities.

However, the failure to conquer Britain certainly played on the wider Roman psyche, with each false start certainly viewed negatively at the time. Even the late-1st century BC poet Horace, usually a supporter of and apologist for Augustus, reflected that (*Odes*, III.5):

> *...Augustus will be deemed a God on Earth when the Britons and the deadly Parthians (also targets for early Imperial Roman expansion) have been added to our Empire.*

This poetic quote is noteworthy for two reasons, both relating to the setting of a very high bar for Augustus to achieve deification. The first is the most obvious. Though Horace fought with the *liberators* on the losing side at the Battle of Philippi in 42 BC against Mark Antony and Octavian, he is usually accused of being a propagandist for the Augustan Imperial project. Some argue this was through the influence of the poet's patron Gaius Cilnius Maecenas, friend and a chief adviser to Octavian and later Augustus, which makes it even stranger that Horace should draw attention here to previous failures. The second is the reference to the Arsacid Parthian empire alongside the Britons. The former, until the arrival of their Sassanid Persian successors, were Rome's principal threat in the east. They were the nearest thing the Republic, and later the Principate Empire, faced to a symmetrical threat. For Britain to analogously be set on this level was high praise indeed, though of the wrong kind given its ultimate fate.

Despite his many successes, Augustus was never to set foot in Britain. In the latter part of his reign, with his attention drawn elsewhere, he instead relied on foreign policy and economic engagement to steadily draw Britain towards the world of Rome. As Moorhead and Stuttard detail (2012, 38):

> *There are more ways to conquer than simply through war. Already the south of Britain was being sucked into the economic sphere of Rome. Roman luxury goods, silver, bronze and glass, began to (increasingly) find their way into the hands of powerful Britons.*

His conservative and risk-averse successor Tiberius (AD 14 to AD 37) also showed no interest in the costly prospect of further military adventure in

Britain. This was instead left to that most unlikely of candidates, his own successor Caligula (AD 37 to AD 41).

By AD 40 the new emperor was desperate for a successful military adventure to bring him the fame and adulation he openly craved. Actually called Gaius Julius Caesar, he'd grown up on campaign with his father Germanicus Julius Caesar, the grandson of Augustus' second wife Livia Drusilla. While there, he'd worn a child's legionary uniform specially made for him, including diminutive *caligae* marching boots, hence his nickname Caligula. Having been made emperor by the Praetorian Guard prefect Naevius Sutorius Macro after Tiberius' death, he now found himself completely unable to live up to the high martial standards set by his Julio-Claudian forebears. Caligula's first foreign policy venture had shocked Rome, in the context of his annexation of the Roman client state of Mauretania in AD 40. This was because, as a precursor, he'd invited its last king Ptolemy to Rome for discussions. Caligula then promptly had him assassinated, for reasons unknown, before snatching his kingdom.

To remedy his growing ills at home Caligula now decided the solution to his problems lay along the Rhine frontier, with Suetonius explaining (*The Twelve Caesars, Gaius*, 43):

> *Gaius had only a single taste of warfare, and even that was unpremeditated. At Mevania [a Roman town in Umbria, now modern Bevagna]...someone reminded him that he needed Batavian recruits for his bodyguard (these his preferred close protection): which suggested the idea of a German expedition. He wasted no time in summoning regular legions and auxiliaries from all directions, levied troops everywhere with the utmost strictness, and collected military supplies of all kinds on an unprecedented scale. Then he marched off so rapidly and hurriedly that the guard cohorts could not keep up with him except by breaking tradition: they had to tie their standards on pack mules.*

However, once in theatre in northern Gaul Caligula was at a loss what to do next with his huge force. His face was saved when a young British noble arrived at his headquarters, accompanied by a few followers. This was Adminius, son of the now ageing Cunobelinus, king of the Catuvellauni. He'd been banished by his father for some unspecified crime, though it's not clear if the young man sought Caligula's backing to become his father's heir, or had simply arrived to ask for sanctuary. The emperor immediately seized on his good fortune, declaring in an extravagant dispatch to the Senate in Rome that the whole of Britain had submitted to him, adding he planned to invade to claim this new fantastical prize for Rome. He then promptly marched his entire force to the north-western coast of Gaul, where he set in train plans for a new campaign of conquest across the English Channel. However, as with Augustus, it was once more not to be. Moorhead and Stuttard take up the story (2012, 41):

> *Plans were made, ships built, supplies sourced and requisitioned, weapons stockpiled, soldiers drilled, all was in place. And then disaster struck. The legionaries gathered on the sea front refused to obey their orders. They would not embark. Not even the threats of the murderous Gaius would induce them to cross the ocean for the nightmare land of Britannia.*

Caligula was furious, though impotent given the entire army was set against the invasion. In a rather ill-thought out attempt to cover up his failure, or perhaps as a punishment for the soldiers, Suetonius says he then ordered the gathered legionaries and auxiliaries to gather sea shells in their helmets and tunic laps from the nearby beaches (*The Twelve Caesars*, *Gaius*, 46). He called this strange harvest the plunder of the ocean and sent it to the Senate as tribute. As a final act he then built the famous Roman *pharos* lighthouse at Boulogne-sur-Mer (Roman Gesoriacum), where extensive harbour works and wharfing had earlier been constructed as part of his abortive invasion. Perhaps realizing he might now be in danger, far from Rome and surrounded by a disgruntled and perhaps humiliated army, he then paid each legionary and auxiliary four gold pieces and then headed quickly back to Rome with his guard. Once there he took his cue from his forebear and namesake Julius Caesar, proclaiming his failed expedition a great success. Celebrations followed, culminating with the Senate awarding him an *ovatio* on his birthday on 31 August. This was a specific form of triumph granted when an opponent was not actually at war with Rome, was considered basely inferior, or where foreign policy success had come without the need to resort to conflict. It seems here the increasingly deluded Caligula really did think gathering pebbles on the Gallic beaches of the English Channel equated to conquering Britain. However, the Roman nobility and people would have none of this nonsense, and only four months later he was assassinated by the acting Praetorian Prefect Cassius Chaerea and another guard officer called Gaius Sabinus.

Enter Claudius

It was left to Caligula's successor, the ill-favoured Claudius, to finally invade Britain and create the new province of Britannia. He came to the Imperial throne in the most unlikely of circumstances. Having fled the killing spree carried out in the Imperial palace by Caligula's faithful Batavian guard after their master's murder, Claudius hid behind a curtain. There he was later found by Praetorian guardsmen searching for the Germans. They pondered what to do with Claudius, eventually deciding to take him to their *Castra Praetoria* camp. There, to his astonishment, the senior officers decided to proclaim him emperor. They expected him to be their puppet, but he was to prove them wrong.

Contemporary sources paint a very unflattering picture of the younger brother of Germanicus, Caligula's father. For example, Suetonius says (*The Twelve Caesars, Claudius*, 3):

> *Claudius' mother, Antonia, often called him 'a monster: a man whom nature had not finished but had merely begun'; and, if she ever accused anyone of stupidity, would exclaim: 'He is a bigger fool even than my son Claudius.'*

Modern sources are equally unflattering, for example Moorhead and Studdart (2012, 42) calling him notoriously absent minded, short sighted, limping and drooling, while Kean (2005) highlights that throughout his education he remained under the same kind of guardianship as would an aristocratic Roman daughter.

However, there was more to Claudius than met the eye. Southern (2013, 56) suggests that, barred from most aspects of political life except token public appointments, he became a scholarly recluse. This certainly set him in good stead when he did become emperor as, defying all expectations, his was one of the more successful Imperial terms of office. In particular, Roman provincial territory grew exponentially in his reign. First defeating a rebellion in the new province of Mauretania, he then invaded Britain in AD 43 as detailed below, where he created perhaps the most unlikely of provinces, before later annexing as Roman provinces Judea in AD 44, Thrace in AD 46 and northern Palestine in AD 49. The latter was particularly important given it created the Roman province of Syria that was to be the bulwark against the Parthians and later Sassanid Persians in the east. He also continued his academic activities, and by the time he died in AD 54 had written 28 history books, his own autobiography and a treatise on Latin.

Back to the beginning of his reign, Claudius knew he needed more than the crushing of a revolt to prove himself a worthy emperor to the political classes and people of Rome. Nevertheless, alighting on Britain as his first target for Imperial expansion seems incredible given the scale of the jeopardy involved. However, two key factors need to be considered here which show it not to be such a strange choice after all. These were that the means were already available to him, and that he was serendipitously presented with a timely motive.

In the first instance, as we have seen above, Caligula had already built a fleet of vessels to carry his army across the English Channel in AD 40. These were still available three years later, and were to provide the core of the fleet of 900 vessels used by Claudius for his AD 43 invasion (Elliott, 2016, 64) these ships later becoming the *Classis Britannica* regional fleet. Further, Caligula had also built the new harbour works detailed above, and stocked row upon row of warehouses with the provisions needed to support his abortive invasion. The non-perishable goods there also remained in place, ready for Claudius to use when he cast his eyes north-westward from Rome.

With these preparations for an invasion of Britain already in place, Claudius was able to act swiftly when the opportunity arose to intervene in there. The trigger was provided by the death in late AD 40 of Cunobelinus. He was succeeded as king of the Catuvellauni by his two sons Caratacus and Togodumnus. These quickly launched a campaign against their Atrebates neighbours in the Thames Valley, who by this time had strong links with Rome. The Catuvellauni were evidently successful as Verica, the elderly king of the Atrebates, fled to Rome where he sought the support of Claudius. However, instead of consolidating their success, Caratacus and Togodumnus overplayed their hand by demanding the extradition of Verica. When this was rebuffed by Claudius, the two British leaders vowed vengeance and soon disturbances broke out in Britain against the Roman merchants already embedded there (*Suetonius, The Twelve Caesars*, 17.1).

It was against this backdrop that Claudius was presented with the opportunity to make his name within the Julio-Claudian dynasty. Suetonius provides detail here, saying (*The Twelve Caesars*, 17.1):

> "*…he decided Britain was the country where a real triumph could most readily be earned.*"

Claudius now had the means thanks to Caligula, and motive thanks to the naïve belligerence of Caratacus and Togodumnus. The scene was now set for one of the greatest amphibious operations in the pre-modern world.

Having committed to the invasion, Claudius set off from the port of Rome at Ostia and was soon in north-western Gaul, where he set up his headquarters in Boulogne-sur-Mer (Suetonius, *The Twelve Caesars*, 17.1). There he gathered his army of conquest, shrewdly appointing the Pannonian governor Aulus Plautius as its commander. Plautius was not only a long-term friend and ally of the Julio-Claudian dynasty, but was also one of the most experienced military leaders in the Empire. He in turn appointed the future emperor Vespasian as his leading legionary *legate*. The invasion force numbered 40,000 men, comprising four legions and 20,000 auxiliaries. The former comprised *legio* II *Augusta, legio* XIV *Gemina* and *legio* XX *Valeria Victrix*, who travelled from their bases on the Rhine frontier, and Plautius' own *legio* IX *Hispana* which travelled with him from Pannonia. Meanwhile, the auxiliaries provided more foot troops and all of the cavalry, the latter vital to military success as Caesar had found in 55 BC when forced to fight in Britain without them. Claudius also ordered 3,000 tonnes of grain to be loaded onto the larger merchant vessels, guaranteeing food for the invasion force for at least three months after its arrival. This was not a reconnaissance in force as with Caesar, but a full campaign of conquest.

Claudius now readied his fleet for the invasion. The vessels built by Caligula, and the additional ones he'd constructed to boost their number to 900, were built in two different ship-construction traditions. Those designed to provide the escort for the fleet, and then provide fire support for the land forces once they were ashore, were normal Roman war galleys, built to a standard Mediterranean design. By this time the most common was the *liburnian* bireme galley, this having taken over from the *trireme* as the dominant type after the conclusion of the late Republican civil wars. These were lighter and more manoeuvrable than earlier types, and much more suited for use in littoral and riparian operations along coastlines and down river systems. Meanwhile, most of the transport vessels employed by Claudius were built in a completely different way. This was in the Romano-Celtic shipbuilding tradition, as used by Julius Caesar in his second incursion to Britain in 54 BC. These featured the same lower freeboards to enable easier disembarkation, banks of oars, large sails, and wider beams to carry bulkier loads and help ride out the rough seas in northern waters. With the local maritime Gallic tribes such as the Veneti, Morini and Menapii long incorporated into the Empire, both Caligula and later Claudius were able to make much use of their noted shipbuilding skills. Claudius was therefore able to utilise a substantial, high quality fleet. To man them he called on the services of his best sailors and marines, those of the *Classis Misinensis* on the Tyrrhenian coast of Italy, many of whom were seconded to north-western Gaul.

Late in the summer all was ready and Claudius ordered the invasion to begin, gambling his reputation and future on the successful conquest of fearsome Britain. However, as with Caligula, all almost came to naught before a single ship had sailed. Once again the legionaries and auxiliaries, wary of crossing terrifying *Oceanus*, refused to board the invasion vessels. The day was saved by the most unlikely of Imperial champions, Claudius' own freedman Tiberius Claudius Narcissus. This former Imperial slave was actually a member of the emperor's *Consilium Principis* main advisory council, and so one of the most powerful men in the Empire. He now stepped forward to address the massed troops, scolding them for their cowardice and disloyalty to the emperor. He then boarded the nearest vessel himself. Shouting *'Io Saturnalia'*, referencing the Roman end of year role-reversing winter festival, the chastened soldiery quickly followed, and the invasion proceeded. Plautius positioned himself in the lead ship, with Claudius remaining in Boulogne-sur-Mer for the time being.

Once persuaded to board, the huge force set sail in three divisions to avoid any congestion when they landed, though Dio (*Roman History*, 60.19) says the weather conditions soon turned against them '…*until a light from the east streaked westwards, in the direction they were sailing*'. This good omen marked a change in meteorological fortunes and soon the fleet was underway again, arriving in Britain uneventfully and unopposed in mid-to-late summer. In this regard the late summer departure of the fleet actually helped the Roman amphibious operation. When the British leaders in the southeast had earlier learned that Claudius was massing an army of invasion in north-western Gaul, they had gathered a large force along the east coast of Britain to oppose any attempted Roman landing. However, by the time Plautius arrived this had been dispersed, the Britons assuming that once more the Romans had changed their minds.

Controversy has long surrounded the exact point where Plautius' force disembarked. Manley (2002, 131) and others have argued in favour of potential landing sites near Chichester and elsewhere. However, given its proximity to the continent, and Roman knowledge of the region gained during Caesar's previous two incursions, I firmly believe the landing site was on the east Kent coast. Others, for example Grainge (2005, 117) in his detailed assessment of the Roman invasions of Britain, agree. If this is accepted, then where were the exact landing beaches for this huge invasion? One candidate would be the beaches between Sandwich and Deal as used by Caesar in 55 BC and 54 BC, though given the huge size of the AD 43 fleet (even accepting it arrived in three waves) a much larger area would have been needed. In that regard, it seems likely that the shelter of the then navigable Watsum Channel to the north of Sandwich, together with the safe harbourage of Pegwell Bay with its broad expanses of beach, would also have been used. As Moody (2008, 141) says:

> *"Given the size of the operation, it is unlikely that a single location can be identified for the Roman landings. More probably, the ships landed where they could, in the network of harbours, beaches and trading ports on the east and western sides of the Watsum and (the) troops secured themselves, by units, over a wide area."*

Wherever the specific landing places were in eastern Kent for this invasion, the locale for the event was later commemorated by the building in the reign of Domitian of a grand monumental arch at Richborough which stood from the later 1st century AD through to the late 3rd century AD, latterly being used as a signal station (Strong, 1968, 72, and see Chapter 6 in this work for detail).

Soon, with his forces and provisions building up ashore but no enemy as yet to engage, Plautius built an extensive ditch and bank fortification to protect his principal beachhead. This has been identified at Richborough, with a section of the vast ditch still visible within the walls of the later Saxon Shore fort there. Over 640m of these defences have been excavated, with the overall site likely to have been playing card in shape, as with a standard Roman marching camp though far larger than normal. Calculations based on its known dimensions suggest a size of up to 57 ha, and from this location it would have sealed off the neck of the then promontory on which the arch and later fort were built. The sophistication of the fortification is indicated by the presence of a gate tower on the western side.

With his forces all now ashore and no enemy in sight, Plautius now began his breakout campaign. In terms of the route taken in modern Kent, Bishop (2014, 2) convincingly argues that rather than build new bespoke roads at this early stage of the initial conquest campaign, the Romans would instead have made use of the extensive network of LIA track ways in the region. I believe the route Plautius would have taken is along the Pilgrim's Way, the well-known prehistoric ridgeway running for much of its length in Kent along the south side of the North Downs. Given the south-facing slopes here, this ensured Plautius' force was exposed to the maximum amount of sunlit daylight as the legionary spearheads snaked their way along the route, helping them stay on the march for longer each day.

As Plautius advanced through northern Kent, he finally tracked down his elusive foe. Once again, as with Caesar, the Catuvellauni were the catalyst for regional native resistance, gathering allies from far and wide across Britain. However, in short order the Romans defeated both Caratacus and Togodumnus separately in two small engagements, after which the Dobunni (a tribe based in the Welsh Marches who'd supplied troops to support the British leaders) became the first of the British kingdoms to sue for peace.

Consolidating for a short period after his victories, Plautius then continued westwards, quickly reaching Bluebell Hill overlooking the Medway Gap where the River Medway cuts through the North Downs. There, instead of continuing along the route of the Pilgrim's Way as it turned north before crossing the winding river at Cuxton, he instead headed directly westwards, aiming to cross at one of two then well-known fording points. These were at modern Snodland and Aylesford, the former marking the tidal reach of the Medway at the time (Kaye, 2015, 232), and both close to each other.

It is here or nearby that I believe the famous river crossing battle described by Dio took place. Indeed, at Snodland local historians have installed two small monuments on the eastern bank of the river opposite the local church to mark the site. Given the importance of Dio's commentary here, it is worth recording in full (*Roman History*, 60.20):

> *(Plautius) advanced farther and came to a river. The barbarians thought that Romans would not be able to cross it without a bridge, and consequently bivouacked in rather careless fashion on the opposite bank; but he sent across a detachment of Germans, who were accustomed to swim easily in full armour across the most turbulent streams. These fell unexpectedly upon the enemy, but instead of shooting at any of the men they confined themselves to wounding the horses that drew their chariots; and in the confusion that followed not even the enemy's mounted warriors could save themselves. Plautius thereupon sent across Flavius Vespasian also and his brother Sabinus, who was acting as his lieutenant. So they,*

> *too, got across the river in some way and killed many of the foe, taking them by surprise. The survivors, however, did not take to flight, but on the next day joined issue with them again. The struggle was indecisive until Gnaeus Hosidius Geta, after narrowly missing being captured, finally managed to defeat the barbarians so soundly that he received the ornamenta triumphalia, though he had not been consul.*

There is much to unpack in this short description. In the first instance, this was clearly a far closer-run battle than Dio would have us believe. It took the Romans two days to force the crossing, even after Plautius' initial stratagem in sending the 'Germans' to swim the river. My interpretation here is that he actually sent them to cross the Medway further downstream, aiming to outflank the Britons, perhaps at a location nearer to modern Rochester. This shows the native forces were perhaps better prepared than Dio describes. The Germans he details have often been identified as Batavian auxiliaries, given such troops similarly swam across the River Po near to Placentia during the civil wars of AD 69 (Southern, 2013, 68). Among the auxilia in Plautius' army these would have been elite warriors, further showing he viewed the Britons on the opposite bank as a serious threat. In terms of such troops swimming in armour, the likelihood is they used inflated pigskins to float across the river, a tactic familiar to the Batavians given their origins in the Rhine Delta (Elliott, 2016, 115).

Whether they were Batavians or not however, the tactic clearly didn't work as it took an extraordinary act of bravery on the part of the officer Geta on the second day of the engagement to turn the tide in favour of the Romans. We know this because of the *ornamenta triumphalia* awarded him. This was the highest award possible for a military officer, and one that in Republican times would have allowed him a real triumph in Rome. In Imperial times it was usually reserved for army commanders, so clearly his actions were dramatic indeed. As Moorhead and Stuttard say (2012, 48):

> *That the Romans' eventual victory hung in the balance, turning on the fierce and determined fighting of Geta's men, suggests a hard-contested bloody struggle.*

With the Romans finally triumphant, the defeated British host withdrew northwards, quickly crossing the Thames where they deployed on the north bank and prepared to fight a second battle defending a major river crossing. Plautius was unrelenting in his pursuit and soon the Roman army was arrayed in force opposite. The location of the ensuing engagement is again a matter of conjecture, with some arguing it was near to modern Westminster (Moorhead and Studdart, 2012, 48). However, in recently published work I have argued in favour of a location further to the east on the line of the medieval Higham-Tilbury ferry. This was the lowest fordable point on the Thames during the Roman period (Elliott, 2016, 116). It also most closely fits Dio's description of it being '*…at a point near where the Thames empties into the ocean and at flood-tide forms a lake*' (*Roman History*, 60.20). If this indeed was the location of the Thames-crossing battle, then Plautius would have reached it by marching north down the Medway past modern Cuxton and Strood, then continuing northwards through modern Higham and Church Street before hitting the line of the Thames.

Viewing the Britons opposite, Plautius once more decided to force a crossing. He again employed the stratagem of crossing the river to flank the Britons, but this time both upriver and downriver of their deployment. This again featured his auxilia '*swimming*' across downriver, but now he also deployed his legionaries to make use of a bridge upriver. This latter must have been a Roman bridge of boats given it is highly unlikely the Britons had the technological capability to build a substantial bridge capable of carrying such a large body of heavily armed men over a major waterway, even taking into account the numerous islands and marshes in the pre-modern Thames.

A key point to note here is that while Plautius hadn't been able to use his fleet in the earlier Medway-crossing battle, given the tidal reach of that river was actually at Snodland at the time and so the battle site too far upriver, he could and did use it to help force the Thames crossing. This not only included the building of the likely bridge of boats, and perhaps ferrying the auxilia rather than they swimming, but also the ships participating in the combat itself. This combination, using ground and naval forces fighting together, proved highly effective and later became a key feature of the Claudian campaigns of conquest.

Dio says that after the two forces had crossed, the Romans '*…assailed the barbarians from several sides at once and cut down many of them…*' (*Roman History*, 60.20). A likely scenario here would see the Britons being engaged on each flank by the troops who'd crossed both downriver and upriver of their position, with *ballistae* and other missile weapons then deployed by the fleet in the Thames to enfilade their serried ranks. Once the Britons were disrupted, the main Roman concentration of legionaries and auxilia then forced the river using known crossing points to complete the destruction of the native army.

Once more the Britons fled northwards, though Dio (*Roman History*, 60.21) says they used their knowledge of the local marshy terrain to make good their escape, with many of the pursuing Romans getting into difficulty and some being surrounded and killed. However, to all intents and purposes this first phase of the Claudian campaign of conquest in Britain was over, with Togodumnus somehow dead and Caratacus fleeing to the west to find sanctuary with the Silures and Ordovices tribes in Wales.

Having successfully crossed the Thames, and about to enter the home territory of the leaderless Catuvellauni, Plautius now paused to consolidate his position. Here he may have taken into account Caesar's difficulties during his two incursions, and been weary of overextending his supply lines. However, this seems unlikely to me given he had his fleet in attendance, able to support his advance from the line of the Thames Estuary and up the coast and down the river systems of modern Essex and Suffolk. Dio, in his commentary, gives a very different reason for the pause. He says (*Roman History*, 60.22):

> *...because of the difficulties he had encountered at the Thames, Plautius became afraid, and instead of advancing any farther, proceeded to guard what he had already won, and sent for Claudius. For he had been instructed to do this in case he met with any particularly stubborn resistance, and, in fact, extensive equipment, including elephants, had already been got together for the expedition.*

There is an unusual hagiographic quality in this comment by Dio, he seeming to indicate that Plautius needed the emperor to help him complete the first season of campaigning in Britain. This presents two problems for the modern historian. First, there is no evidence elsewhere that Plautius had any difficulty in the Thames engagement other than controlling the pursuit of the routed Britons across the marshes. Second, as we will see, there was no other subsequent set piece engagement. To my mind, this is therefore a clear example of well thought out Imperial propaganda. Claudius and Plautius had agreed the emperor would travel to Britain in time to take the final submission of their opponents, and this he did.

As an aside here Dio says Claudius was in Rome when he received Plautius' request to join him in Britain (*Roman History*, 60.21). I believe this highly unlikely given it would have taken some 10 days using maritime transport and horse relays for the dispatch to get to Ostia using the fastest routes. Then a short period would have been needed to make preparations for Claudius' departure, before a likely 24-day journey for the Imperial retinue to arrive in Britain at its fastest pace. It is highly unlikely Plautius would have waited this length of time to finish off his defeated enemy. The experienced general knew this might give them time to regroup. Further, given the campaign began in late summer, any journey from Rome to Britain for Claudius would have taken place in the Autumn when conditions on both land and sea would have been more problematic. As detailed earlier, Suetonius in his much briefer description of Claudius' engagement in Britain indicates he travelled to Boulogne-sur-Mer at the beginning of the campaign, and I believe that is where he waited until Plautius was ready for him to join him.

When Claudius did arrive in Britain, the Romans lost no time in driving home their advantage to bring the campaign to a swift conclusion. First, as a propaganda exercise, Dio says Claudius arrived with elephants in his retinue (*Roman History*, 60.21). Given the last time the Romans had used trained war elephants was a century earlier, it is likely these were beasts from the emperor's personal menagerie, or those destined for use in the arena. Plautius then targeted the now leaderless Catuvellaunian capital Camulodunon in a lightning strike, with any remaining resistance quickly crushed. The Catuvellauni finally defeated, they and ten other British confederations and tribes now voluntarily submitted to Roman rule. It is at this point Tacitus says the province of Britannia was founded, with Plautius becoming its first governor (*Agricola*, 14.11). The army then acclaimed Claudius as *imperator* several times, allowing him to later hold a triumph in Rome, this number an unheard of precedent given only one acclamation was usually reserved per individual campaign.

Having achieved his career-defining conquest, Claudius didn't stay in his new province for long. First he gave Plautius instructions to continue campaigning, given only the southeast had to that point been conquered. Then, after only 16 days he crossed back to Boulogne-sur-Mer, before taking an overland route back to Rome given the increasingly difficult sea conditions this late in the year. However, he had no such concern for his son-in-laws Magnus and Silanus who Dio (*Roman History*, 60.21) says he sent back to Rome by the fastest means to carry the news of his great victory to the Senate and people there. The former quickly granted him the title *Britannicus*, confirmed his triumph, and voted there should be an annual festival to commemorate this most unlikely of conquests given their previous qualms about Claudius. Further, two triumphal arches were erected in his honour which detailed his success in Britain, one in Rome itself and one in Gaul (most likely Boulogne-sur-Mare given its key role in the campaign). Finally, by the time Claudius himself had arrived back the returning hero, the Senate had also given the title *Britannicus* to his two-year-old son Tiberius Claudius Caesar. Claudius' dramatic gamble had paid off, with his name now secure as one of the leading members of Julio-Claudian pantheon. However, the Roman campaigns of conquest in Britain were far from over.

Chapter 5

Early Conquest Campaigns AD 43–AD 61

In Rome the Claudian invasion of AD 43 was considered a great success, with at least part of fearsome Britain tamed and incorporated into the world of Rome as a new province. However, the Empire had a voracious appetite for territory it deemed *pretium victoria* (worth the conquest), and no time was lost in the rapid growth of Imperially-controlled land there. This chapter tells the story of these first breakout campaigns, with the legions of Rome expanding out from existing provincial territory in the South East to conquer the South West, the Midlands, the northeast up to the Humber estuary, the Welsh Marches, and later to invade Wales.

First Breakout

At the point Claudius left his new province it only comprised south-eastern Britain. However, the emperor made it very clear to Plautius before his departure that his newly conquered territory must be expanded swiftly. The new governor responded immediately, guided by the tribal landscape set out before him. Already the territories of the Cantiaci, Catuvellauni and Trinovantes had been assimilated by Rome to establish the core province. Looking further afield, the Romans now followed a familiar pattern of Imperial conquest. First, those confederations and tribes politically closest to Rome became client kingdoms. This was a formal process where the king or queen of the nation in question became a *clientes* of the Empire, in a procedure called *rex sociusque amicus* (translating as becoming an official king/queen, ally and friend of Rome). Such kingdoms continued to function 'independently', but under the guidance of Rome, and often with Roman troops deployed in their territory. These arrangements were usually with a specific king or queen rather than the kingdom itself, the latter more often than not being incorporated into the Empire after the ruler's demise (Southern, 2013, 75). In Britain, at the point of the initial breakout campaigns from Claudius' original province, known *clientes* there included the Regni on the south coast, the Atrebates in the Thames Valley (both possibly under the same ruler by this time, thought to be Tiberius Claudius Cogidubnus, an heir of Verica), the Iceni in north Norfolk and perhaps the Brigantes in the north.

Before launching his first campaign Plautius tasked *legio* XX *Valeria Victrix* with building a fortress at Camulodunon, where he also established a *colonia* for retiring veterans. Their rear secure, the legionary spearheads then set out in short order, using corridors of safe passage through the client kingdoms where necessary to target those British confederations and tribes yet to submit to Rome. Each of the three remaining legions headed in a different direction, with Plautius' own *legio* IX *Hispana* advancing north. Skirting the territory of the *Iceni*, it soon reached the River Nene in modern Cambridgeshire where it established a vexillation fort at Longthorpe (Roman name unknown). This built, the legion continued north to found another vexillation fort at Leicester (Roman *Ratae Corieltauvorum*) on the River Soar. Finally, it then headed north-east to the lands of the Coritani above the Wash where it built the full legionary fortress at Lincoln on the River Witham. There the IXth legion was based for a generation, with its legionaries certainly leaving their mark, for example in the form of funerary inscriptions. A fine example is the tombstone of legionary Gaius Saufeius, found at the corner of Salthouse Lane on the High Street in the modern city. The inscription (RIB 255) on his fine two-metre tall limestone monument reads:

> *To Gaius Saufeius, son of Gaius, of the Fabian voting-tribe, from Heraclea, soldier of legio IX, aged 40, of 22 years' service: he lies here.*

If Saufeius' tombstone is contemporary with the IXth legion's stay in Lincoln then here is a warrior that, given his 22 years' service at death, could easily have taken part in the Claudian invasion itself, and the subsequent breakout campaign.

Meanwhile *legio* XIV *Gemina* headed north-westwards deep into the Midlands, establishing vexillation forts at Great Chesterford (Roman name unknown), Mancetter (Roman *Manduessedum*) and Alchester (Roman name unknown). Finally, and most famously, *legio* II *Augusta* under the future emperor Vespasian (AD 69 to AD 79) struck out for the still-hostile South West. Suetonius (*The Twelve Caesars*, *Vespasian* 4) goes into great detail here, telling us that he:

> *...fought 30 battles, subjugated two warlike tribes [the Durotriges and Dumnonii], captured more than 20 oppida [fortified native urban centres], and took the Isle of Wight.*

Vespasian's speedy westward advance was greatly aided by his use of the British fleet to provide close support in the littoral zone along the coast and down the river systems. This included exercising military control there, scouting and raiding ahead of the land forces, carrying out all of the logistical heavy lifting, and building fortified harbours to supply the troops as they advanced (Elliott, 2016, 120). An extreme example of this was the capture of the Isle of Wight early in Vespasian's campaign. Analogously this would have featured an AD 43 Claudian-style invasion in microcosm, with the fleet displaying all of its military roles to facilitate the swift conquest of this significant landmass opposite the vital Solent waterway.

Archaeological data supporting the rapid progress of Vespasian's offensive from that point comes in the form of large-scale Claudian-period storage buildings and Claudian pottery on the site of the later Roman settlement of *Clausentum* (today a suburb of Southampton) at the tip of the Bitterne Peninsula. From here supplies arriving via the regional fleet would have been ideally placed for forward deployment up the River Itchen to the advancing legions and auxilia. Vespasian's ongoing progress can be tracked today by each new coastal base he established during his westward progression. The next step from Bitterne can be found at Wimborne in Dorset where he built an early vexillation fortress with an associated port and storage facility (this time on Poole Harbour). Weymouth Bay would then have been the location of the next fleet base given its proximity to the major military engagement site at Maiden Castle, where Vespasian's legionaries famously stormed the extensive hill fort defended by the Durotriges. Then heading deep into Dumnonian territory, a key fleet base was established at Topsham, immediately to the south of the later legionary fortress and *civitas* capital of Exeter (Roman *Isca Dumnoniorum*, of which it became the port). After four seasons of intense campaigning, with Vespasian using this combination of land based shock troops supplied by his new series of fortified harbours, the South West was conquered and incorporated into Britannia.

Plautius returned to Rome in AD 47, accompanied by Vespasian. The Romans could be forgiven for thinking at this point that the conquest of Britain was following the same pattern as Caesar's conquest of Gaul. Soon they expected the whole main island of Britain to be filling the

Emperor's *fiscus* treasury with taxes as one large province. However, nothing could be further from the truth, with years of campaigning still to come and the conquest of the far north ever problematic.

At the point of Plautius' departure, the territory of the new province had been greatly expanded. Britannia now comprised the region below a line from the River Severn to the River Trent, excepting the territories of the Regni, Atrebates and Iceni client kingdoms. This new stop line is often called the 'Fosse Way Frontier' after the major Roman road that later ran along its length from the legionary fortress at Exeter to that at Lincoln. This route way almost certainly derived the name by which it was later known from the Latin word *fossa*, meaning ditch. This not only reflects its origins as the late AD 40s stop line of the initial Roman campaigns of conquest in Britain, but also indicates that for at least some of its length the ditched barrier remained visible hundreds of years later. Back to the late AD 40s, along the 'Fosse Way Frontier' a number of vexillation forts were built, for example at Newton-on-Trent and Great Casterton (Roman names unknown), joining already established bases including Longthope and Leicester. These forts later became logistics bases for the next phase of conquest.

By this time manifestations of *Romanitas* had begun to emerge across conquered territory, with the former native British nobility encouraged to learn formal Latin, wear togas on official business and invest in grand stone-built public building enterprises, conveniently for the Romans funded with loans from the leading Senatorial families back in Rome. More practically, given the always-urgent need to make a new province pay its own way, Roman patterns of local Government were also imposed. As Oosthuizen (2019, 27) details:

> *The (new) administration of Roman Britain was based on a set of nested hierarchies: broadly speaking from vicus, a small local centre (as opposed to the vici civilian settlements associated with Roman forts), to pagus, the locality, to civitates, a region often reproducing a prehistoric territory (as for example with the Cantiacii in modern Kent).*

The next governor in Britain was called Publius Ostorius Scapula, he arriving just as winter set in in AD 47. His first task was to pacify those areas already conquered by Rome below the 'Fosse Way Frontier', in the first instance disarming any Britons still under arms. This included the client kingdoms there and prompted the first revolt against the new Roman presence in Britain, this among the Iceni in north Norfolk. The rebels there fortified themselves in a promontory with a narrow entrance, sometimes identified as Stonea Camp in the Cambridgeshire Fens, later the site of a Roman agricultural Imperial Estate (Potter and Jackson, 1982, 118). Ostorius knew there was real danger here as a native victory could begin to unravel the Roman conquests in Britain to date. He advanced swiftly on the rebels and defeated them in short order, only needing his auxiliaries to do so with his cavalry fighting dismounted.

Ostorius now turned his attention to the expansion of Imperial territory north and west of the 'Fosse Way Frontier' stop line. First he campaigned against the Deceangli tribe in north-western Wales, with the Roman fleet deploying to the Dee Estuary to protect his littoral flank and supply his troops along the coast and down the local river systems. To support this extensive campaign, the governor built a large 18 ha legionary fortress-sized supply base at Rhyn Park in modern Shropshire on the English side of the River Ceiriog. However, his campaigning in Wales was cut short when he was called away to deal with a disturbance among the northern Brigantes.

This large confederation, whose name translated as 'High Ones' or 'Hill Dwellers', had yet to feel the might of Rome. Their territory covered a huge region in the north, including modern Yorkshire excepting the east coast, Lancashire, Cumbria, Northumberland and south-western Scotland. Their power is evident in the size of the pre-Roman tribal capital located at Stanwick in North Yorkshire, this an enormous *oppida* enclosing almost 300 ha surrounded by 9km of ditches and ramparts (Moorehead and Stuttard, 2012, 93). Given the scale of his opponents here Ostorius took no chances, marching north with a large force of legionaries and auxilia, swiftly wiping out any opposition and then putting to death the ringleaders.

Matters in the north resolved, Ostorius then returned to Wales where this time he targeted the Silures and Ordovices tribes in the south and centre who between them were still harbouring the fugitive Caratacus. First Ostorius redeployed *legio* XX *Valeria Victrix* from Colchester to Kingsholm near modern Gloucester where he built a vexillation-size fort. This location became a key site for the various campaigns of conquest in Wales, given it was the lowest easily bridgeable point on the River Severn, while also being navigable for the sea-going transport vessels of the fleet. Once the campaign was underway, with the XXth legion driving hard into the territory of the Silures, the governor then deployed *legio* XIV *Gemina* to the Welsh Marches. From there they opened a new front against the Ordovices. Progress for both legions and their auxiliaries was slow, but eventually Roman military prowess prevailed with the tribes submitting after Caratacus was defeated when the Romans assaulted the fortified site he was defending deep in Ordovician territory. The rebel leader fled once more, this time leaving behind his wife and daughter to be captured by the Romans. Heading north, in AD 51 he eventually arrived at the court of Cartimandua, now the queen of the Brigantes. Here she was presented with a dilemma. The Roman conquest of Britain was still in its early years, with resistance still evident in many areas, even below the 'Fosse Way Frontier'. To that end, handing him over to the Romans would be an embarrassing loss of face to those Britons still fighting Rome. However, after the failed unrest in Brigantian territory at the beginning of Ostorius' governership (the event which may have placed her on the throne there) she was clearly aware of the military might of the Empire. In the end she made the pragmatic choice to hand the former leader of the Catuvellauni over to the Romans in chains. Caratacus was later presented to Claudius, with the emperor deciding to spare him. He was allowed to live out the rest of his life in Rome where he made a positive impression on the nobility and people there. Meanwhile, Tacitus (*The Histories*, 3.45) says Cartimandua was rewarded with great wealth for her support for Rome.

Back in Wales, if Ostorius thought the region pacified then he couldn't have been more wrong, for the Silures now rose in revolt. The governor made it known he intended to exterminate the whole confederation as a punishment, this unsurprising given Rome's usual attitude to recalcitrant foes. As Mattingly says (2006, 89):

> *A key ingredient in the Roman approach to war was their ruthless attitude, which frequently extended to their use of exemplary force. Rebellious peoples were slaughtered or enslaved without qualms, massive resources being poured into the crushing of even small groups of dissenters.*

On this occasion this was a mistake, as with nothing to lose the Silures now fought a vicious guerrilla campaign (Southern, 2013, 88). On one occasion they inflicted a major defeat on the Romans, ambushing a sizable force of legionaries when they were building a marching camp. In this engagement Roman losses were heavy, with the *praefectus castrorum* camp prefect, eight centurions and hundreds of soldiers killed. However the Silures then made a mistake, being drawn into a set piece encounter when, having ambushed a Roman foraging party, Ostorius arrived with a sizeable force of legionaries and wiped out the Britons there. Despite this setback the Silures still refused to submit, knowing the fate that awaited them. The conflict fizzled on unresolved, its ultimate outcome the death of Ostorius in AD 52, worn out by years of campaigning in Wales and the north.

Britannia's next governor was Aulus Didius Gallus, who relocated *legio* XX *Valeria Victrix* to a new legionary fortress at Usk (Roman *Burrium*) in south-eastern Wales, *legio* XIV *Gemina* to a similar new fortress at Wroxeter, and *legio* II *Augusta* to the existing vexillation fortress at Gloucester. Both the new sites were specifically chosen for the access provided to the Bristol Channel by the Rivers Usk and Severn respectively, with maritime supply remaining vital to Rome's continued military success in its Welsh campaigning. This observation is reinforced by the next two forts built as the campaign continued, at Chepstow on the mouth of the River Wye and Cardiff on the River Taff.

The gruelling Welsh campaign continued throughout the AD 50s, with the use of three complete legions showing the intensity of the campaigning there. However, the most noteworthy event of Didius' time as governor in Britain was his intervention in Brigantian territory again. There, in the mid AD 50s, a schism occurred between Cartimandua and her husband Venutius. We have no insight into what caused this, but we do of the outcome, he being banished from the northern kingdom. Soon he was raising a force to invade the queen's territory. This was a serious threat to the Roman client kingdom, with Tacitus (*Annals*, 12.40) calling him the leading British military leader now Caratacus had been captured. Didius realized the queen was under threat and quickly intervened. At first he sent auxiliaries, but soon realized he'd misjudged the seriousness of the threat. He therefore deployed a full legion to the north, either *legio* IX *Hispana* or *legio* XIV *Gemina*, and soon the situation was under control after a series of decisive clashes, with Venutius again banished. The queen later divorced him and married his armour bearer, a man called Vellocatus.

It is around this time that we have an interesting insight into how the Romans were viewing the seemingly unending campaigns of conquest in Britain. This is in the form of a comment by Suetonius, who says that after Claudius died in AD 54 the new emperor Nero (AD 54 to AD 68) for a time considered abandoning the province given the ongoing cost the campaigning there (*The Twelve Caesars*, *Nero*, 18). He eventually decided his forces would stay and the province continue, though only because he feared the negative publicity if he withdrew.

Didius departed back to Rome in AD 57 and was replaced by Quintus Veranius Nepos, a noted military leader with a hard-man reputation. Here, Nero had clearly determined that if Rome was to stay in the main island of Britain then all resistance in Wales must be crushed once and for all. However, the new governor only had time to lead a few skirmishers against the still recalcitrant Silures before he died in office. His replacement was one of the truly great British governors, Gaius Suetonius Paulinus, appointed by Nero in AD 58. Another seasoned military leader, he set to work in his new province immediately, picking up where Verianus had left off in Wales. First, to consolidate his position in Silurian territory he built a series of forts to secure the key valleys in the interior that the natives had been using to access the rich farmlands along the coast. Then, in AD 60, he targeted the region he determined to be the real centre of resistance to Roman power in Wales. This was the Island of Anglesey, deep in the heart of Ordovician territory, the mysterious island that was home to the druids, leaders of LIA religion in pre-Roman Britain. It was also a place of refuge for the thousands of Britons fleeing the gradual scouring campaigns of the Romans, not only in Wales but elsewhere in the main island of Britain.

As with Vespasian's conquest of the Isle of Wight a decade earlier, here Paulinus staged a Claudian invasion in miniature, with an army of around 20,000 men. This included *legio* XIV *Gemina*, most of *legio* XX *Valeria Victrix* and an equivalent number of auxiliaries. The governor was a meticulous planner and built hundreds of flat-bottomed boats in the estuary of the River Dee to transport his legionaries and auxilia foot troops across the shallow Menai Straight, with the auxiliary cavalry swimming across. However, his amphibious assault was heavily opposed, despite the war galleys from the regional fleet enfilading the landing zone with *ballistae* and other missile weapons. Tacitus here provides a detailed description of the desperate engagement, saying (*Annals*, 14.29):

> *On the beach stood the adverse array, a serried mass of arms and men, with women flitting between the ranks. In the style of Furies, in robes of deathly black and with dishevelled hair, they brandished their torches; while a circle of Druids, lifting their hands to heaven and showering imprecations, struck our troops with such an awe at the extraordinary spectacle that, as though their limbs were paralysed, they exposed their bodies to wounds without an attempt at movement. Then, reassured by*

> *their general, and inciting each other never to flinch before a band of females and fanatics, they charged behind the standards, cut down all who met them, and enveloped the enemy in his own flames. The next step was to install a garrison among the conquered population, and to demolish the groves consecrated to their savage cults: for they considered it a duty to consult their deities by means of human entrails.*

So far so good for the new governor. However, next he faced an existential threat to the survival of the province from a totally unexpected direction. This was the AD 60/61 revolt of Boudicca, queen of the Iceni in north Norfolk.

The Boudiccan Revolt

The blood-soaked rebellion of Boudicca is arguably the most famous event in the story of the Roman occupation of Britain. It almost ended the Roman presence in the islands here and saw the legionaries and auxilia fighting in the most extreme conditions. Defeat would have meant the destruction of four whole legions, on a scale even larger than the loss of Varus' three legions in the Teutoburg Forest in Germany in AD 9.

The context behind this dramatic event was the earlier death of the Iceni king Prasutagus, Boudicca's husband. A Roman client king, in his will he left his kingdom to his two daughters and also to Nero. As detailed above, ruling *clientes* of the Romans usually left their kingdom entirely to the Romans after their deaths, and the emperor reacted predictably when he heard news of Prasugatus' unusual arrangement. The dead king's will was ignored and the territory of the Iceni quickly folded into the expanding province of Britannia. It is now that Boudicca enters history, with Dio describing her appearance as very much the warrior queen, he saying (*Roman History*, 62.2):

> *She was very tall and stern; her look was penetrating; her voice harsh; a mass of auburn hair fell to her hips and around her neck was a heavy golden torc; she wore a patterned cloak with a thick cape over it fastened with a brooch.*

Boudicca protested against the treatment of her kingdom. Tacitus says the Roman response was brutal in the extreme (*The Annals*, 14.31). He details Iceni territory was pillaged by centurions, the dead king's household ransacked by slaves, Boudicca lashed and her two daughters raped. It is worth noting here that Dio gives a completely different and far more mundane reason for Boudicca leading her revolt, he saying (*Roman History*, 62.2):

> *An excuse for the revolt was found in the confiscation of the sums of money that Claudius had given to the foremost Britons; for these sums, as Decianus Catus, the procurator of the island, maintained, were to be paid back. This was one reason for the uprising; another was found in the fact that Seneca (a leading statesman in Rome), in the hope of receiving a good rate of interest, had lent to the islanders 40,000,000 sesterces that they did not want, and had afterwards called in this loan all at once and had resorted to severe measures in exacting it.*

Whatever the cause, the result was incendiary in the extreme. Tacitus has Boudicca address her people, setting them on course for savage rebellion, the queen saying (*The Annals*, 14.35):

> *It is not as a woman descended from noble ancestry, but as one of the people that I am avenging lost freedom, my scourged body, the outraged chastity of my daughters. This is a woman's resolve; as for men, they may live and be slaves.*

Dio also has the queen exhort the masses to revolt, grasping a spear and then saying (Roman History, 62.3):

> *Have we not been robbed entirely of most of our possessions, and those the greatest, while for those that remain we pay taxes? Besides pasturing and tilling for them all our other possessions, do we not pay a yearly tribute for our very bodies? How much better it would be to have been sold to masters once for all than, possessing empty titles of freedom, to have to ransom ourselves every year! How much better to have been slain and to have perished than to go about with a tax on our heads! Yet why do I mention death? For even dying is not free of cost with them; nay, you know what fees we deposit even for our dead. Among the rest of mankind death frees even those who are in slavery to others; only in the case of the Romans do the very dead remain alive for their profit. Why is it that, though none of us has any money (how, indeed, could we, or where would we get it?), we are stripped and despoiled like a murderer's victims? And why should the Romans be expected to*

display moderation as time goes on, when they have behaved toward us in this fashion at the very outset, when all men show consideration even for the beasts they have newly captured?

Soon Boudicca's ferocious insurrection had ignited most of the South East above the Thames against the Romans, giving credence to Dio's reasoning behind the revolt, with all of the local aristocracy affected, not just those of the Iceni. Marching south at the head of an army 120,000 strong according to Dio (*Roman History*, 62.2), she first targeted the then provincial capital at Colchester. The nearest Roman legion was *legio* IX *Hispana* in the Midlands, still holding the north-eastern line of the 'Fosse Way Frontier'. Its *legate* Quintus Petilius Cerialis, a future governor in Britain, moved quickly to lead a large force comprising vexillations of legionaries and auxiliaries to intercept Boudicca. This arrived too late to save Colchester which by that point had already been torched with great loss of life, a large number burned alive as they sought shelter in the Temple of Claudius there, built to celebrate Plautius' earlier victory. Cerialis' force was then decisively defeated by the main British army, with the *legate* fleeing for his life alongside his cavalry, he leaving his legionaries to their fate. They then remained incongruously holed in up in a nearby fort until the insurrection had been defeated.

In Wales, Paulinus abandoned his immediate plans to integrate north Wales into the province after his defeat of the druids there as soon as he heard of Boudicca's revolt. The governor immediately headed south-east along the route of Watling Street, the key military trunk road running from the legionary fortress at Wroxeter in the Welsh Marches through St Albans to London, and then onwards to Richborough on the east Kent coast (today the A5 and A2 broadly track its route). He was accompanied by *legio* XIV *Gemina*, some vexillations from *legio* XX *Valeria Victrix* and a few auxiliary units including two *alae* of cavalry. Reaching High Cross in modern Leicestershire where Watling Street crossed the Fosse Way, Paulinus then sent for the Exeter-based *legio* II *Augusta* to join him. However, the unit's *legate* and second-in-command were away, with its *praefectus castrorum* in charge. Called Poenius Postumus, he ignored the call, bringing shame on the legion. Clearly he thought the province was about to fall and wanted to stay on the River Ex from where he could evacuate his troops if necessary. Meanwhile, some stragglers from *legio* IX *Hispana* also found their way to Paulinus, giving him a total force of around 6,000 legionaries from the three legions, 4,000 foot auxiliaries and around 1,000 mounted auxiliaries.

At this point Tacitus has Paulinus marching in person to London, the recently-founded major trading port on the River Thames, from where the provincial procurator Catus Decianus had fled to Gaul as Boudicca and her growing force continued its march south towards the town. It is useful to quote the historian in full at this point, given the real sense of jeopardy he presents as the new province fell into chaos (*The Annals*, 14.33):

> *Paulinus…with wonderful resolution, marched amidst a hostile population to Londinium, which, though undistinguished by the name of a colony [it was styled by the Romans a municipium mercantile town], was much frequented by a number of merchants and trading vessels. Uncertain whether he should choose it as a seat of war, as he looked round on his scanty force of soldiers…he resolved to save the province at the cost of a single town. Nor did the tears and weeping of the people, as they implored his aid, deter him from giving the signal of departure and receiving into his army all who would go with him. Those who were chained to the spot by the weakness of their sex, or the infirmity of age, or the attractions of the place, were cut off by the enemy.*

The key reference here is that which describes the local population as hostile when Paulinus was marching down Watling Street through Leicestershire and Hertfordshire, to my mind confirming the Catuvellauni certainly, and most likely the Trinovantes to their east, had joined the Iceni in the great revolt. In these circumstances Paulinus' force would have been constructing defended marching camps at the end of each day's march as they travelled southeast. It is therefore unlikely that if Paulinus did indeed travel in person to London, he took his whole army. More likely he would have travelled with a bodyguard of auxiliary cavalrymen, or even more likely have sent an advance guard to assess the situation with authority to order an evacuation if needed.

In the event, when Boudicca did arrive in London, any remaining Romans or Romano-British were butchered and the town burned to the ground. Boudicca then targeted the new *municipium* of St Albans (Roman *Verulamium*), razing this also. The primary sources say that 80,000 were killed in the three sacking events by this point, indicating the scale of the insurrection and its rank savagery. However, the stage was now set for Roman retribution, and on a devastating scale.

By this point Boudicca's force had grown to 230,000, though only 120,000 were still likely warriors. This was an enormous force to keep in the field and she knew that a meeting engagement with Paulinus would be needed quickly to keep her army and its swelling number of dependent camp followers together. She also knew that if the governor was defeated, the Romans might abandon the province for good. Boudicca therefore advanced northwest along Watling Street to seek out the Roman army. As she progressed she received intelligence about the size of Paulinus' force, and no doubt felt the outcome of the forthcoming battle was a foregone conclusion.

In that she was wrong, as the wily Paulinus was ready for her and chose the place to make his stand very carefully. This was in a bowl-shaped steep defile, with woods on either side and rear and an open end facing Watling Street, Boudicca's line of advance. The woods protected his flanks and limited the frontage of the line of battle, negating the British superiority in numbers, playing to the martial superiority of his own legionaries. The exact location of the battle is unknown, though all of the leading candidate sites are along the line of Watling Street, hence the engagement often being referred to as The Battle of Watling Street. These sites are at Mancetter, High Cross where Paulinus had awaited the arrival of *legio* II *Augusta* in vain, Church Stowe in Northamptonshire and Markyate in Hertfordshire. All four sites also have a significant water source, essential with so many engaged in the battle.

Paulinus deployed his legionaries and auxilia uphill of the Britons. He divided his foot troops into four main bodies with a centre, left and right flanks, and with a reserve to the rear of the centre. He then positioned an *ala* of auxiliary cavalry on either extreme flank hard against the woods there, where he finally deployed field defences for additional protection. Dio says he then addressed his legionaries and auxilia as the huge British force approached. He has him say (69.2):

> *Up, fellow-soldiers! Up, Romans! Show these accursed wretches how far we surpass them even in the midst of evil fortune. It would be shameful, indeed, for you to lose ingloriously now what but a short time ago you won by your valour. Many a time, assuredly, have both we ourselves and our fathers, with far fewer numbers than we have at present, conquered far more numerous antagonists. Fear not, then, their numbers or their spirit of rebellion; for their boldness rests on nothing more than headlong rashness unaided by arms or training. Neither fear them because they have burned a couple of cities; Exact from them now, therefore, the proper penalty for these deeds, and let them learn by*

actual experience the difference between us, whom they have wronged, and themselves.

Boudicca deployed her enormous force opposite, though in much denser formation, with the chariots in front manned by her own elite warriors. So confident were the Britons of victory that the families of the warriors joined the baggage train at the rear of her battle line to watch events unfold. She now exhorted her own army to more slaughter, then opened the battle with a wild uphill charge with both the chariots and foot warriors. The former rode across the front of the Romans, hurling insults and javelins, before turning square on to close for hand-to-hand combat. The foot troops followed close behind. Soon Boudicca had lost control of her army as each noble and warrior strove to get to grips with the Romans.

By way of contrast, the discipline of the legionaries and auxilia now shone through. The battle proper began with the Roman artillery opening fire as soon as the Britons were in range, first the *ballistae* and then the *scorpiones*. Given the nearby proximity of the various logistics bases being used by the Romans as they campaigned in Wales, it seems likely there were a larger number of artillery pieces available to Paulinus than usual. Further, having chosen his battlefield, it is certain he would also have set range markers down to ensure the accuracy of his artillery bombardment. Then, as the range narrowed, auxiliary archers and slingers also joined the barrage. By this point the Britons, increasingly disordered by the concentrated missile fire, had begun their ascent up the steep hillside towards the main Roman deployment. At that point, *en masse* the legionaries released their lighter *pila*, 6,000 iron-barbed javelins arcing high in the air in a steep parabola and then dropping on the heads of the Britons, many without helmets. The auxiliary infantry joined in with their own *lancea*. Then, at point blank range as the flagging Britons reached the Roman lines, the legionaries unleashed their second, heavier *pila*. These flew in a flat arc, hammering into the front ranks of Britons who came to a shuddering halt in a tangle of dead horses, overturned chariots, bodies and wounded.

Paulinus saw the British advance falter and seized his chance to take the initiative. He now ordered the legionaries to move forward in a series of *cuneus* (swine head) wedge formations, with centurions and standard bearers to the fore. The auxiliaries followed on the flanks. Swords were drawn and shields set hard forward. The wedges then charged downhill into the dense mass of Britons, causing slaughter everywhere and forcing the natives into a huge, desperate crush where the warriors couldn't use their weapons.

A massacre now ensued as the Britons broke and tried to run away. However, they were trapped on the field by the surrounding families and baggage train. All were hacked down where they stood, the slaughter desperate.

The result was a mighty victory for Paulinus, with Tacitus saying (*Annals*, 14.35):

> *The troops gave no quarter even to the women: the baggage animals themselves had been speared and added to the pile of bodies. The glory won in the course of the day was remarkable, and equal to that of our older victories: for, by some accounts, little less than eighty thousand Britons fell, at a cost of some four hundred Romans killed and a not much greater number of wounded. Boudicca ended her days by poison; while…Postumus, camp-prefect of the second legion, informed of the exploits of the men of the fourteenth and twentieth, and conscious that he had cheated his own corps of a share in the honours and had violated the rules of the service by ignoring the orders of his commander, ran his sword through his body.*

Dio's account of Boudicca's fate differs, he saying that after the battle (*Roman History*, 62.12):

> *Boudicca fell sick and died. The Britons mourned her deeply and gave her a costly burial; but, feeling that now at last they were really defeated, the survivors scattered to their homes.*

The Romans then quickly drafted in 2,000 more legionaries from Germany together with 1,000 auxiliary cavalry and eight units of auxiliary foot to help stamp out the last flames of resistance. This was carried out with such vigour in the Iceni homelands of north Norfolk that the region remained for many years under-developed compared to the rest of the province, with some of the urban plots in the later *civitas* capital at Caistor St Edmunds (Roman *Venta Icenorum*) never used.

Thus ended the Boudiccan revolt, with the province now secured for another 340 years. However, Paulinus didn't receive the plaudits he might have expected. This was because the absent procurator, Decianus hiding in Gaul, was quickly replaced by the emperor Nero with a new man named Gaius Julius Alpinus Classicianus. The latter was critical of Paulinus' post-revolt punitive actions against the Britons, fearing it might spark another revolt. He reported this to the emperor who sent his own freedman Polyclitus to conduct an investigation. Though we don't have the full details of its findings, the investigator did report that Paulinus had lost some ships from the regional fleet. This excuse was used to relieve him, he being replaced by the more conciliatory Publius Petronius Turpilianus as governor. However, Paulinus does not seem to have returned to Rome in disgrace as a lead *tessera* found there features both his and Nero's names alongside symbols of victory, and a man with his name was nominated as consul for AD 66. Nevertheless, the Romans had been badly rattled by the rebellion, and in my view if Paulinus had lost his battle Britannia would have fallen, with the Romans perhaps unlikely ever to return.

Consolidation

With a degree of calm restored to Britain, rebuilding and repair began, with consolidation once more the order of the day. In the first instance, the provincial capital was moved from the *colonia* at Colchester to the *municipia* of London on the north bank of the Thames. This triggered a rebuilding programme there, paid for by the Imperial *fiscus* treasury, the first manifestation being the construction of the 1.5 ha Neronian fort at modern Plantation Place on Fenchurch Street. This was found during rescue excavations by Museum of London Archaeology (MOLA) in the early 2010s. The fortification was a timber and earthwork structure, similar in design to a standard Roman marching camp though more robust in its construction. It was enclosed by double ditches each 1.9m wide and 3m deep. Hingley (2018, 62) provides more detail, saying:

> *Dominating a strategic point of high ground, the fortification was close to the major road junction and the early marketplace above the bridgehead. Its northern ditches cut through the main north-west road of early Roman Londinium and it is unclear why this road was put out of use. This fortified enclosure overlay timber buildings…burned during the Boudiccan uprising and the rampart itself contained charred timbers and burnt mud bricks that were reused from destroyed buildings.*

The fort could accommodate 500 troops and was occupied for around 10 years. Within its walls were located a granary, latrine and cookhouse, with the soldiers housed in tents rather than permanent wooden or stone-built structures. Its construction was a statement to any natives in the region that Rome was here to stay, and from that point the rebuilding of Roman

London progressed quickly. By the end of the decade a variety of fine buildings had been built on the high ground around Cornhill, including a new *basilica* and *forum* and temples to the Imperial Cult and the Capitoline Triad. Meanwhile, on the riverfront beneath modern Cannon Street railway station an impressive governor's palace was built.

The governors who followed Paulinus in the AD 60s are often criticized for not living up to his martial prowess. However, as Jones & Mattingly (1990, 71) argue, the likes of Turpilianus and his own successor Marcus Trebellius Maximus were clearly obeying a new set of orders, not to continue the expansion of Roman-controlled territory but to re-garrison the province, and complete the pacification of the natives in the newly conquered territories north of the 'Fosse Way Frontier.' It is worth reflecting here that the Romans had only been in Britain for a generation following the Claudian invasion, and many areas within the new province were still coming to terms with their new fate. As Mattingly says (2006, 91):

> *The activities of the Roman army in the conquest phase will have had a profound impact on the peoples of Britain. Even in a professional army like the Roman one, the collateral damage to civilian communities was undoubtedly high.*

However, this pacification programme was clearly successful, as by the mid-AD 60s Nero was able to pull the veteran *legio* XIV *Gemina* out of the line in Britain for redeployment to Syria for service against the Parthians.

By this time the territory of the new province had greatly expanded beyond the 'Fosse Way Frontier' stop line of the late AD 40s. Below it the various client kingdoms, including the Regni, Atrebates and Iceni had now been subsumed into Roman controlled territory. Above it, to the northeast, the lands of Coritani south of the Humber were also now part of the province, and perhaps even land belonging to the Parisi to their north. The lands of the Dubonni and Cornovii in the Welsh Marches were now also part of the province, providing the springboard for the numerous campaigns in Wales, some more successful than others. Evidence this region became a new frontier zone for the campaigns in Wales is evident with the construction of two new branches of Watling Street from Wroxeter, one heading south to the legionary fortress at Caerleon and one north to the Dee Estuary where shortly a legionary fortress would be built at Chester (Roman *Deva Victrix*).

All of the above detail enables us to roughly establish the northern frontier of the province of Britannia as the AD 60s came to an end. This was now on a line from the River Dee on the west coast to the Humber Estuary on the east, excepting the territory of Wales whose final conquest remained elusive. However, as the decade came to an end, Roman priorities switched from consolidation to conquest once more, with the new focus the far north. Soon the legions were again on the move.

Chapter 6

Later Conquest Campaigns AD 62–AD 193

The early Roman campaigns of conquest in Britain reached their climax in the AD 70s and 80s when successive warrior governors launched legionary spearheads deep into the far north. These culminated with Agricola declaring the whole main island of Britain conquered. However, without the political will back in Rome to maintain the huge military presence needed to secure the region of modern Scotland, Roman forces were soon moving back south once more, where the northern frontier eventually settled on the Solway Firth-Tyne line. From that point onwards the now unconquered far north proved a never-ending source of trouble for the province in the south, with multiple conflicts north of the border throughout the 2nd century AD.

Here, I initially detail the campaigns of the governors Marcus Vettius Bolanus, Cerialis, Sextus Julius Frontinus and Agricola as Brigantian territory in the north, then Wales, and finally the far north were the targets of Roman conquest campaigns. Next I examine the trouble that broke out in the north of Britain around the time of the accession of Hadrian in AD 117, followed by his visit to Britain in AD 122 and the construction of Hadrian's Wall. Finally, I consider the ongoing Roman campaigns in the far north during the reigns of Antoninus Pius (including the building of the Antonine Wall), Marcus Aurelius and Lucius Verus, and lastly Commodus (AD 180–AD 192). The latter sets the scene for Chapter 7 where Septimius Severus' enormous conquest campaigns in the early 3rd century AD are examined in full.

The Campaigns of Bolanus, Cerialis, Frontinus and Agricola

The post Boudiccan-revolt policy of consolidation in Britain continued until the suicide of Nero in AD 68, this leading to the dramatic Imperial power struggle known as the 'Year of the Four Emperors' in AD 69. This was the Principate Empire's first period of civil war, with sequentially from June AD 68 Galba, Otho, Vitellius and finally Vespasian claiming the throne. The latter's ultimate victory ushered in the Flavian Dynasty, and it was this event that provided the impetus for a new series of conquest campaigns in Britain.

As soon as Vespasian became emperor the veteran of the Claudian invasion had to deal with a number of insurrections that had broken out across the Empire during the 'Year of the Four Emperors'. One involved Britain directly, and one indirectly. In the case of the former, this was a second revolt by the Brigantian queen Cartimandua's former husband Venutius. Taking advantage of the chaos back in Rome, the exile successfully deposed Cartimandua, she again asking Rome for help (Tacitus, *Histories*, 3.45). By that time Bolanus had replaced Trebellius as governor, and the new incumbent headed north immediately. However, he was only able to muster a force of auxiliaries, with some believing the legions in Britain at the time had become unreliable given the civil war back in Rome. This force managed to extract Cartimandua to safety back within the borders of the province to the south. The troops then campaigned further north in Brigantian territory, with the poet Statius (*Silvae*, 53 - 56) having Bolanus campaigning in the 'Caledonian Plains'. This indicates the governor had penetrated the Scottish Borders, the farthest north the Romans had ventured in force to that date. However, despite this success, no meeting engagement took place and, with only his auxiliaries to hand, Bolanus was eventually forced to withdraw leaving Venutius in power. Southern provides a useful summary of Bolanus' campaign, saying (Southern, 2013, 121):

> *At best, from the archaeological evidence, it can be said that Bolanus contained the situation, but was unable to embark on full conquest of the north, while the whole Roman world held its breath, waiting to find out who would finally emerge as emperor.*

Meanwhile, the insurrection that indirectly involved Britain was the Batavian Revolt in the Rhine Delta led by Gaius Julius Civilis in AD 69, again at the height of the 'Year of the Four Emperors.' Here, the *Classis Britannica* transported *legio* XIV *Gemina* (newly returned to Britain by Vitellius after it had sided with Otho against him) back to the continent to help put down the uprising. This is an important event in the history of the regional fleet given it is the first time it is actually called the *Classis Britannica* (Tacitus, *Histories*, 4, 79, 3). However, the mention here is ignominious as, having arrived in the Rhineland, the legion's *legate* Fabius Priscus marched his troops inland to attack the neighbouring

Tungri and Nervii tribes who were supporting Civilis. In so doing, he left the fleet at anchor and unguarded, excepting its own *milites*, where it became an easy target for the Canninefates, another regional tribe supporting Civilis. Tacitus says that nearly all of the *Classis Britannica*'s vessels were captured or destroyed during a sustained attack on the anchorage (*Histories*, 4, 79, 3). However, Rome being Rome, once Civilis' revolt had been successfully dealt with all the losses were made good, and it continued in service until the mid-3rd century AD.

Back in Britain, Bolanus never got a second chance of glory in the north. With Vespasian now emperor, he cast around to find a suitable target for early conquest, keen to usher in his new dynasty with a swift victory. He alighted on the Brigantes. The first new governor, Bolanus' replacement, was the Cerialis who we first met infamously when he fled from Boudicca after defeat in her sanguineous revolt. This proved the low point in his progress along the *cursus honorum* career path for Roman aristocrats, and by the time of the 'Year of the Four Emperors' he was a leading military commander again, fighting alongside his kinsman Vespasian and playing a key role in the latter's success. His reward was command of the Roman forces that defeated Civilis in the Batavian Revolt, after which he was promoted to the governorship in Britain. He arrived in AD 71, bringing a new legion with him. This was *legio* II *Adiutrix*, an interesting choice given it had been created by Vespasian from the *milites* of the *Classis Ravennate* in Ravenna in AD 70 after their support for him in the 'Year of the Four Emperors'. These troops, as with Cerialis, were therefore totally loyal to the Flavians, and their deployment to Britain illustrates the importance the new emperor placed on securing new victories there.

Once in Britain Cerialis headed north immediately to set about Venutius and the Brigantes (Tacitus, *Agricola*, 17). In the first instance he ordered *legio* IX *Hispana* out from its legionary fortress at Lincoln into Yorkshire where the troops constructed a new fortress at York, deep in Brigantian territory on the River Ouse. He then moved *legio* II *Adiutrix* into the vacated fortress at Lincoln to act as a strategic reserve. Next, Cerialis split the *Classis Britannica* into two divisions, one on the west coast which gathered in its old hunting ground in the estuary of the River Dee, and another on the east coast off the Humber Estuary. The former was to support a drive north along the west coast by the *legio* XX *Valeria Victrix*, whose loyalty the Flavians continued to suspect following the 'Year of the Four Emperors'. Vespasian had therefore replaced its commander with Agricola, who makes his first appearance in Britain here. Meanwhile, the latter was to support a similar drive up the east coast by the units of the *legio* IX *Hispana* led by the governor himself, Cerialis taking command of his old legion once more. Finally, before the campaign began, Cerialis redeployed part of *legio* II *Adiutrix* from Lincoln to the River Dee where a new vexillation-sized fort and naval facility was built at Chester, with the double aim of providing a base for the west-coast division of the *Classis Britannica* and to secure Agricola's left flank from any insurgency in north Wales.

Clear here is the vital importance of the *Classis Britannica* to the success of Cerialis' campaign against the Brigantes, for example in controlling the littoral zone to secure the exposed maritime flanks of the legionary spearheads, providing the transport and supply function along the coast and down the river systems to keep the land forces moving, and to scout ahead to provide timely intelligence of any gathering opposition. The parallels of this campaign with that of Vespasian along the south coast in the late AD 40s are remarkable, not least with the combination of the land forces following routes along the coast supported by a strong naval presence, with again military harbours created along the route as the advance continued. We have strong archaeological data to support this, showing such harbours being built at Wilderspool, Kirkham, Lancaster (later the site of a vexillation fort), Ravenglass and Kirkbride on the west coast (in addition to Chester), and Brough-on-Humber (later the regional *civitas* capital of the Parisi, Roman *Petuaria*) and South Shields (Roman *Arbeia*) on the east coast.

Cerialis' campaign followed a familiar pattern, with each legionary spearhead heading inland to subdue the native tribes of the Brigantian confederation on arrival at each estuary and river. Thus, rivers like the Dee, Esk, Ellen and Wampool on the west coast, and the Humber, Tees and Tyne on the east provided highways along which the invading Romans took the fight to the enemy. Soon, Cerialis and Agricola began to wrestle regional control from the Brigantes piece by piece. The progression of this campaign is well evidenced by the multitude of vexillation forts built as the operation unfolded, with the end never in doubt given the scale of Roman commitment. The final British stand was at the Brigantian capital Stanwick, with the Romans totally victorious and Venutius killed. Our primary sources are silent at this point regarding Cartimandua so it is unclear whether she regained her crown or not, but we do know that by the time Cerialis returned to Rome in AD 74 the whole of the north of England (and potentially the southern Scottish Borders) was occupied by Rome, with the province extending its frontier further north than ever before.

The next soldier governor was Frontinus, another Flavian favourite who'd fought for Vespasian in the 'Year of Four Emperors'. Famed in his lifetime as a military man of letters, he composed a book on strategy called *Strategems*, this heavily used as source material for the later and more famous *Tactics* by Aelian. Frontinus arrived in Britain with the north for now pacified and so turned his attention back to the unfinished business in Wales. There, despite the campaigns of Ostorius, Didius, Verianus, and Paulinus, the native tribes were still proving troublesome, especially the Silures in the southeast. Deploying *legio* II *Augusta* from its base in Gloucester where it had been based since the mid AD 60s, Frontinus mounted a lightning campaign using the River Severn and Bristol Channel to protect his left flank, where once again the regional fleet played a major role in the now very familiar roles of littoral control, transport and scouting. Within three years all opposition in the south of Wales had been crushed, with a new string of forts built to help enforce the rule of Rome. A number of these were on riverine estuaries, including locations such as Caerhun, Carmarthen, Caerarfon, Lougher, Conwy, Pennal and Neath. Finally, to secure the region even more firmly he permanently redeployed the *legio* II *Augusta* from Gloucester to Caerleon on the River Usk, where they proceeded to build the famous legionary fortress and harbour to oversee southern Wales and the Bristol Channel. He similarly tasked *legio* II *Adiutrix* with developing the vexillation fort and harbour at Chester into a full legionary fortress to keep an eye on northern Wales. However, this region continued to be troublesome and was the initial target of our next and greatest soldier governor, Agricola. His fame, and our knowledge of his campaigns today, owes much to the public relations exercise carried out on his behalf by his son-in-law Tacitus. One of the finest Roman historians, he detailed a number of aspects of the history and nature of early-occupied Britain in his *Annals* and *Histories*. However, it is his narrative regarding the campaigns of his father-in-law in his *Agricola* that is most relevant here.

Arriving in the late summer of AD 77, Agricola immediately launched a savage offensive against the Ordovices in response to their near annihilation of a detachment of Roman cavalry. Within a month he'd hacked his way through to the Isle of Anglesey, once more a centre of native opposition to Rome, surprising the Britons with a lightning assault and completely defeating them. He then consolidated his position, completing what Paulinus had started 17 years earlier, with Wales finally pacified. Then in AD 78 the new governor turned his attention to the north, spending a year targeting any remaining resistance among the Brigantes to ensure his rear would be secure, with his eye now on the unconquered far north. This campaign included building a ring of new vexillation forts around the newly incorporated territory (Tacitus, *Agricola*, 20) up to the Solway Firth-Tyne line.

Finally, in AD 79, Agricola launched his first assault across the northern frontier into the Scottish Borders. This campaign followed the same pattern as that of Cerialis against the Brigantes, with two spearheads forging northwards, one on the west coast and one (led by *legio* IX *Hispana*) on the east. As always in these campaigns of conquest in Britain, the *Classis Britannica* was on hand just off the coast of each thrust to fulfil its littoral control, transport and scouting roles, with Moorehead and Stuttard (2012, 103) saying that:

> *In fact, the fleet was to play a vital role throughout the course of the campaign, sailing ahead to reconnoitre harbours, shadowing the troops as they pressed forward on land, shipping supplies up from the south. Just as importantly, it was a useful tool in Agricola's arsenal for psychological warfare, as the sight of Roman galleys plying up and down the…coast of Scotland, using its sea lanes and its anchorages and beaches as if they were their own, struck fear into the Caledonians' hearts.*

Agricola's first season north of the border was relatively problem free, with the remains of a number of marching camps showing the progress of his campaign. At Newstead on the River Tweed near modern Melrose a more substantial fort was also built, near to the site of the capital of the Selgovae tribe. Tacitus says that by the time the campaigning season had ended, the eastern coast spearhead had reached as far north as the River Tay (*Agricola*, 22). The governor's exploits were also well regarded back in Rome, with Dio (*Roman History*, 66.20) saying the new emperor Titus (who had succeeded his father Vespasian the same year) was given his 15th salutation by way of celebration.

Agricola was a seasoned warrior and knew it was imperative not to overstretch his lines of supply, even with the fleet in support. He therefore spent the next campaigning year in AD 80 consolidating his position in the Scottish Borders, the Romans occupying the region up to the Clyde and Forth line and possibly beyond. In this year many of the marching camp sites there were fortified for permanent occupation, and a road system with supply bases built. The principal route later became

Dere Street. Military harbours were also constructed, these at Kirkbride, Newton Stuart, Glenluce, Stranraer, Gurvan, Ayr and Dumbarton on the west coast, and Camelon on the east. Further north, the key fort, supply base and fortified harbour at Carpow on the Tay may also have been first constructed at this time.

The only region in the Scottish Borders still holding out against the Romans was modern Dumfries and Galloway in the southwest, where the indigenous Novantae had been bypassed. These became the target of Agricola's next campaign in AD 81. Gathering the east coast units of the *Classis Britannica* together, he launched an amphibious assault with himself in the lead ship (Tacitus, *Agricola*, 24), either northwards across the Solway Firth from the occupied south coast or westwards across the River Annan in Dumfries and Galloway (some translations of the *Agricola* specifically name the Annan). Once again the combination of land and naval forces proved highly successful, with the Novantae totally defeated.

At this point Tacitus (*Agricola*, 24) has the governor consider a campaign against Ireland, he saying:

> *The side of Britain that faces Ireland was lined with his forces. His motive was rather hope than fear. Ireland, lying between Britain and Spain, and easily accessible also from the Gallic Sea, might serve as a very valuable link between the provinces forming the strongest part of the Empire. It is small in comparison with Britain, but larger than the islands of the Mediterranean. In soil and in climate, and in the character and civilization of its inhabitants, it is much like Britain; and its approaches and harbours have become better known from merchants who trade there. A Scots prince, expelled from his home by a rebellion, was welcomed by Agricola, who detained him, nominally as a friend, in the hope of being able to make use of him. I have often heard Agricola say that Ireland could be reduced and held by a single legion with a fair-sized force of auxiliaries: and that it would be easier to hold Britain if it were completely surrounded by Roman armies, so that liberty was banished from its sight.*

This is a most interesting passage given it seems to indicate that, just as Britain was a source of trouble when conquering Gaul, so Ireland was for Britain when the Empire was trying to conquer Wales and the far north. Certainly it would have been the most likely place for refugees escaping the Roman campaigns of conquest in Wales and western Scotland.

The lion and the lamb. The experience of Roman conquests as experienced by native Britons throughout the Roman occupation. Corbridge Museum, site of Roman *Coria*, the most northerly town in the Roman Empire.

The legions of Roman Britain left their mark across the whole of Imperially occupied territory in Britain. This image of a boar is a symbol of Chester-based *legio* XX *Valeria Victrix*, found in Corbridge.

Above left: The emperor Hadrian, for ever associated with Roman Britain through his building of the wall which carries his name running from the Solway Firth to the Tyne.

Above right: The Imperial troubleshooter Publius Helvius Pertinax, later to briefly become emperor, who served in Roman Britain three times. Early in his career he was an officer with *legio* VI *Victrix* in York, then commanded an auxiliary unit on Hadrian's Wall, and finally in the AD 180s was governor here.

Later Roman Britain featured a number of usurpers who tried to seize the Imperial throne. However, only one succeeded in becoming the emperor of the entire Roman Empire, Constantine the Great. The legionaries of *legio* VI *Victrix* in York declared him emperor in July AD 306. Today the event is commemorated with this statue, sited next to York Minster.

The view of the Aylesford bend on the River Medway from Bluebell Hill on the North Downs, the likely site of the river crossing battle during the Claudian invasion of Britain in AD 43.

Above and below: The Roman campaigns of conquest in Britain were facilitated by a sophisticated network of military roadways which later became the province's key trunk roads. Above, Ermine Street (courtesy of Francis Tusa) heading from London through Lincoln to York, and below, Dere Street running from York to the Firth of Forth.

Above left: An altar from Corbridge, set up by the individual in charge of managing the granaries there during Septimius Severus' *expeditio felicissima Brittannica* campaigns in the far north of Britain in AD 209 and AD 210.

Above right: A number of Roman soldiers who served in Britain are known by name, through inscriptions on their tombstones. Here, Lucius Duccius Rufinus, signifer standard bearer of the IXth legion, who was buried in York.

One of the most important inscriptions from Roman Britain. An inscribed limestone slab dating to AD 108, originally installed above the newly stone-built southeastern *Porta Principalis Sinistra* gate at the legionary fortress in York. This is the last time the enigmatic *legio IX Hispana* is mentioned before it disappears from history.

Roman legionary in classic *lorica segmentata*, as featured on a panel from a lost Arch of Marcus Aurelius, reused on the later Arch of Constantine.

Right: Over half of the Principate Roman military establishment was comprised of auxiliaries. Here foot troops are seen on the Arch of Septimius Severus in Rome.

Below: That most Roman of military formations, the legionary *testudo*, seen here on the Column of Marcus Aurelius in Rome.

Auxiliary cavalry played a key role in all of the Roman campaigns of conquest in Britain. Here they are shown in action in the Marcomannic Wars on the Column of Marcus Aurelius in Rome.

Late Roman legionaries on contemporary panels on the Arch of Constantine. Note the large round body shields which by this time had replaced the classic *scutum*.

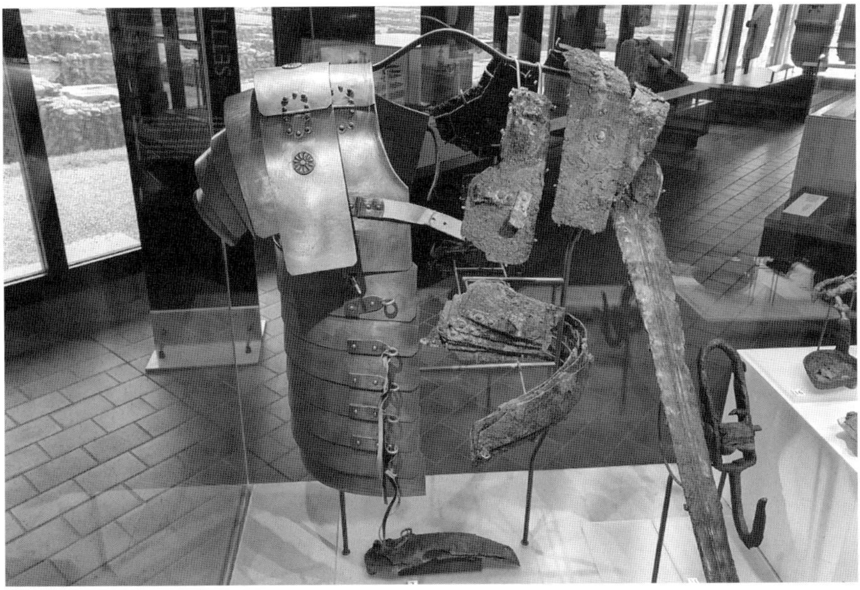

In the Principate phase of Empire the most common form of legionary armour was *lorica segmentata*, this comprising linked bands and plates of iron. This armour evolved over time, with that at top from Corbridge an earlier style and the replica at bottom from Newstead (Roman *Trimontium*) a later and less sophisticated type. The replica is displayed in the Trimontium Trust Museum, Melrose, Scottish Borders.

A variety of Imperial Gallic helmet replicas in the Trimontium Trust Museum, Melrose, Scottish Borders. These provided excellent head protection for Roman legionaries in the Principate-era campaigns of conquest in Britain.

A variety of Roman spear and javelin heads recovered during excavations by Museum of London Archaeology on the banks of the Walbrook, a key stream which bisected Roman London. Now displayed in the London Mithraeum museum there.

Late Republican legionary of the Caesarian period. The legionaries who accompanied Caesar to Britain in 55 BC and 54 BC would have appeared like this, wearing long *lorica hamata* chain mail hauberks. (© *Graham Sumner with permission of Thomas Kurtz, mules-of-marius.com*)

Legionary of the early Empire wearing *lorica segmentata* banded iron armour. Many of the troops accompanying Aulus Plautius to Britain in AD 43 would have appeared like this. (© *Graham Sumner*)

A Roman *equites* auxiliary cavalryman on patrol in the far north of Britain. (© *Graham Sumner*)

A trader's details are checked before she crosses the *vallum* of Benwell fort on Hadrian's wall during the reign of Hadrian. (© *Graham Sumner*)

Above left: Severan legionary figure painted by the author. By the time of the Severan campaigns of conquest in Britain a change had begun to take place in the panoply of these elite warriors in the Roman army, indicated here by the replacement of the *pilum* with a long spear.

Above right: Late Roman *equites cataphractarii* figures painted by the author. Such heavily armoured lancers would have been a key component of the field armies of the Dominate phase of the Empire, including in Britain.

Left: Late Roman legionary or *auxilia palatina* figures painted by the author, accurately depicting *lorica hamata* chainmail armour, oval body shields and *spatha* swords. Note the *draco* standard.

The Roman campaigns of conquest in Britain featured a number of huge legionary fortresses used to house the legionaries who conquered and then pacified each targeted region. Here, the barrack blocks and ovens at the legionary fortress at Caerleon in south-eastern Wales.

The sequence of five defensive ditches at the Roman fort site at Ardoch near Braco in Perthshire. Originally Flavian, it formed a key part of the Gask Ridge series of watch towers and signal stations.

Fortifications in Roman Britain became more sophisticated as the occupation progressed. Here, the multangular tower which formed the west corner of the legionary fortress at York. (Roman *Eboracum*)

Left: One of two huge granaries at Roman Corbridge, built to help supply the Severan campaigns in the far north.

Below: The *aedes* shrine which housed the legionary standards beneath the Principia headquarters building of a Severan military compound at Corbridge.

The Flavian and Antonine fort site at Roman *Trimontium* near Melrose in the Scottish Borders. In the distance, the entire far hillside was the location of the vast marching camp built by Septimius Severus for his early 3rd century AD campaigns of conquest in the far north.

After the demise of the *Classis Britannica* regional fleet in the mid-3rd century AD, Roman Britain increasingly relied on a series of coastal citadels for maritime defence, these in a chain later called the forts of the Saxon Shore. Here, that at Burgh Castle in Norfolk.

Later Roman campaigning in Britain was often defensive in nature, designed to counter frequent raids into Imperial territory by Scots from Ireland, Attecotti, Picts and Germans. By this time many of the key towns in Roman Britain had significant defensive wall circuits. Examples can be seen here at St Albans (above) and Caerwent (below). (Roman *Venta Silurum*)

Further, it may well be that Tacitus is only telling us half of the true story here, and for evidence of that we need to briefly return to Chester. There, the legionary fortress is particularly grand in its design and, covering 25 ha in area, larger than any other Roman fortification in Britain dating to the later 1st century AD. Additionally, remains have been found within its walls of buildings usually associated with a provincial capital, in addition to the usual utilitarian structures of a legionary fortress. This may indicate that at one stage Agricola considered Chester to be the chosen location of the provincial capital of a larger combined province featuring both Britain and Ireland. Given the building work had already started on these unusual buildings within the fortress, perhaps Agricola's plans in that regard were more advanced than Tacitus indicates. Certainly he had the means to invade with the west coast fleet available. If this had gathered in Loch Ryan or Luce Bay in Galloway, then it would only have to travel 32km to reach Belfast Lough in today's Northern Ireland. Such a dramatic intervention would certainly have required Imperial approval. However, it seems that if Agricola did ask for permission for this new venture, the new emperor Domitian refused. The third Flavian emperor had little interest in Britain at this stage, his initial focus being on the development of the *limes Germanicus* series of border fortifications along the Rhine. Moorehead and Stuttard (2012, 103) argue that the decision not to invade Ireland was Agricola's biggest regret during his time as governor in Britain.

Agricola received new orders from Rome at the beginning of AD 82 to focus back on the far north again. This time, as the legionary spearheads advanced well beyond the Clyde and Forth line, they focused on the east coast given the inhospitable terrain of the Highlands and Islands to the west. Tacitus (*Agricola*, 25) is clearer here than at any other time about the vital role played by the *Classis Britannica*, detailing it being used to transport troops from the south to replace casualties, harassing the enemy-occupied coast to disrupt economic activity, and maintaining tight control of the littoral zone along the coast and down the river systems. He also highlights the hazards faced by the fleet in the waters so far north, with its frequent storms and unforgiving tides. We have direct evidence of such dangers back in occupied Britain, with the tombstone of an unnamed *optio* of the regional fleet at Chester. According to the epigraphy on his memorial, he died in a storm off the east coast of Scotland at this time. Tacitus (*Agricola*, 26) adds that, as the campaign progressed inexorably northwards, the two distinct arms of the Roman military began to share the same fortified camps. This is perhaps the best example in our primary sources we have showing the army and fleet working so closely together, whether legionaries, auxilia or *milites*.

To this point most of the native resistance to Agricola's campaigns in the far north had been in the form of guerrilla warfare, they withdrawing glen by glen and loch by loch. Now however, given the success of the governor's combined arms approach, they began to risk open encounters. Tacitus has them attacking military installations, and it is in this context we have the last ever historical mention of the famous IXth legion. This references a specific incident when Agricola's legionary spearheads were driving hard through native territory. Tacitus says (*Agricola*, 27):

> *The natives of Caledonia turned to armed resistance on a grand scale…They went so far as to attack our forts, and inspired alarm by taking the offensive…But just then Agricola learned the enemy were about to attack in several columns. To avoid encirclement by superior forces familiar with the territory, he likewise divided his own army into three parts and so advanced. As soon as the enemy got to know of this they changed their plans and massed for a night attack on the IXth legion, which seemed to them the weakest. Striking panic into the sleeping marching camp, they struck down the sentries and broke in. The fight was already raging inside the camp when Agricola was warned by his scouts of the enemy's march. Following closely on their tracks, he ordered the speediest of his cavalry and infantry to harass the assailants' rear and then had his whole army join in the battle cry; the standards gleamed in the light of dawn. The Britanni were dismayed at being caught between two fires, while the men of the IXth took heart again: with their lives now safe they could fight for honour. They even effected a sally, and a grim struggle ensued in the narrow passage of the gates. At last the enemy broke under the rival efforts of the two armies, the one striving to make it plain that they had brought relief, the other that they could have done without it.*

After this Agricola took no chances, tasking *legio* XX *Valeria Victrix* with building the legionary fortress at Inchtuthill on the north bank of the River Tay in Perth and Kinros. He then began to build a naval logistics chain of fortified harbours northwards towards the Moray Firth, this matching the well-known marching camp sequence as his legionaries and auxilia penetrated deep into native territory. South to north above the River Tay these naval installations were located at Monifieth, Dun, Aberdeen, and finally Bellie in

Moray itself. This construction programme concluded the fourth northern campaigning season, with Agricola garrisoning his forts and fortified harbours in the far north for the winter and the Britons moving their women, children and elderly to places of safety. Tacitus (*Agricola*, 28) adds one more interesting detail here, showing the Romans didn't have everything their own way. He says that a cohort of Usipi auxiliaries recruited from Germany mutinied for reasons unknown and, murdering their centurion, stole three *liburnian* biremes. Tacitus (*Agricola*, 28) enigmatically described the ships as '*…a ghostly apparition as they sailed along the coast…*' while making their getaway, they eventually crossing the North Sea before coming to various kinds of grief on the north German coast due to the ineptitude of the crews.

Agricola's fifth and final campaign in the by now very far north took place in AD 83. It marked the culmination of his ambitions to subdue the entire main island of Britain and, given the resistance he had encountered the previous year, he took no chances, fielding the largest force available. This numbered up to 30,000 men, including legionaries, auxiliaries and the *milites* of the *Classis Britannica.*

In the first instance Agricola deployed the fleet forward once more ahead of the legionary spearheads to raid up and down the coast as far north as the Moray Firth. His aim was to force a decisive meeting engagement. In this he was eventually successful, with the famous Battle of Mons Graupius taking place in the Grampians below the Solway Firth. While the exact location of this encounter isn't known, a series of large 44 ha marching camps heading north along the Highland Line, and then onwards from the Mounth uplands up to the Moray Firth (these specifically from Raedykes to Muiryfold), have now been identified as Agricolan (Hodgson, 2014, 41). This route is believed to lead to the battle's general location. Wherever it specifically occurred, the engagement was decisive with the total defeat of the Caledonians despite they having an uphill advantage. Tacitus (*Agricol*a, 37) adds Agricola only had to use his auxiliary foot to effect victory, his legionaries held in reserve, with the native army suffering 10,000 casualties compared to 360 on the Roman side.

His victory secure, Agricola led his troops on a punitive expedition in the Grampians and the Moray and Buchan Lowlands below the Moray Firth. He then tasked squadrons of the *Classis Britannica* with completing a circumnavigation of Britain, with Tacitus saying (Agricola, 10):

> *The Roman fleet now sailed round the furthest shores for the first time, and so established that Britain is an island. At the same time it discovered*

> *and overthrew some islands, called the Orkneys, which until then had been unknown. Thule (possibly Iceland) too, was sighted.*

The defeat of the natives complete, Agricola claimed in dispatches to Domitian that the entire main island of Britain had been conquered. To further cement control of the north, a series of forts and fortlets were then built to seal off the various Glens in the Highlands, in much the same way trouble had been contained in the conquest of Wales. Today these are called Glenblocker forts. To celebrate complete victory Domitian then ordered the construction of a Carrera marble-clad 25m high monumental arch in Richborough on the east Kent coast to mark the place where the successful Claudian invasion had landed.

However, Agricola's great success was not to last, with Domitian recalling him sometime between AD 83 and AD 85. When he arrived back in Rome he was initially feted, with the emperor awarding him a statue and triumphal decorations. However, he soon fell from Imperial favour and never again held high military or civil office, dying in AD 93. By this time his great achievements in the far north had begun to unravel as Rome gradually lost interest there, perhaps because of the lack of economic potential at the time. Within four years of Agricola's departure the forts cutting off the Highland line had been evacuated and the devastated local population had begun to trickle back south. Then the legionary fortress at Inchtuthil was abandoned before it was fully completed, with *legio* XX *Valeria Victrix* redeploying south to Chester where it replaced *legio* II *Adiutrix* after the latter was redeployed to the Balkans. Similarly, while patrolling in the waters of the far north no doubt continued to maintain control of the littoral zone there, the *Classis Britannica* headed south. Thus as the end of the 1st century AD approached, the fleet found itself principally operating out of the harbours at Chester on the west coast and South Shields on the east.

Before his departure Agricola had set in place his main legacy in Britain, this the 61km long Stanegate road (named after 'stone road' in Northumbrian dialect) running from Carlisle (Roman *Luguvalium*) in the west to Corbridge (Roman *Coria*) in the east, through the natural gap formed by the valleys of the Rivers Irthing and Tyne. The Stanegate was a substantial military trunk road almost 7m wide, and as Roman troops gradually headed south or elsewhere from the far north, it became the northern border of the province. However, to the north there remained the unfinished business of conquest. This was now set to trouble the Roman presence in the south for much of the next century.

More Trouble in the North

As the 2nd century AD began, the mood in the far-flung province of Britannia was one of rare stability. Economically, it had begun to take on the geographical shape set to dominate its structure for much of the rest of the occupation, with the south and east below a line drawn from the Severn to the Humber a fully productive and economically integrated part of the Empire which provided a steady return to the Imperial *fiscus*. However, above this line the north and west remained a border territory where the whole regional economy was geared towards maintaining the large military presence deployed there to maintain the northern frontier. This included vexillations of the three legions still deployed in Britain, all by now settled into the legionary fortresses that were to be their homes for the rest of their stay in Britain. These were *legio* II *Augusta* in Caerleon, *legio* XX *Valeria Victrix* in York and *legio* IX *Hispana* in York (the latter only for a short stay, as we will see). The legions were joined by numerous units of auxilia, many based in a new series of vexillation forts constructed along the Stanegate frontier, a good example being that at Vindolanda. Meanwhile a new series of forts and fortified harbours were built to house the *Classis Britannica* along the east and south coast, examples being those at Dover, Lympne and Pevensey.

Britain remained a quiet province through the reign of Trajan, his attention focused on his two campaigns in Dacia and later the east. The only significant epigraphy relating to the wider military presence in Britain from this period is an inscribed limestone slab dating to AD 108. This was originally installed above the newly stone-built south-eastern *Porta Principalis Sinistra* gate at the legionary fortress at York. It was found in 1854 by workmen digging a deep drain seven metres beneath King's Square in the city. Now in the Yorkshire Museum, it originally formed the centre section of a monumental inscription that, once reconstructed by the best scholars of the day, was translated as below (RIB 665):

> *The Emperor Caesar Nerva Trajan Augustus, son of the deified Nerva, Conqueror of Germany, Conqueror of Dacia, Chief Priest, in his twelfth year of tribunician power, acclaimed imperator six times… (built) through the agency of the ninth Hispana legion.*

This reference is iconic given it is the last time *legio* IX *Hispana* is mentioned in existence before it disappears from history.

Looking at the wider province, trouble in the unconquered far north was never far away. It next broke out with the accession of Hadrian in AD 117 when the *Historia Augusta* (*Hadrian*, 5.1-2) says there was widespread trouble across the Empire. The advent of a new emperor was often met with unrest, as for example earlier with Vespasian. That was certainly the case with Hadrian, who was in Syria with Trajan when the latter died and so well away from Rome where his elevation was met with discontent among the Senate and people. Specifically, in Britain, the *Historia Augusta* (*Hadrian*, 5.1-2) says that '*…the Britons couldn't be kept under control.*' The noted Roman rhetorician Marcus Cornelius Fronto also detailed this event when writing in the AD 160s to his former pupil Marcus Aurelius, saying that the heavy casualties suffered by the Romans in the Rome-Parthian War at that time were comparable to those suffered at the beginning of Hadrian's reign in Britain (Birley, 2005, 118). Epigraphy also references a dramatic event in the north of Britain at this time, in the form of the funerary monument to Titus Anneus, a centurion of the I *Tungrorum* auxiliary cohort. His tombstone at the vexillation fort at Vindolanda references him being killed '*…in the war…*' (Southern, 2013, 175). Other contemporary evidence at Vindolanda is also instructive, in the form of the famous writing tablets excavated there. Specifically, tablet number 164 references '*…nasty little Britons…[Brittunculi].*' This certainly shows there was no love lost between Rome and the natives of northern Britain, whether in the province itself or north of the frontier. Further, a coin dating to AD 119 features Britannia for the first time ever, this on the rear. On the coin the iconic figure is depicted in a typically martial manner, with spear and shield seated on rocks. Moorhead and Stuttard (2012, 124) say it conjures an image of a rugged, warlike province. This is certainly the impression given by contemporary writers. The coin may represent an issue minted to celebrate a Roman military triumph in the far north of Britain.

This troubling level of insurgency, which Moorhead and Stuttard (2012, 124) say threatened the very survival of the province, required the creation of a special task force. This is referenced on the career inscription on the tombstone of Titus Pontius Sabinus found in Farrentino (Roman *Farrentinum*) in Italy (CIL X.5829). Though it mostly details the high offices he later achieved, the most interesting reference is that which states that while he was serving as the *primus pilus* senior centurion of *legio* III *Augusta* in the province of Germania Inferior (note this legion was normally stationed in North Africa so he may have been commanding a vexillation deployed out-of-theatre) he was seconded by the emperor Hadrian to command an emergency task force which the inscription calls the *expeditio Britannica*. This featured vexillations from three legions, these being *legio* VIII *Augusta* and *legio* XXII *Primigenia*, also from Germania Inferior, and *legio* VII *Gemina* from Hispania Tarraconensis. This gives a likely force size of around 3,000 men, it being unclear from the inscription if more troops were also drawn from the vexillation he himself originally commanded. That would increase the legionary force to nearer 4,000 men, almost the size of a full legion, giving real context to events in Britain when the expedition took place. The legionaries may also have also been joined by auxiliaries given another inscription from an altar found at Maryport in modern Cumbria references one Marcus Maenius Agrippa who, when commander of the *cohors* I *Hispanorum* auxiliary cavalry regiment, was tasked by Hadrian to lead them on an *expeditionem britannicam*. Southern (2016, 23) says that these deployments indicate '*…a disaster of some considerable proportions*'. To provide context, the last occasion when such reinforcements had been required in Britain was in the wake of the Boudiccan Revolt in AD 60/61, when the then-new province nearly fell.

This narrative that trouble broke out in the north of Britain at the beginning of Hadrian's reign begs the question who the protagonists were. Certainly the Brigantes, only recently pacified and residing in the military frontier zone (and with some of their peoples still likely living beyond the northern border) are candidates for revolt. Southern (2013, 175) says a specific reason behind any antagonism here may have been forced conscription into the Roman military. This would have been into auxiliary units, with the conscripted troopers then having to serve abroad, well away from their homes. She describes this process as '*…neither gentle or welcome…*' Such a move, when added to the heavy economic dislocation in the north following the earlier conquest campaigns there, may have been the tipping point leading to widespread insurrection. The cause of the trouble may also have come from north of the frontier, with any of the confederations and tribes there candidates for conflict with Rome, the opportunity for glory and plunder in the province to the south perhaps too tempting given Imperial attention was turned towards Rome. It may well be that any northern conflagration involved both the Brigantes and the peoples north of the border, one sparking the other into revolt. This clearly overwhelmed the extensive Roman military presence there, with some speculating it was this event that provides the context for the mysterious disappearance of *legio* IX *Hispana*. This is a reasonable hypothesis to consider given the legion was the most northerly in the province, and therefore first responder to any crisis there. Whatever the case, Sabinus' and Agrippa's *expeditio Britannica/expeditionem britannicam* was a success in the short term, with peace in the north restored temporarily. However, the crisis had attracted Imperial attention, with the troublesome province soon to receive a rare visit from a sitting emperor, he also arriving with a new governor and legion.

Fortifying the Northern Frontier

When Hadrian became emperor he switched the focus of Roman foreign policy from conquest to consolidation. As the *Historia Augusta* details (*Hadrian*, 5.1-2):

> *When he took over the Empire, Hadrian reverted to an earlier policy, devoting his energies to keeping the peace throughout the world.*

The new emperor determined that the Empire had extended as far as it could while remaining a single homogenous unit, and now began to withdraw from regions he thought not worth the cost of maintaining a military presence. These were principally in the east, where he abandoned Trajan's conquests in Mesopotamia. Hadrian then decided to travel the breadth of his wide Empire, eventually arriving in Britain in AD 122 as part of his tour of the northern *limes*.

When Hadrian arrived in Britain, despite the earlier success of the *expeditio Britannica/expeditionem britannicam*, there were again signs of trouble. The *Historia Augusta* (*Hadrian*, 11.2) says he '*...corrected many things...*' and then quotes the poet Florus as saying '*...I do not want to be Caesar, to walk among the Britons...*' (*Hadrian*, 16.3). The emperor also had issues with the military in the province, given an altar found in the Tyne references the discipline he imposed on the legions, while coins minted to commemorate his visit also show him addressing the *exercitus Britannicus*, this broadly translating as the military in Britain. The inference here is that he gave the legions some kind of dressing down. Contextually, this might relate to the fate of *legio* IX *Hispana* if indeed it had been defeated/disbanded in the earlier northern insurrection, while another theory relates to the so-called 'Hadrianic War in London.' Here, hundreds of severed heads in the upper reaches of the Walbrook Valley, a severe city-wide conflagration and the building of the Cripplegate vexillation fort, have been interpreted as evidence of major unrest in the provincial capital, perhaps involving the military (Perring, 2017, 46).

A further indication that all wasn't well in Britain when Hadrian arrived was the arrival of the new governor who travelled with him. This was Aulus Platorius Nepos, previously the governor of Germania Inferior, he replacing the previous incumbent Quintus Pompeius Falco. The latter had been one of Hadrian's early provincial appointments. For some reason, by AD 122 the emperor had decided on a change. The new governor was an interesting choice given he was a close friend and ally of Hadrian, they both belonging to the same Sergia *gentes* tribe. He was also an experienced military leader. His deployment to Britain was therefore a purposeful move by the emperor who wished to place a loyal strongman in charge of a province still clearly riven with issues.

The final new arrival with the emperor and his new governor was *legio* VI *Victrix*, this also travelling from Germania Inferior. The newly arrived legion was highly experienced, having been founded by Octavian in 41 BC at the height of the final round of Republican civil wars. It first fought at the siege of Perusia in northern Italy in that year, where lead slingshots have been found featuring the legion's stamp, before engaging Pompeian forces in Sicily and then taking a leading role in the naval Battle of Actium in 31 BC when Octavian finally defeated Mark Antony and Cleopatra. The legion then served extensively in Spain in the final stages of the Roman conquest of the Iberian Peninsula, where it founded the legionary fortress of León. For this it was awarded its first cognomen, *hispaniensis* (confusingly, given the legion it replaced in York). There it was to remain for a century, before deployment to the Rhine frontier at the end of the 'Year of the Four Emperors' in AD 69 when it then participated in the campaign to defeat the Batavian Revolt. Afterwards it was granted its second cognomen *Victrix* by Vespasian. The legion remained in Germania Inferior, redeploying to Neuss where the troops rebuilt the legionary fortress there after it had been destroyed by Civilis. It next helped defeat the rebellion of Lucius Antonius Saturninus, governor of Germania Superior, against the emperor Domitian in AD 89, before relocating to Xanten (Roman *Colonia Ulpia Traiana*) at the end of the 1st century BC, where it also rebuilt the fort there. Vexillations were then sent to accompany Trajan in his Dacian campaigns, before it finally travelled to Britain. On arrival it headed directly for York where it replaced the disappeared IXth legion as the incumbent, remaining there for the rest of the Roman occupation.

However, Hadrian's greatest legacy in Britain was the building of the 135km-long wall that carries his name along the Solway Firth-Tyne line. Its construction was a key feature of his wider ambition to fully fortify the northern *limes* in Britain, along the Rhine and down the Danube. The accepted version of events regarding the building of Hadrian's Wall has him ordering its construction to physically secure the northern border on his arrival in AD 122, after the earlier insurrection had been put down. However, new evidence is beginning to emerge which shows that its initial construction might actually have begun well before he came to Britain, with sections prepared for him to view as part of his tour of the northern frontier (Graafstall, 2018, 80). If this new theory is correct, it seems he was unimpressed with what he found in Britain as at least some parts of the new frontier fortification were radically altered after his visit, a key change being the building of major forts along its length including those at Birdoswald, Housesteads and Chesters. Whenever the wall was actually built, what is clear about Hadrian's Wall is the vast cost in terms of material and manpower needed to complete it. This forensically highlights the seriousness of the earlier conflagration in the north of the province, perhaps backing the view that *legio* IX *Hispana* may have met a grim fate there.

Hadrian's Wall was anchored in the west at Bowness-on-Solway (site of the Roman fort of *Maia*) on the Irish Sea, and in the east at Wallsend (Roman *Segedunum*) on the Tyne. For much of its length it ran with the line of the Stanegate Road to its rear. As finally completed after Hadrian's visit, the wall was threaded with watchtowers and milecastle fortlets (in addition to the larger forts detailed above), commonly two of the former between each of the latter. The western part was initially constructed from compacted turf blocks, these later being replaced with stone. This was the section built first, and quickly, giving insight perhaps into the direction of the principal threat during the earlier insurrection. Meanwhile, the eastern section was constructed as new from stone, with 3.7 million tonnes of sandstone and limestone eventually used for the facing alone. The wall featured a north-facing fore-ditch, where this was possible, and additionally a large *vallum* constructed to its immediate south. The latter included a broad flat-bottomed ditch up to 3m deep, this up to 6m wide at the top and 2m wide at the bottom, with a mound up to 6m wide on either side. This provided rearward defence for the wall and suggests that the Romans continued to be wary of any further agitation among the Brigantes.

Hadrian left Britain in late AD 122 to tour Gaul and Spain. He never returned, and though his visit can be declared a success given the period of relative peace that followed (excepting the 'Hadrianic War in London' if this took place), fortifications continued to be built in the province. These included a series of coastal defences along the Cumbrian coast around the promontory of the Lake District, consisting of a network of mile-forts and watch towers similar to those of Hadrian's Wall, all occupying prominent positions with views out into the Irish Sea. Clearly, the threat of raiding from that direction was growing in importance. Similarly, we see around this time the construction of similar fortifications on the north-eastern coast. A prime example is the fort at Newcastle (Roman *Pons Aelius*) overlooking the Hadrianic bridge over the Tyne there, this built on the line of Hadrian's Wall to protect the docking facilities further upriver at Wallsend and South Shields.

Hadrian died in AD 138, the event ushering in further serious unrest in the north of Britain, despite the huge investment in fortifications there. Within a year his successor Antoninus Pius had ordered renewed campaigning in the province, with the new governor Quintus Lollius Urbicus sent north with Imperial orders to pacify the region. This was clearly a huge undertaking given he first oversaw a significant upgrading of the logistical infrastructure in the region to support his new northern campaign. This included the refurbishment of key fortifications at sites such as Corbridge, Risingham (Roman *Habitancum*) and High Rochester (Roman *Bremenium*). Once ready, Urbicus then launched his campaign into the Scottish Borders. The route taken north of Hadrian's Wall can be tracked through the refurbishment of the old Flavian forts, for example Newstead near Melrose, and the building of new ones. Any native opposition was quickly overcome, further indicating the size of the force involved.

We actually have direct evidence of the severity of this campaign, this in the context of recently published research regarding the 7 ha hillfort site at Burnswark in Dumfriesshire. Here, a debate has taken place as to whether data previously considered (from antiquarian and 1960s archaeological excavations) showed an actual Antonine-period Roman siege at the site or that the site was actually an example of a Roman siege training exercise. The key items of interest were the north and south Roman siege camps there, and also a plethora of ballista bolts/balls and lead slingshots found at the site. To reach a conclusion either way the Trimontium Trust recently carried out a new review of the existing research and also secured fresh data, the latter based on a systematic metal-detecting survey to identify more lead sling shots (with a view to plotting their scatter) and also experimental archaeology regarding the use of slings in siege warfare (Reid, 2016, 22). The results of this research suggest yet another grim interpretation for the activities of the Romans north of the frontier, with the two camps now being seen as a real-world tactical response to the topography in the context of a full siege, and the widespread scatter of sling shots and other missiles (and their quality) suggesting deadly intent. As Reid (2016, 26) says, the evidence shows that:

> *there was a massive missile barrage at Burnswark. This was not just restricted to the gateways, but extended along a full half kilometre of native rampart. The simplest explanation for this distribution is that the defenders on the hilltop were suppressed by a hail of sling bullets with an accurate range of 120m and the stopping power of a modern handgun, as well as ballista bolts, and arrows. This presumably covered an attacking force sweeping out the three huge gateways and storming the hilltop. Such a combination of missile troops and conventional infantry is likely to have been brutally effective.*

There we have yet again the use of the word brutal with regard to Roman activity in the far north of Britain. Further, one other factor adds even more insight into the awful experience of the native Britons on the receiving end of this devastation. This is because some of the slingshots were hollowed out with a 4mm hole through their centre, this designed to make a screeching noise when slung. This is an early example of psychological warfare on the battlefield, bringing to mind the screaming sirens of diving Junkers Ju-87 Stukas during the Blitzkrieg early in World War 2, adding to the misery of those on the receiving end.

Urbicus' advance was also accompanied by the renovation of the Flavian military harbours that had supported the campaigns of Agricola, and again the construction of new ones. In the Clyde these included Lurg Moor and Bishopton, while on the Forth they included Inveresk, Cramond and Carriden. Inveresk, where Dere Street crosses the River Esk before heading westwards to Cramond, is particularly important in the context of this campaign as two contemporary pieces of epigraphy in the form of altar dedications have been found there, one to Apollo Grannus, the deity of mineral and thermal springs who was associated with healing. These were placed there by Quintus Lusius Sabinianus, the British procurator at the time. The presence here of the official tasked by the emperor with making the province pay is important as it indicates a desire to maintain a permanent presence in the north of Scotland, and indeed it is at this time that the Antonine Wall was constructed on the Clyde-Forth line bringing at least the Scottish Borders within the province of Britain. This event was important enough to be referenced in the *Historia Augusta*, which says that the Emperor (*Antoninus Pius*, 5.4):

> *...defeated the Britons through his legate Lollius Urbicus, and having driven back the barbarians, he built another wall, of turf.*

As with Hadrian's Wall the Roman military built the new fortification, with the whole of the *legio* II *Augusta* and vexillations from the *legio* VI *Victrix* and *legio* XX *Valeria Victrix* involved. The wall, called the *vallum Antonini* during the occupation, was built from slabs of turf set on stone foundations with a wooden palisade running along the northern side, it representing the northernmost fortified frontier in the entirety of the Roman Empire. The Antonine Wall was around 63km in length, was some 3m in height and 5m in width, and featured a 5m deep ditch running along the northern side. Construction began in AD 142 and took about 12 years to complete, with the final wall protected by 16 forts (two of which were, at least in part, stone built), with small fortlets set between them in a similar manner to the system used on Hadrian's Wall. Yet despite the colossal effort needed for its construction the wall was abandoned in the late AD 150s, with the 7,000 strong garrison relocating back to Hadrian's Wall which was then renovated. The evacuation was overseen by the governor Gnaeus Julius Verus.

During the time the wall was occupied trouble again erupted in the far north, and at some stage in the AD 150s military reserves were once more urgently summoned to Britain from the legions and auxilia based in Germania Superior and Inferior (possibly under Verus, the event then marking his arrival as governor). These troops recorded their arrival in dedications to Antoninus Pius on a shrine erected next to the bridge over the River Tyne which also mentioned vexillations of the three resident British legions. This new trouble in the north is also attested by the minting of coins in Rome dating to AD 154–155 which show Britannia in mourning. Finally, Greek geographer and traveller Pausanias (*Guide to Greece*, 8.43.4) also mentions Antoninus Pius depriving the Brigantes of territory. This may indicate that the trouble in the north at this time was from a threat at least partly much further south than the Antonine Wall, perhaps reflecting native discontent that the regional economy was still bent on supporting the exceptionally large military presence there. One should note here that this reference could also be a misunderstanding by Pausanius, with the Brigantes he mentions actually located in Raetia near modern Bregenz in Austria. Interestingly, Verus' next but one replacement Sextus Calpurnius Agricola ordered the *vallum* to the rear of Hadrian's Wall filled in, which could indicate that any internal threat from the Brigantes had been removed.

Some military presence did remain further north for a while, as happened in the immediate period following the post-Agricolan Scottish withdrawal. Some of the forts may have been garrisoned as late as the AD 190s, when it has been argued troops from *legio* VI *Victrix* dedicated an altar to the god Mercury at the fort at Castlecary on the line of the old Antonine Wall.

Further military activity is then evident in AD 169 at the time of the death of co-Emperor Lucius Verus, with the *Historia Augusta* (*Marcus Aurelius*, 22.1) again referencing trouble in Britain, although no further details are given. However, six years later the *Classis Britannica* transported 5,500 Iazyges Sarmatian heavy cavalry to the province where they were based at the Ribchester (Roman *Bremetennacum*) vexillation fort in modern Lancashire to help defend the northern frontier.

Later in the 2nd century AD, trouble again erupted along the northern border during the reign of Commodus. Dio (*Roman History*, 77.12) explains that by this time the various tribes in modern Scotland had coalesced into two main confederations. These were the Maeatae and Caledonians, and given their importance to all of the subsequent Roman campaigns of conquest in Britain, it is worth setting out here in full his early description of them (*Roman History*, 77.12.1-4):

> *The Maeatae live next to the cross-wall which cuts the island in half, and the Caledonians are beyond them. Both tribes inhabit wild and waterless mountains and desolate and swampy plains, and possess neither walls, cities, nor tilled fields, but live on their flocks, wild game, and certain fruits…their form of rule is democratic for the most part, and they choose their boldest men as rulers. They go into battle in chariots, and have small, swift horses; there are also foot soldiers, very swift in running and very firm in standing ground. For arms they have a shield and a short spear, with a bronze apple attached to the end of the spear shaft, so that when the enemy is shaken it may clash and terrify the enemy; and they also have a dagger. They can endure hunger and cold and any kind of hardship; for they plunge into swamps and exist there*

for many days with only their heads above water, and in forests they support themselves upon bark and roots, and for all emergencies they prepare a certain kind of food, the eating of a small portion of which, the size of a bean, prevents them from feeling either hunger or thirst.

The hunger-preventing food described here has been identified as the heath pea (*lathyrus linofolius*) by Dr Brian Moffat (2000, 13) of the Soutra Aisle research centre.

This is a fascinating paragraph for many reasons, but in the first instance shows what a troublesome opponent both confederations would have been for the legions of Rome. This was a very hardy enemy, capable of sustaining military campaigns for a long period in the worst of climatic and geographical conditions. As will be seen in Chapter 7, it seems that both of the Severan incursions in the north were met with intense guerrilla resistance rather than any kind of meeting engagement. However, if the above paragraph is to be taken even partially at face value, Dio also appears to be saying that here also was an opponent capable of standing up symmetrically to the world of Rome, with a seemingly steady spear-armed shield wall and an elite aristocracy riding in swift chariots (perhaps they not being as democratic as he describes).

Meanwhile, Dio's reference to a '*…cross-wall…*' is usually interpreted as referencing the Antonine Wall, despite it having been abandoned by the time he wrote the above. This is based on the known areas where the Romans later campaigned in the far north. This would place the Maeatae either side of the Clyde-Forth line and perhaps even further north above the River Tay, broadly populating much of the Midland Valley, with the Caledonians beyond them in the upper reaches of the Midland Valley and into the Highlands. The names of two hills in this region have in the past been used to show the most northerly and southerly spread of the Maeatae in this interpretation, the former being Dumyat Hill in the Ochils overlooking Stirling

Back to the narrative, the Caledonians and almost certainly the Maeatae breached Hadrian's Wall in AD 182 and headed south along Dere Street, destroying the forts at Halton Chesters (Roman *Hunnum*), Rudchester (*Vindobala*) and Corbridge, with a Roman general being killed in the process. Commodus responded decisively, ordering the British Governor Ulpius Marcellus to counter-attack in force. This campaign seems to have been successful given three epigraphic inscriptions (one at Corbridge and two from Carlisle) speak of successful action beyond Hadrian's Wall at this time (Southern, 2012, 229). Confirmation comes in AD 184 when Commodus received his seventh acclamation as *Imperator* and took the title *Britannicus*.

However, this success came at a price. Given the large military presence needed to maintain the northern border in Britain, and the province's distance from Rome, it continued to be troublesome. Further, the three legions in Britain, *legio* II *Augusta* in Caerleon, *legio* XX *Valeria Victrix* in Chester and *legio* VI *Victrix* in York, had by this time developed a reputation for volatility. In AD 180 Marcellus had to put down some kind of revolt among the legionaries, earning a reputation as a strict disciplinarian. Worse then followed after his victory in the north, with the legions breaking out in a full rebellion against him later in AD 184. Overthrown, he was recalled to Rome in disgrace. The legions then tried to appoint a legate called Priscus as a usurper governor but he refused, with Dio (*Roman History*, 73.9) having him say *'I am no more an emperor than you are soldiers.'* At this point Dio says the legions then selected a delegation of 1,500 soldiers (he calls them 'javelinmen') to travel to Rome to denounce the Praetorian Prefect Sextus Tigidius Perennis to Commodus over some slight they felt he'd caused them. Dio (*Roman History*, 73.9) says they went on to accuse Perennis of plotting against the emperor, and after some convincing by his advisors, Commodus believed them. Perennis was handed over to the British soldiers and killed along with his wife, two children and sister. It should be said that this sounds a most unlikely tale, though Birley (2005, 169) suggests one explanation is that the legionaries were part of a task force established to round up deserters who were becoming endemic at the time in Gaul and Spain. He adds this may have seemed a good way of dealing with some of Britain's most mutinous legionaries, and the whole story does fit with the often-chaotic nature of Commodus' reign. A further hypothesis is that the troops were the *beneficiarii consularis* or *beneficiarii procuratoris* seconded from the legions in Britain to serve on the staff of the governor and procurator in London, in which case the delegation may have had some kind of official capacity.

Whatever the truth, the emperor then moved to restore order in Britain again. First he ordered the legates of the three British legions to be cashiered, and then unusually replaced them with equestrian-rank officers promoted from within their ranks (Kulikowski, 2016, 63). He then, as a stopgap, appointed Marcus Antius Crescens Calpurnianus as a temporary governor. Birley (2005, 171) argues this may have been because, with the three legionary legates deposed, he may have been the only senatorial-level aristocrat left in the province. Unsurprisingly, the Maeatae and Caledonians decided to take advantage of the disruption and attacked the frontier again in early AD 185. However, they were quickly defeated, with coins being minted to celebrate victory in Rome.

Later the same year Commodus appointed his key Imperial trouble-shooter, Publius Helvius Pertinax, as the new full time governor in Britain. The son of a manumitted slave, this Roman everyman had risen improbably through the ranks of the military to be one of its most successful commanders. Elevated to consul after great success in the Marcomannic Wars, he next became the go-to governor in the most challenging border provinces, for example Syria. Commodus now turned to him to finally bring calm to troublesome Britannia. Once in post Pertinax got to work straight away. His top priority was to bring the legions to heel, and like Marcellus he followed a very strict line in discipline. Again this seems to have backfired, for although he won over two of the legions, the other mutinied. The *Historia Augusta* (*Pertinax*, 3.6) says the trigger was actually his turning down an offer to usurp Commodus. It says simply:

> *They wished to set up some other man as emperor, preferably Pertinax himself.*

Whatever the cause, the mutiny was a serious event, the troops ambushing him and leaving him for dead with his bodyguard slain. The *Historia Augusta* (*Pertinax*, 3.9) then says he punished the legion very severely, perhaps by ordering a decimation whereby one legionary in ten was executed by his fellow soldiers. This seemed to work, with Dio (*Roman History*, 73.9) saying Pertinax eventually 'quelled' the mutiny.

There is some controversy about how Pertinax's time as governor in Britain ended in AD 187. The *Historia Augusta* (*Pertinax*, 3.10) says he next '*…petitioned Commodus to be excused from the governorship…*', blaming the legions who, it adds, were still hostile to him. This is at odds with Dio's earlier comment about Pertinax pacifying them. However he left Britain though, Pertinax was soon back in Rome where his next position was another promotion, this a further stepping stone on his way to being the first of the Imperial incumbents in the 'Year of Five Emperors' in AD 193.

The chaos in Rome that year was the catalyst for the final round of military action in Britain in the 2nd century AD. The year began with the assassination of Commodus on New Year's Eve. Pertinax, by then the city prefect, was quickly made emperor by the Praetorian Prefect Quintus

Aemilius Laetus and Eclectus, the court Chamberlain. He proved a popular choice with most of the Senators and people of Rome given his plans to overturn the grossly self-indulgent policies of his predecessor. However, he fell foul of the Praetorian Guard who had gotten used to an easy life under Commodus, and only three months later they assassinated him. The leading Senator Didius Julianus then shamefully won the throne through a bidding war with the guard, though he wasn't to last long either. Septimius Severus, a native of Lepcis Magna in North Africa, was governing Pannonia Superior at the time. He fell like a Sword of Damocles on Rome after his mentor Pertinax was assassinated. By the year's end he was the last man standing in the Imperial capital, with Julianus killed by the Senate even before Severus' arrival in Rome. That left only two challengers to his claim to the throne. These were the Syrian governor Pescennius Niger and the British governor Albinus. Prioritising Niger as the bigger threat, Severus proclaimed Albinus his *caesar* to secure the west. He then fought a year-long campaign in the east against Niger, finally defeating him at the Battle of Issus in May AD 194. Severus then turned his attention to the eastern frontier and the Parthians. However, his plans there were curtailed when news reached him that Albinus had usurped in Britain. Herodian (*History of the Roman Empire*, 2.15) is explicit that Severus' earlier appointment of Albinus to be his *caesar* was a simple ruse to buy time to defeat Niger. Matters came to a head in autumn of AD 196 when word reached Albinus that Severus now felt secure enough to appoint his elder son Caracalla *caesar*, and specifically to be his successor. The British governor saw the writing on the wall and decided to take the initiative, minting his own coins on which he styled himself a full *augustus*, and then usurping. The move was popular in Britain, with Herodian (*History of the Roman Empire*, 3.7.1) describing scenes of revelry. However, soon sobering news reached him that Severus was on his way to stamp out the rebellion. Albinus moved quickly, gathering the three British legions and a significant number of the auxiliaries from the province. Together they were ferried by the *Classis Britannica* to Gaul. There, Albinus gathered a huge force to challenge the emperor, the two armies meeting at the titanic Battle of Lugdunum in AD 196 which, though close run, Severus eventually won.

With Albinus now dead Severus' immediate response was to send military commissioners to Britain to bring the military there back under his full control, in the first instance installing his supporter Virius Lupus as the governor. Southern (2013, 237) says that when the latter arrived in AD 197 he found the province in chaos once more, and quickly set about restoring order. However the Caledonians, soon to be joined by the Maeatae, lost no time in causing more trouble, clearly sensing an opportunity given the diminished Roman military presence. With a new invasion across Hadrian's Wall now in prospect, and with no reserve troops to call upon given the Emperor's focus by that time on Parthia in his second eastern campaign (see Chapter 7), Lupus had few options and opted to secure peace along his northern borders with massive payments of money (Dio, *Roman History*, 76.5). However, this only bought a short period of stability, and the next development, as this paid-for-peace slowly collapsed, leads elegantly to the next chapter which covers Septimius Severus' enormous attempts to conquer the far north of Britain in the early 3rd century AD.

Chapter 7

Septimius Severus in Scotland

In this chapter the Roman campaigns of conquest in Britain reach their crescendo with Septimius Severus' two enormous invasions of the far north in AD 209 and AD 210. In these he led a force of 57,000 legionaries, auxiliaries and *milites* of the regional fleet, the largest force ever to campaign in Britain. His second surge north is also infamous given he ordered a genocide in the lowlands of modern Scotland.

In this chapter I first consider why Severus mounted these two colossal shock-and-awe invasions north of the frontier, called the *expeditio felicissima Brittannica* by contemporary audiences. I then detail the planning for his 'Severan surge', before considering the composition of the emperor's vast army as it gathered in York, the town which became the Imperial capital for the last three years of his life. Finally I describe the two campaigns in detail, including an analysis of the brutal strategy he employed to subjugate the Maeatae and Caledonian native confederations who came to bitterly regret attracting his attention.

Why Did Severus Invade Britain

In AD 207 the great warrior emperor Septimius Severus was bored in Rome. After securing the throne by defeating of Albinus in AD 197, Severus had turned his attention back to the east and Parthia. His campaign there proved a great success, with his forces sacking the Parthian capital Ctesiphon in AD 198. Before leaving, Severus then expanded the *limes Arabicus* along the eastern frontier, in the process constructing new fortifications in the Arabian Desert including those at Azraq (Roman *Basienis*) in Jordan and Dumah al-Jundal (Roman *Dumata*) in modern Saudi Arabia. He then toured his eastern provinces, a process that lasted four more years, before returning to Rome in AD 202 where he celebrated his *decennalia* with a victory games and oversaw the marriage of his eldest son Caracalla. He stayed only briefly, the native North African never comfortable among the political classes there, and later the same year returned to his native Lepcis Magna in Africa Proconsularis. There he initiated an energetic building programme, this including a new *forum* and *basilica*, colonnaded streets and a new harbour. Late in AD 202 he then launched a campaign against the Garamantes Berber tribe who were causing trouble along the *limes Tripolitanus*. There, *legio* III *Augusta* under the *legate* Quintus Anicius Faustus had been fighting an intensive campaign to prevent raiding into rich farmlands of Tripolitania on the North African coast, with steps already underway to further fortify the border. Typically, Severus now took matters in hand and launched a campaign that penetrated far to the south of the *limes*, capturing several significant oasis settlements including Cydamus, Gholaia, Garbia and the Garamantes capital of Garama, the latter over 600 km south of Lepcis Magna. He then incorporated much captured territory into Africa Proconsularis, and further fortified the border. This campaign over, Severus continued his travels westwards in North Africa, spending time in Numidia where he again expanded Imperial territory by annexing the settlements of Vescera, Castellum Dimmidi, Gemellae, Thabudeos, Thubunae and Zabi. Then, reluctantly, he returned to Rome again.

This most military of men was never happy in the Imperial capital, with its constant political machinations and temptations. However, a new opportunity soon presented itself for further martial adventure. This was in Britain, where as the 3rd century AD began renewed conflict again broke out in the north. Severus, brooding in the Imperial palace, was apparently angry when news reached him that the governor Lucius Alfenus Senecio was winning wars in the province while he was reduced to leading a campaign in the Apennines against a bandit uprising (Dio, *Roman History*, 76.10.6). The emperor was further displeased by the way his sons Caracalla and the younger Geta were behaving in Rome, indulging in a life of luxury clearly at odds with the old warrior's martial nature. Forever squabbling, the former was already displaying the psychotic tendencies that were to later cost his younger brother his life. Severus therefore jumped at the chance when Senecio wrote to him in AD 207 with alarming news. Herodian, our only source here, describes the letter thus (*History of the Roman Empire*, 3.14.1/2):

> *the governor of Britain informed Severus by dispatches that the barbarians there were in revolt and overrunning the country, looting and destroying virtually everything on the island. He told Severus that he needed either a stronger army [usually interpreted as a request*

> *for more troops] for the defence of the province or the presence of the Emperor himself. Severus was delighted with this news: glory-loving by nature, he wished to win victories over the Britons to add to the victories and titles of honour he had won in the East and the West.*

Given Herodian's known inaccuracies in his life of Severus, the veracity of this account and the very existence of Senecio's letter needs to be considered in the first instance. Birley (1999, 172) highlights that the classical historian was well known for the use of the rhetorical *topos*, a stock formula such as a pun, proverb, cause and effect or a comparison. We have two specifically relevant instances of this where he utilised the existence of a letter similar to Senecio's from other provincial governors in his later work to justify Imperial expeditions. These were with regard to Syria and Mesopotamia, and to Illyria. In the former case, the dramatic events described in the letter requiring the emperor's attention actually date to five years earlier than the communiqué, a fact that leads Birley to reject Herodian's narrative regarding Senecio's letter as pure invention (1999, 172).

However, if we were to take Herodian's story at face value, then context is very important as we consider this famous request, given it is so often the starting point for narratives regarding the *expeditio felicissima Brittannica*. After the period following Albinus' usurpation attempt when the new governor Lupus had had to weather severe agitation along the northern border by buying the invaders off with huge subsidies, Rome was again starting to assert its authority in the north. By way of example, we know that Lupus and succeeding governors (including, latterly, Senecio) had started the restoration of a number of the installations along Hadrian's Wall, with auxiliaries used to build a new granary at Birdoswald. They also refurbished defences further south at Corbridge (Frere, 1974, 171), and restored buildings at Chesters and Housesteads. Meanwhile, a victory dedication by the *Ala* I *Astorum* under Senecio's governorship at Benwell indicates military success on his part, this thought to relate to events in AD 206 when Dio (*Roman History*, 77.10.6) references victories in Britain (this likely the source of Severus' irritation detailed above). However, all of this positive activity seems to have changed in a very short space of time, with some kind of calamity in the north, and perhaps even further south if we take Herodian's interpretation of Senecio's request at face value. Given we have no data to allow us to interpret what this crisis in AD 207 actually was, the request and the Emperor's very rapid, seemingly over-the-top response requires further consideration.

In the first instance, Herodian's reference to the emperor being '... *delighted...*' seems pretty clear cut, especially in the context of his concerns with the behaviour of his sons in Rome. A blunt reading of the primary sources indicates that the threat was sudden, very real, and that when presented with the opportunity to intervene Severus couldn't wait to get stuck in. However, others have raised issues with taking Herodian at face value, over and above Birley's wider reticence regarding the letter. Wilkes (2005, 213) for example has questioned why Severus would trouble himself with a disturbance on the fringes of Rome's most remote province for the last three years of his life (given the primary sources also tell us that the emperor didn't think he would return alive once he committed to the expedition). Meanwhile, Rankov (2009, 170) suggests Severus was actually far more concerned with re-establishing his authority over the military in Britain given it had been the seat of Albinus' earlier attempt at usurpation. He says:

> *the expedition [was] ... as much concerned with re-establishing the loyalty of the army as with dealing with barbarian incursions or the conquest of Scotland for its own sake.*

In this interpretation the letter from Senecio (if it existed) might therefore have been part of a plan concocted to give Severus an opportunity to carry out an expedition he wouldn't normally have had a motive for. This is an interesting argument given Severus had already sent his commissioners to Britain in the immediate aftermath of his victory over Albinus, and at the same time temporarily combined the command of the regional fleets in the west under one commander (Elliott, 2016, 25). Further, it was his commissioners who initiated the building of the land walls of Roman London, to remind the elites in the provincial capital who the boss was. Matters with the military must have become very strained indeed if all of the above had failed to the extent that the emperor had to come up with some kind of diplomatic ploy. However, as Hodgson (2014, 35) counters:

> *If the loyalty of the British army was really the only issue, one wonders why Severus left it so long: he was freed up from his eastern wars by AD 201. Rankov may be right to sense Severus' long-standing*

> *fear of disloyalty in Britain, but wrong to dismiss the seriousness of the 'barbarian incursions'.*

Hodgson goes on to speculate that perhaps the commissioners had instead failed to overcome problems that originated with the weakening of the British garrison after Albinus had taken his best army troops to their defeat at Lugdunum in AD 197. Given the size of the losses it would certainly have taken time to rebuild the military strength of the recalcitrant province, although another factor may have been Severus responding to his own near usurpation by deliberately leaving the garrison undermanned (and the province therefore inadvertently vulnerable). It is worth noting here that although it was later under Caracalla that the single province was divided into two, namely Britannia Superior in the south and Britannia Inferior in the north, planning for this almost certainly began under Severus (Elliott, 2016, 20). One thing is very clear here. This was a province he didn't trust.

Meanwhile, Bidwell has carried out an examination of the archaeological data regarding the garrisons in the northern forts of the province in the final years of the 2nd century AD and also the beginning of the 3rd, he concluding that evidence at Bainbridge (Roman *Virosidum*), South Shields and Bowes (Roman *Lavatris*) does seem to show the military there below full strength both in terms of numbers and its cadre of commanders (Bidwell, 2012, 69), even though as we have seen above the rebuilding of physical military structures was taking place under Senecio. Following this narrative, Severus' concerns about Britain as a continuing hotbed of potential revolt may have led to a situation where the Maeatae and Caledonians sensed an opportunity, their appetites already wetted by their being bought off with massive bribes in their previous incursions. As Hodgson (2014, 36) says:

> *The silver denarius subsidy hoards, evident in the archaeological as well as the literary record, are a clear enough attestation of how seriously Rome took her northern neighbours in Britain, and the expense to which she was prepared to go to manage them.*

Such hoards persisted longer in the far north of Britain than on the continent (they generally ceasing there around AD 194 after Severus' elevation to Emperor), showing that even though reconstruction had begun along the northern frontier under the governors who succeeded Albinus, the Empire at this time still found it easier to buy off their troublesome northern neighbours. Thus, with the northern frontier still denuded of an appropriate garrison (even as the infrastructure was being rebuilt to accommodate newcomers), the Maeatae and Caledonians may have looked to the south for easy pickings.

We are therefore left with a number of motives to consider for Severus' extraordinary decision to commit the vast sums of manpower and cash needed for his *expeditio felicissima Brittannica*. These are:

- Severus, whether Senecio's letter existed or not, was itching to get away from Rome and return to the field, a warrior bored in the Imperial capital and concerned about the behaviour of his two sons. In that context, he may have been looking for an opportunity for martial endeavour, and in the most extreme interpretation manufactured one.
- Another factor here was Severus' legacy. A long-term sufferer from chronic rheumatic gout, he was not a well man by this time (and indeed, as detailed above, did not expect to return from his British expedition), and would not have wanted to leave unfinished business in the form of unrest in Britain. In that regard, all Roman emperors (no matter how successful) knew they would be judged against the glory of the first emperor Augustus, and Severus would have been keenly aware of the words of the late-1st century BC poet Horace that Augustus would only be judged a God if the Britons and Parthians were defeated (see Chapter 4 for full quote). In that context, from Severus' perspective, he had dealt with the Parthians. All that was left were the troublesome northern Britons.
- Clearly, even after the attentions of the emperor's commissioners, all was not well with the garrison in Britain. Although the rebuilding of military infrastructure was taking place, the northern border was still undermanned after Albinus' usurpation. Whether this was a deliberate policy by Severus who feared an internal threat there rather than an external one from further north, or was simply the natural outcome of the difficulties in rebuilding a garrison force much denuded by Albinus, is unclear.
- Finally, and a factor much overlooked by many commentators, are the motivations and behaviour of the protagonists. The Maeatae and Caledonians had already been heavily engaged along the border throughout the previous generation at various times from the AD 180s, and had been bought off with enormous quantities of portable

> wealth in the AD 190s. That in itself must have caused enormous friction among their own elites, already coalescing into larger and larger political units through the cultural impact of close proximity to the Empire. It may therefore have been the case that their leaders, now permanently on the lookout for a military distraction to the south, saw the opportunity for a profit-making raid to keep their warriors occupied. Further, another factor for consideration here involves a possible harvest shock (crop failure) in the early 3rd century AD in Scotland. Given the emergence of the two confederations detailed above in the late 2nd century it seems reasonable to suggest that the population in the region was growing, and there were now more mouths to feed. We also know that the weather at the time of the two Severan campaigns in the north was unusually poor. We might therefore speculate that the latter could have impacted crop yields, leading to a need for the native leaders north of the frontier to head south to feed their growing populations.

My own view here is that we are looking at a combination of factors, presenting all of those involved with a unique set of circumstances that together led to what followed. The warrior confederations north of the border were getting a taste for vast wealth and looking for an opportunity for easy plunder (and may have been hungry), the northern border for some reason was undermanned, and the emperor was on the prowl for war and mindful of his legacy. Whether triggered by the arrival of Senecio's letter or provincial news in another form (whether real or engineered), the scene was therefore set for Imperial shock and awe writ large.

Planning the Campaign

Whatever the reason behind Severus' decision to launch a new campaign of conquest in Britain, he jumped at the chance to take the field one last time. Prior to departure, his first action was to gather any senior individuals in Rome with knowledge of Britain to provide close council. These included Lupus, his trusted first governor in Britain after the defeat of Albinus, and the recently returned Gaius Valerius Pudens, Senecio's immediate predecessor. Other likely candidates included Gaius Julius Asper, patron of the province of Britannia in Rome, and Polus Terentianus, Severus' ally in the 'Year of the Five Emperors' who was earlier *legate* of *legio*

II *Augusta* in Caerleon. Another former legate of this elite legion close to hand was Silius Plautius Haterianus, while another candidate was Antius Crescens Calpurnianus, the *quindecimvir sacris faciendis* responsible for the maintenance of temples in Rome at the time who, as detailed in Chapter 6, was briefly acting governor in Britain under Commodus.

As the year progressed the emperor began the detailed logistical planning for his *expeditio felicissima Brittannica*. The first step was to bring together the key military leaders and advisors who would accompany him. Birley (1999, 175) says there is no evidence that he took any of those with whom he initially sought counsel, perhaps preferring a younger team to join him in what he knew would be an arduous expedition. Those we do know accompanied him in his senior team included two senatorial *comites* (Imperial military companions), namely Julius Avitus Alexianus (the brother in law of the empress Julia Domna) and Gaius Junius Faustinus Postumianus, the recent governor of Lower Moesia and a fellow North African who would take over as governor in Britain upon the expedition's arrival (an interesting appointment, perhaps reflecting a fall from grace for Senecio after his urgent request for help). Others who joined the top team for the expedition included Sextus Varius Marcellus of Apamea, the new procurator for the province, this appointment again indicating all was not well in Britain. This was another safe pair of hands from a Severan perspective, he being the son-in-law of the above Julius Avitus Alexianus, married to Julia Domna's niece Julia Soaemias (these the parents of the future emperor Elagabalus). Meanwhile, also accompanying the emperor was the Praetorian Guard prefect Aemilius Papinianus. We also know of two others named in the senior military team from inscriptions regarding their job titles, but whose actual names are now lost to us. One is detailed on a sandstone altar found at Corbridge who was assigned the key role of managing the granaries and logistics base there, while another is found in Rome, this being the individual assigned to lead the *Classis Britannica*. The former is a key figure in the narrative of the Severan invasions of Scotland as it is in the context of his inscription (RIB 1143) that we get the reference to the *expeditio felicissima Brittannica*. In full, this important dedication reads:

> *[...]norus [...pr]aep(ositus) cur(am) agens horreorum tempo[r]e expeditionis felicissi(mae) Brittannic(ae) v(otum) s(olvit) l(ibens) m(erito).*

This translates as:

> *...]norus..., officer in charge of the granaries at the time of the most successful expedition to Britain, gladly and deservedly fulfilled his vow.*

Having set in place the military leadership for the campaign, Severus now turned to the members of his Imperial administration who would accompany him, given York would become the most unlikely of Imperial capitals for the last three years of his life. First however, he moved to ensure stability in Rome and the wider Empire while he was away. We have some detail here, his planning having a distinctly North African feel to it, with key provinces left in the hands of his kinsmen, supporters and friends. For example, Pannonia Superior was under the governorship of Egnatius Victor while Germania Superior was being governed by Aiacius Modestus Crescentianus, both North African natives, while the legionary *legate* in the key Danubian frontier province of Pannonia Inferior was Septimius Castinus, likely a family member. Other key postings were allocated to trusted former military colleagues. For example, Coele Syria (Severus having divided the province of Syria into two military/administrative units), the vital province in the east, was governed by Marius Maximus, another North African, who had been a legionary legate under Severus' brother Geta when the latter was governor of Moesia Inferior in AD 193. Severus' plans were clearly meticulous given that, even after his death in AD 211 in York, the Empire within and outside its borders remained remarkably quiet (despite Caracalla's purge of his father's inner circle as soon as the latter had passed away, and his later 'terror' in Rome).

Having secured his rear, Severus now gathered his team of Imperial advisors and confidants. These included his *Consilium Principis* main council, the *ab epistulis* head of secretariat, *rationalis summarum* head of the *fiscus* Imperial treasury, and large numbers of his own Imperial freedmen and slaves from his *familia Caesaris*. Of the latter we know specifically of two. These were Castor the court chamberlain, and Euodus who had previously been Caracalla's tutor. The emperor was also joined by his close family including Julia Domna, Caracalla and Geta, the latter two probably the first on his list of attendees given his keenness to remove them from the sensual diversions of Rome. Key Senators who were not already part of his inner circle also joined.

As AD 207 slipped into AD 208 Caracalla and Geta were both appointed as consuls in Rome, they holding office for the third and second time respectively. By this time his elder son had been 'joint' emperor for a decade, with Geta remaining as the junior 'most noble Caesar'. Coins were then minted showing the Emperor riding off to war, though we know from the primary sources that he was actually carried in his litter for most of his journey (and indeed later when on campaign in Britain) given the gout he was suffering from. The sources also indicate that his two sons set off first, reaching the continental coast before him, probably with their own entourage. The majority of the huge Imperial party took things more slowly given the enormous baggage train travelling with the emperor.

The orders for the mobilisation of the military units making up Severus' force were actually sent out across the Western Empire earlier in AD 207, using the *cursus publicus* state-run courier system. Given their early notice, all units so ordered were therefore ready to move at the beginning of AD 208, coinciding with Severus' departure from Rome. It is in this context that we can see the northern regional fleets (by now back under individual command) gathering off the major ports on the continental coast of Gaul, ready to start ferrying the troops to Britain. This would have commenced from the Spring in AD 208, with many being sent direct to the north of the province through Brough-on-Humber from where they headed to York to await the Emperor. Others would have landed further north at Wallsend and South Shields, either making camp there or travelling back south to York, while others still would have sailed through the then Great Estuary in East Anglia to Caistor St Edmunds, or travelled up the Thames Estuary before beginning the long march north along Ermine Street. However, Severus and his large entourage would certainly have entered Britain through the Imperial Gateway at Richborough in Kent, essential given he would have wanted to put his stamp on the formerly recalcitrant province from the word go. The image of the ageing and ailing Emperor, who was 63 by this time, being carried through Domitian's monumental arch in a sedan chair is an enigmatic one, although one wonders if he might have made the effort to hobble through under his own power given the importance of the expedition to him. Either way, he had arrived and the *expeditio felicissima Brittannica* was under way.

The Composition of the *expeditio felicissima Brittannica*

We can determine the composition of the 'Severan surge' by cross-referencing the various units known or inferred to have participated by the primary sources, archaeological data and informed modern commentators.

For example, given that one of the Prefects of the Praetorian Guard, Aemilius Papinianus, was part of the Severan leadership team for the expedition, it seems highly likely that at least part (and probably a significant portion) of this elite fighting force participated. Severus would certainly not have travelled without his own guard. It should also be remembered that by this time the Praetorians were composed of veterans from the Danubian frontier after Severus had reformed the body shortly after he'd become emperor, in the process doubling its strength. It was therefore an elite fighting force designed for battle, not simply the palace guard that had enjoyed the high life under Commodus. The *equites singulares Augusti* Imperial guard cavalry, also doubled in size when Severus reformed the Praetorian guard, were also part of his entourage, while another ready source of troops was *legio* II *Parthica* based in *Albanum* 34 km from Rome, many of whose legionaries would also have joined him in his *expeditio felicissima Brittannica* (Birley, 2005, 200). This was one of the three Parthian legions raised by Severus for his second eastern campaign, and the only one to travel back to Italy with him. As detailed in Chapter 1, at this time most legions were based in legionary fortresses around the frontier of the Empire, so it was highly unusual for Severus to choose to base this one so close to the Imperial capital. The implication is clear enough, the legion a reminder to the political classes of Rome who was in charge. Meanwhile, it has also been speculated that one of the urban cohorts from the *cohortes urbanae* in Rome may also have joined Severus' force.

Other units receiving notification in AD 207 to prepare to journey to Britain were the legions and auxilia based along the northern frontiers of the Empire, with Birley (1999, 175) saying that:

> *The Rhine and Danube armies will also, it is clear, have contributed to the expedition...It may well be that several whole legions were sent, although it is more probable that vexillations only were detached.*

It seems likely given the size of his eventual force that the legions along the Rhine and Danube were stripped down to the bare minimum to hold the frontier, and one can imagine large amounts of tribute being paid to the tribal confederations north of the border to encourage their peaceable intentions while the emperor was in Britain.

Once in the province these legionaries would have been joined by those of the three British legions based there at the time, these still *legio*

II *Augusta* based at Caerleon, *legio* VI *Victrix* at York and *legio* XX *Valeria Victrix* based at Chester. The British legions seem to have performed well during the Severan campaigns here, with for example *legio* VI being awarded the commemorative title *Britannica Pia Fidelis* (based on tile stamps from Carpow) and *legio* XX being similarly styled *Antoniniana* by Caracalla after the death of his father. To this elite force of troops we can then add the auxiliaries, still a prominent component of the Principate armies of this period. Either based in Britain, or being ordered to the province to accompany the Severan expedition, Moorhead and Stuttard (2012, 162) estimate their numbers at a huge 35,000, though I estimate this figure at slightly less given the huge number of guards and legionaries deployed for the campaign. We know specifically of one of the units engaged in this regard, this being *cohors* V *Gallorum* whose presence has been identified at South Shields and Cramond, both key supply depots for the *expeditio felicissima Brittannica*.

Overall, this gathering of military units from across the west implies a total force of around 50,000 front line troops mustered for the campaigns in the north of Britain, this figure corresponding to the calculation referenced by Moorhead and Stuttard (2012, 162) that the granaries at South Shields could hold enough grain to feed 50,000 men for two months, and also the seemingly random figure chosen by Dio (77.12.2) when referencing casualties in the campaign. The gathering of such an enormous force was a dramatic undertaking by the emperor, he effectively creating what would later in the Empire be called a field army.

As a final point here, to this figure of 50,000 we can then add the 7,000 naval *milites* of the *Classis Britannica* which would have played a vital role controlling the littoral flank of the campaign (including along the river systems), scouting ahead of the legionary spearheads, patrolling once territory had been pacified and (perhaps most importantly) transporting men and supplies.

The Severan Campaigns of AD 209 and AD 210

At this point, while Severus was making his final plans in York, a delegation arrived from the far north to sue for peace, not surprising given the overwhelming force they now knew was about to be unleashed upon them. However, the emperor was in no mood for compromise. Even if he had been, realistically this was not an option considering the size of military force he had gathered there. Herodian (*History of the Roman Empire*, 3.14.4) says that instead he wanted to:

> *"...prolong his time in Britain and not return hurriedly to Rome, while entertaining his ambition to add to his victories and titles by a campaign against the British, so he sent the delegates away empty-handed, and put everything in order for war."*

This also fits in well with the earlier analysis regarding his motives for the *expeditio felicissima Brittannica,* which included a desire to stay away from Rome and seek out further martial glory. Thus, whatever his opponents in the north hoped to achieve in trying to negotiate, they failed. An apocalypse was now set to descend on them.

All Roman thoughts now turned to the campaign. With 50,000 men in the field, plus the 7,000 *milites* of the regional fleet to hand, Severus knew the key to the success of his plans to conquer the far north of Britain was a colossal logistics operation. To that end the eastern maritime flank was vital, with Severus planning a never-ending conveyor heading north from South Shields with food and supplies, this stopping off at the old fort, supply base and militarized harbours at Cramond on the Forth and Carpow on the Tay, both refurbished once the campaign commenced. From there the emperor then planned for the carried materials to be trans-shipped to smaller riverine vessels which would then use the regional river systems to transport their goods to the troops on the front line and in the rear. Under this meticulously planned operation the plan was for the vessels to then return with any booty, prisoners soon to be slaves, and the wounded (of which there were many in these two campaigns), before the whole process would start again.

With the logistic plans in place, Severus and his senior command team then devised their overall campaigning strategy. This was simple but brutally effective. In the first instance, the entire army was to cross the frontier *en masse* and head north along the well-trodden route of Dere Street in the Spring of AD 209. This would hammer through the Scottish Borders as one massive homogenous force, cauterizing all before it and in the immediate vicinity. Here, given the vast scale of his operation, Severus expected the local tribes to quickly sue for peace. We have direct evidence of this in the archaeological record, for example at the Flavian vexillation fort at Vindolanda. Here the large Antonine structure, whose remains are visible today, was demolished by Severus and replaced with a levelled platform set out in a Roman street grid pattern. Along the length of the roadways LIA round houses were then set out. It seems here that the emperor built a concentration camp to house the refugees escaping his predations to the north.

Severus planned for the enormous Roman force to stay together throughout its surge through the Scottish Borders along Dere Street. Then, once it reached the Firth of Forth at Inveresk, it was to turn west and find a bridging point. At that point the plan was for the force to divide into two. The larger, with two-thirds of the legionaries and auxilia under the fitter Caracalla, was to head northeast along the Highland Boundary Fault (effectively the Highland line) to seal off the fertile upper Midland Valley from the Highlands, building Glenblocker forts as they passed each glen. At the same time the *Classis Britannica* was to seal off the eastern coast of modern Scotland. Then, once the local population was trapped and had nowhere to go, Severus with the remaining third of the army was to launch a legionary spearhead over the Forth directly through Fife, crossing the River Tay into the upper Midland Valley where it would eviscerate all before it.

All preparations in place, Severus waited for the weather to improve. However, it did not, with the whole campaign set to play out in atrocious conditions. By late Spring his troops were growing restless, so Severus decided enough was enough and launched the massive 'Severan surge' across the frontier. At first it was a great success, smashing all before it. As the Romans advanced, an enormous supply train in tow and with the emperor and Caracalla in their midst, outriders from the auxiliary cavalry *alae* ranged far and wide to protect the flanks of the advance and provide a scouting function, no doubt raiding recalcitrant native settlements wherever possible. At the end of each day's march a single, huge marching camp almost 70 ha in size was built to house the whole force. Today we can track the progress of Severus' route through the Scottish Borders by the crop marks and archaeological remains they left. These enormous camps, all tracking Dere Street and heading south to north, are located at (Jones, 2011, 103):

- Newstead V
- St Leonards (the largest at a full 70 ha)
- Channelkirk
- Pathhead III

Soon the region up to the Forth, at least in the east, was completely subdued. Reaching Inveresk, Severus then continued along Dere Street as it turned westwards to track the extensive waterway. At some point on the south shore a bridge was then built to allow the force to cross the Forth, with the former Antonine Wall heading west to the Clyde also repaired and re-manned with a view to protecting Severus' rear once the Roman force advanced further north.

As to the crossing, the exact location has never been found and there is some debate about where this would have been, and what type of crossing it was. What we can say definitively is that a bridge crossing did take place. The principal data used here to determine the bridge type (and that later discussed for the Tay) is based on contemporary coin evidence. Robertson (1980, 137) definitively identified these coins as a gold *aureus*, bronze *asses* and bronze medallions of Severus from AD 208, which all feature an image of a permanent monumental bridge, and a small coin or medallion of Caracalla dated to AD 209 featuring a bridge of boats. Although he misdated it to AD 208, Reed (1975, 92) earlier described the Caracallan coin, saying it:

> *…shows a bridge of boats (with Caracalla and his father marching over it) with the legend Traiectus underneath, [it being] similar to a bridge on coins of Marcus Aurelius of AD 172, showing his crossing of the Danube.*

One of the locations suggested by this coin would have been a crossing of the Forth at South Queensferry near Edinburgh, divided in the middle by Inch Garvie, where the Forth Railway Bridge now stands. Reed (1975, 92) goes on to make the case that a bridge of boats up to two kilometres in length (possibly up to 500 boats, impressive considering the overall size of the *Classis Britannica* was 900 vessels) was constructed under Caracalla's authority, hence it being on his coin. He says that archaeological data emerging at the time of his writing also supported this hypothesis, he arguing that the location of the Severan marching camp at Auchtermuchty in Fife on a line from North Queensferry to Carpow indicates a road on that line (see below for more detail). Reed (1975, 95) cites Dio (*Roman History*, 77.40) as a primary source when the latter details:

> *…as he advanced through the country he experienced countless hardships in cutting down the forests, levelling the heights, filling up the swamps, and bridging the rivers…*

Reed chose to interpret this in the context of a road-building exercise northwards along this line in Fife, the route Severus was to take with the third of the force he commanded. South Queensferry is also close to the important supply base at Cramond to the east on the line of Dere Street. Other options suggested for the Severan Forth crossing include further upriver northeast of the Antonine Wall fortress of Camelon (on the river Carro, a Forth tributary), and also at Alloa and even Stirling. However, Reed's earlier hypothesis does make sense given the strategy I earlier detailed.

Moving on, having reached its crossing point the 'Severan surge' divided as planned, with Caracalla leading his two thirds of the army across the bridge onto the northern shore of the Forth. His legionary spearhead most likely comprised the three British legions, used to campaigning in this theatre, together with the British auxilia. Vexillations of legionaries and auxilia from the Rhine and Danube would have provided support. Caracalla stuck rigidly to the emperor's plan, launching his blitzkrieg lightning strike southwest to northeast along the Highland Boundary Fault, building the sequence of 54 ha marching camps as he went. These formed the basis of the Glenblocker forts that were constructed once Caracalla reached the coast. Yet again we can track his route based on the cropmarks and archaeological remains they left behind, these located at (Jones, 2012, 113):

- Househill Dunipace near Falkirk, presumably the stopping off point before crossing the Forth
- Ardoch 1 at the fort site at the south western end of the Gask Ridge
- Innerpeffray East
- Grassy Walls
- Cardean
- Battledykes, Oathlaw
- Balmakewan
- Kair House

The marching camp at Kair House was built adjacent to Bervie Water, only 13km southwest of Stonehaven on the coast, with the Highland line visibly converging with the sea there. The Highlands and the route northwards to the Moray and Buchan Lowlands beneath the Moray Firth were now sealed off, as was the coast by the Classis Britannica, leaving the Maeatae and Caledonians living in the upper Midland Valley trapped and in great peril. It also seems likely that at this time the Flavian Gask Ridge system of watchtowers and signal stations was brought out of retirement to act as a link between the marching camps/Glenblocker forts to the north and Severus with his reserves on the Forth. All was now set for the emperor to deliver his coup de grâce.

Severus now gathered his force and crossed the Forth. This likely comprised the Praetorian Guard, other guard units, troops from *legio* II *Parthica* and the Rhine legions, and more auxiliaries. He headed directly north, crossing through Fife, a region heavily settled by the Maeatae who the emperor swiftly subjugated, with two 25 ha marching camps showing his route. These are at:

- Auchtermuchty
- Edenwood

Severus quickly reached the River Tay at Carpow where the earlier fort, supply base and fortified harbour had already been rebuilt, ready for use when he arrived. Here he built another bridge to cross into the upper Midland Valley. Reed has argued that the Severan coins and medallions featuring a permanent monumental bridge and dated to AD 208 (see above) could be related to a new stone-built crossing here, but this view was later rebutted in detail by Robertson (1980, 137). I agree with the latter interpretation given that, to my mind, this was far too early in the campaign to build such a structure. The coins might therefore refer either to a pre-existing stone-built bridge there (Flavian or Antonine, very unlikely), or more likely the bridge over the River Ouse at York or the River Tyne crossing at Newcastle, if this bridge is in Britain at all. My preference at Carpow is yet another bridge of boats, as argued by Robertson (1980, 137) for this location, in addition to that across the Forth. In this context the Caracallan coin of AD 209 then references both, possibly in a generic context for all major river crossings associated with the campaign.

As detailed above, Reed (1975, 95) suggested that to link the Forth and Tay crossings a road was built through Fife. He argued that this ran from North Queensferry (the northern footing of his Forth bridge of boats) to Auchterderran (where he cites antiquarian reports of a marching camp and the finding of a coin of Pertinax, as detailed above first of the incumbents in the 'Year of Five Emperors' in AD 193), then on to Loch Leven where a Severan coin hoard was found in 1851 at Portmoak, and finally onwards to the known marching camp sites at Auchtermuchty and Edenwood and thence to Carpow. To be clear, no road has actually been found to date along this route. However, given the often marshy nature along its proposed length, it might be here that the primary source references to log-built roads being built refer.

Back to the campaign narrative, by the time the bridge at Carpow was ready, all within the upper Midland Valley who hadn't been able to escape west or north were now trapped and at the mercy of the Romans. Severus then struck north across the Tay bridge into the soft underbelly of native resistance, initially driving hard inland before turning eastwards and heading for the coast where he met up with the larger force under Caracalla, perhaps at Inverbervie on the coast near the marching camp site at Kair House (Kamm, 2011, 126). Such a strategy may explain the brutality of this campaign, given the natives had literally nowhere to run, the Romans ravaging the whole upper Midland Valley. In such circumstances the native Britons had no chance to coalesce into a single homogenous fighting force (most primary sources reference there being no single meeting engagement), with resistance to the Romans reduced to localised, vicious guerrilla warfare.

At this point it is worth considering the experience of battle in this most gruelling of campaigns. As mentioned previously, the Severan campaigns in the far north were grim for all protagonists. As detailed the weather was worse than usual, and the terrain proved particularly difficult for the Romans. Our best account comes from Dio (*Roman History*, 76.13), which I set down in full below given the crucial insight it provides:

> *as he (Severus) advanced through the country he experienced countless hardships in cutting down the forests, levelling the heights, filling up the swamps, and bridging the rivers; but he fought no battle and beheld no enemy in battle array. The enemy purposely put sheep and cattle in front of the soldiers for them to seize, in order that they might be lured on still further until they were worn out; for in fact the water caused great suffering to the Romans, and when they became scattered, they would be attacked. Then, unable to walk, they would be slain by their own men, in order to avoid capture, so that a full fifty thousand died [clearly a massive exaggeration, but indicative of the difficulties the Romans faced]. But Severus did not desist until he approached the extremity of the island.*

Herodian's account (*History of the Roman Empire*, 3.14) also highlights the difficulty the Romans faced in pinning the Britons down, he saying:

> *frequent battles and skirmishes occurred, and in these the Romans were victorious. But it was easy for the Britons to slip away; putting their knowledge of the surrounding area to good use, they disappeared in the woods and marshes. The Romans' unfamiliarity with the terrain prolonged the war.*

The reference to battles in the latter quote has been interpreted by most as indicating small engagements, in the context of the subjugation of the upper Midland Valley. In fact, only one primary source seems to overtly detail major engagements, with Orosius (*Seven Books of History Against the Pagans*, VII.17) speaking in his brief reference to the Severan campaigns in the far north of '*…great and serious battles*'. However, of all of the various sources here, Dio is the clearest and most relevant (with Orosius for example writing in the early 5th century AD) and it is his insistence that Severus '*…fought no battle and beheld no enemy in battle array…*' that I choose here to follow. As Moorhead and Stuttard (2012, 164) argue, a century of studying the strategy and tactics of the Romans had taught the native Britons to avoid a formal engagement if at all possible, with Herodian (*History of the Roman Empire*, 3.14.) saying their guerrilla tactics '*…told against the Romans and prolonged the war*'.

The nature of the opponents also counted against the Romans, as evidenced by the Dio quote in Chapter 6 regarding the hardiness of the Maeatae and Caledonians. They were clearly far more experienced to a life of living rough in their indigenous terrain when required, with Herodian (*History of the Roman Empire*, 3.14) saying they dispensed with breast plates and helmets '*…which would impede their movement through the marshes*'. However, despite the grim nature of the campaign, ultimately the size and rapidity of the Roman campaign was successful, with the enemy defeated and the entire regional economy devastated (Hodgson, 2014, 48). Soon the Maeatae and Caledonians were suing for peace, desperate to preserve what was left of their local economy and population. By this time the Romans were also keen to wrap things up given the enormous cost to the Imperial *fiscus* treasury of keeping such a huge force in the field, while the steady stream of casualties (note Dio's improbable figure of 50,000) from guerrilla activity had also begun to tell on the morale of troops. Additionally, the ageing Severus was exhausted by this point. He therefore decided to agree terms with his equally fatigued enemy. This may have been unpopular with his military leadership and some of the troops, as Dio next tells the famous tale of an attempted Imperial fratricide by the increasingly ambitious Caracalla. Once more this a passage important enough to be presented in full (*Roman History*, 76.14):

> *Antoninus (Caracalla) was causing him alarm and endless anxiety by his intemperate life, by his evident intention to murder his brother if the chance should offer* [discussed later in the chapter], *and, finally, by plotting against the emperor himself... (thus) when both were riding forward to meet the Caledonians* [and presumably Maeatae], *in order to receive their arms and discuss the details of the truce, Antoninus attempted to kill his father outright with his own hand. They were proceeding on horseback, Severus also being mounted, in spite of the fact that he was weakened by infirmity in his feet, and the rest of the army was following; the enemy's force were likewise spectators. At this juncture, while all were proceeding in silence and in order, Antoninus reined in his horse and drew his sword, as if he were going to strike his father in the back. But the others who were riding with them, upon seeing this, cried out, and so Antoninus, in alarm, desisted from his attempt. Severus turned at their shout and saw the sword, yet he did not utter a word, but ascended the tribunal (where the peace was to be signed), finished what he had to do, and returned to headquarters. Then he summoned his son ... ordered a sword to be placed within easy reach, and upbraided the youth for having dared to do such a thing at all and especially for having been on the point of committing so monstrous a crime in the sight of all, both the allies and the enemy. And finally he said: "Now if you really want to slay me, put me out of the way here; for you are strong, while I am an old man and prostrate. For, if you do not shrink from the deed, but hesitate to murder me with your own hands, there is Papinian, the* [Praetorian] *prefect, standing beside you, whom you can order to slay me; for surely he will do anything that you command, since you are also emperor." Though he spoke in this fashion, he nevertheless did Antoninus no harm ... on the present occasion he allowed his love for his offspring to outweigh his love for his country; and yet in doing so he betrayed his other son, for he well knew what would happen* [once he himself was dead].

If this isn't a literary device by Dio, who was later very critical of Caracalla as emperor, then the narrative seems pretty clear that Severus here only just survived an assassination and usurpation attempt. The peace was signed nevertheless, and on terms favourable to Rome, with the native Britons ceding much territory to the Empire (perhaps up to the Antonine Wall line, and even Fife given Carpow's evident ongoing use: Dio, *Roman History*, 76.13). Severus next proclaimed a famous victory, with he and his two sons given the title *Britannicus* and celebratory coins struck to commemorate this. Campaigning, at least in the short term, was over, and to apparent Imperial satisfaction. Dio (*Roman History*, 76.16.5) even adds an anecdote here about Julia Domna, saying that after the peace had been agreed she had a conversation with the wife of a Caledonian leader named Argentocoxus in which they compared the sexual customs of their respective cultures.

With garrisons left in the far north Severus, Caracalla and the military leadership headed south to winter in York, and were still there in May AD 210, given Birley (1999, 185) highlights a letter sent in their names in response to an inquiry by a lady called Caecilia dated to the 5th of that month. However, clearly the terms which had so satisfied the Romans in AD 209 were not so agreeable to at least the Maeatae (probably the recipients of the most extreme experiences of the AD 209 campaign) as in AD 210 they revolted again. Birley (1999, 186) suggests one of the issues here was that a key tribal centre may have been near to the later Pictish capital site at Abernethy, very close to the Roman supply base and bridge at Carpow, and it may latterly have dawned upon the native Britons that the Romans in the region were determining to stay for the long term, settled deep in the Maeatae heartland. One can only guess at the sad fate of the Roman garrisons in the far north as the revolt gathered pace, and Severus reacted with fury. Once more he determined to march north, and this time to finish the job for good.

Sadly for the emperor ill health got the better of him and he delegated overall command of the ensuing campaign in AD 210 to the now apparently-forgiven Caracalla. However, before the troops left Dio says the emperor addressed his massed army, this leading to one of the darkest episodes in British military history if true. The historian, who we should remember was a contemporary of Severus and who knew him well, puts the following words in his mouth as he spoke to the soldiers (*Roman History*, 77.15):

No: we are not going to leave a single one of them alive, down to the babies in their mothers' wombs – not even they must live. The whole people must be wiped out of existence, with none to shed a tear for them, leaving no trace.

These words are actually a quote from Homer's Iliad (6.57-9) by Agamemnon to his brother Menelaus when asked how to deal with Trojan prisoners. Though clearly a literary device by Dio, the implication is clear. The historian is saying that Severus gave the order to kill every native Briton the Romans came across in the second campaign. To provide context here, it has already been noted in this work that when faced with a recalcitrant foe the Romans would often order a brutal response, for example with Ostorius and the Silures as detailed in Chapter 6. However, this was on a different scale entirely. Ostorius' example was with regard to a specific tribe or confederation, but Severus' shocking command was targeted at an entire people. The emperor was, in effect, ordering a genocide. As we will see, he may have succeeded.

We have less detail of this second campaign under Caracalla excepting it seems to have been an exact replica of the first, though with no quarter given to the native Britons, not even the non-combatants. It was certainly successful again from a Roman perspective, given more commemorative coins of Caracalla, and this time his brother Geta, were minted in Rome celebrating their British victory. However, as ever when the Romans campaigned in the far north of Britain, fate intervened. This was because, in a freezing February in AD 211 in York, Severus died. His death, when he'd finally succeeded in conquering the far north of Britain to his satisfaction, is one of the great turning points in the history of the British Isles. This is because it seems he was willing to commit the resources to maintain a significant military presence there. Further, given that recent archaeological research shows the AD 210 genocide may really have taken place (with settlement in the Midland Valley a shadow of its former self and reforestation on a large scale occurring on previously fertile farm land), the regional threat was significantly diminished. It would stay so for another 80 years before trouble in the north of Britain is mentioned again by contemporary sources (see Chapter 8).

However, with the emperor's demise, Caracalla and Geta couldn't wait to get back to Rome. The emperor had hoped they would form a new Imperial diarchy, as with Marcus Aurelius and Lucius Verus, but in this they failed their dead father miserably. By the year's end Caracalla had killed his brother, or had him killed, with Geta bleeding to death in their mother Julia Domna's arms. The new emperor then set about a new round of proscriptions in Rome of a gruesome scale to match those of Sulla in the early 1st century BC, with many Severan family members and supporters killed as Caracalla moved to secure his hold on the Imperial throne. Back in Britain, without the political will of Severus to keep the troops in place in the far north, the 50,000 men gradually returned to their own bases. The northern border was then re-established on the line of Hadrian's Wall once more, which was extensively repaired, and here it would remain for the remainder of the Roman occupation of Britain. Thus, for all of Severus' Herculean efforts to conquer the far north of Britain, it all came to naught. From that point, when the Romans did return to campaigning in the far north of Britain at the end of the 3rd century AD, their ambitions were much diminished, with no intention to stay.

Chapter 8

Later Campaigns in the Far North

For those with a love of the Roman campaigns of conquest, Britain is the gift that keeps on giving. This is because, as seen in earlier chapters, the far north was never fully conquered, continually requiring a much larger military presence than otherwise needed. This was to be tested to breaking point in the late 3rd and 4th centuries AD as time and again Roman occupied Britain was wracked with both usurpations, and also invasions from the far north by the now emergent Picts. The latter were later joined by Scots from Ireland, Attecotti from south-western Scotland and Germanic pirates from lands far to the north of the *limes* along the Rhine.

In this chapter I detail the last two major campaigns of conquest (or rather re-conquest) in Britain. These were that of the western Caesar Constantius Chlorus in AD 296 to defeat the North Sea Empire of Carausius and Allectus, and that of *Comes* Theodosius (often called Theodosius the Elder given he was the father of Theodosius I) in AD 367 to defeat the so-called 'Great Conspiracy'. Other serious military operations did occur in this period, and are covered here, though we know less about them. However, I begin with political developments in Britannia in the immediate aftermath of Septimius Severus' campaigns in the far north, and then cover the impact of the devastating 'Crisis of the 3rd Century' in Britain.

Before beginning this dramatic chapter, which takes the story of Roman Britain to the very brink of its collapse in the early 5th century AD, I make two brief comments on key sources. Firstly, I frequently make use of the *Notitia Dignitatum* list of key late Roman military offices across the Empire. This was almost certainly compiled in the late 4th and early 5th centuries AD, and so is most applicable to that period. However, given it reflects many of the changes to the Roman military initiated by Constantine I (see Chapter 1), I believe it also remains applicable earlier in the 4th century AD. Additionally, another key source for the second half of the 4th century AD is Ammianus Marcellinus, a Roman soldier and historian who wrote a lengthy history of Rome called the *Res Gestae* (from the Latin '*things done*'). This originally covered the period from the accession of Nerva (AD 96 to AD 98) to the death of Valens at the Battle of Adrianople in AD 378. Sadly, only the section covering events between AD 353 and AD 378 survives, this known to us today as his *Late Roman History*. Ammianus Marcellinus is a particularly important source for the activities of *Comes* Theodosius in Britain in AD 367/ 368. However, it should be noted he wrote this account in the reign of the latter's son, which clearly influenced his objectivity given he was broadly a supporter of the emperor. Nevertheless, he is the best primary source we have for this period, and with that health warning in mind I use him freely here.

A Land Divided

The first major development in Britain following the Severan campaigns in the far north, and the later military withdrawal to the line of Hadian's Wall, was the formal division of the province into two. These were called Britannia Superior, with its capital in London, and Britannia Inferior, with its capital in York. Though this significant structural change was carried out in the reign of Caracalla, it is likely planning began under Septimius Severus given his mistrust of the province following the usurpation of Clodius Albinus. That was certainly the case in the province of Syria which he divided in his own lifetime, into Syria Coele and Syria Phoenice, following his troubles with its governor Pescennius Niger after his seizure of the Imperial throne in AD 193. Though the naming of the two new provinces in Britain simply reflects their physical position rather than status (as for example with Germania Superior and Inferior), that in the south was certainly the senior given its governor was of consular rank, while the governor in the north was of praetorian rank. The former had control of *legio* II *Augusta* in Caerleon and *legio* XX *Valeria Victrix* in Chester, while the latter directly commanded *legio* VI *Victrix* in York in addition to his day-to-day administrative duties.

The location of the physical border between the two new provinces is unknown, though likely ran along a horizontal line somewhere between Chester to the south and Lincoln to the north. As Southern (2013, 254) points out, it wasn't an impermeable barrier, with vexillations from the two southern legions still forward-deploying north to help man the northern frontier. We have direct evidence of this in the archaeological record, with for example inscriptions noting both helping rebuild the fort at Netherby (Roman name unknown) north of Hadrian's Wall around AD 219.

A factor to note here easing the creation of the new northern province was York's recent use as the Imperial capital under Septimius Severus, with all of the physical infrastructure of Imperial control no doubt still in place. Its elevation in importance, with the creation of Britannia Inferior, may have been the catalyst for the upgrading of its status from a *municipium* mercantile town to a *colonia* veterans' colony.

The Impact of the 'Crisis of the 3rd Century' in Britain

Despite his dramatic interventions in the far north of Britain at the end of his life, Septimius Severus' real legacy here and elsewhere in the Empire was negative in the extreme. This was because the collapse of his dynasty ushered in the ruinous 'Crisis of the 3rd Century' that brought the whole Empire to the point of collapse. The phrase is commonly used to describe the final phase of the Principate Empire, beginning with the assassination of Severus Alexander (the last Severan emperor) by his own troops in AD 235, and lasting until the accession of Diocletian in AD 284. Such was the damage to the political, economic and social structure of the Empire by the crisis that its nature had to fundamentally change, and from this time we talk of the Dominate Empire. This referenced a much more authoritarian style of Imperial control, with the name itself based on the word *dominus* meaning master or lord in Latin. Gone was the conceit of the Principate with the Emperor the principle citizen of the Empire but still *'one of us'*. Now, with control of the military and political classes vital to the survival of the Empire, he became more akin to an eastern potentate.

The 'Crisis of the 3rd Century' featured a complex series of major issues that strained the Empire to its limit. These included:

- Frequent civil war following the murder of Severus Alexander, with a troubled Imperial succession continually a catalyst for internal conflict. As Mattingly (2007, 226) details:

> *There were over 20 recognised emperors and numerous co-regents and usurpers between AD 235 and AD 284, few of them dying peacefully in their beds. Precariously ruling emperors and usurpers alike gathered troops to…stamp out rivals.*

- Widespread conflict, with significant invasions of Imperial territory by opponents whose contact with Empire had precipitated a level of critical mass previously absent (Heather, 2013, xv). In the west this included significant raids by the Germanic Franks, Iuthungi, Alamanni and others across Rhine and Danube that penetrated deep into the Imperial interior. The combined effect of these incursions was to create a real sense of fear within wider Roman society, and a lack of confidence in the military that Mattingly (2007, 226) argues had not existed before. Ultimately, recognising the threat to Rome itself, Aurelian (AD 270 to AD 275) built the 19km Aurelian Walls in Rome to replace its Servian predecessor. Meanwhile, in the east, a far more significant development proved even more destabilising, and for far longer. Over a two-year period from AD 224 Ardashir I of Persia had defeated his Parthian overlords, bringing the Sassanid Persian Empire into being. By the onset of the 'Crisis of the 3rd Century' this had matured into a true symmetrical threat to the power of Rome. In particular, Ardashir's son Shapur I proved a mighty opponent, humbling the Roman military time and again at the height of the crisis.

- Pestilence, particularly the devastating '*Plague of Cyprian*' which afflicted the Empire from around AD 250 until after AD 270. This pandemic originated in the east and is thought to have been a virulent form of smallpox which claimed 5,000 lives a day in Rome at its height (Stathakopoulos, 2007, 95), though more recent research argues it was either a form of bubonic plague, or a particularly lethal strain of measles (Breeze and Hodgson, 2020, 32).
- Economic depression as Imperial expansion slowed and ceased (Cornell, 1993, 168). Combined with the multiple shocks to Roman society detailed above, this led to major disruption in the availability of coinage, which itself was continually devalued in terms of silver content throughout the crisis. One outcome was a rise in the use of poor-quality forgeries to compensate. The lack of understanding in the ancient world of basic state-level economics is evident in the various responses to this financial crash, for example Aurelian's attempt to replace all coinage in circulation in the early AD 270s with new improved issues which nearly bankrupted the Empire.

In Britain the changed nature of Empire post the 'Crisis of the Third Century' is evident in a variety of ways, all linked to the political, economic and social dislocation caused by its multifarious impacts. For example,

Southern (2013, 250) highlights a dearth of inscriptions being set up in the province from this time. This tracks a broader phenomenon, namely the effective ending of that most Roman expression of *Romanitas*, the building of grand stone-built structures by societal elites. Even the few such buildings that were constructed from this time are very different in nature. A prime example is the palace at Peter's Hill in London associated with the usurpers Carausian and Allectus (see below), while another is a large structure found in the *canaba* at York dated to the later 3rd century AD. Unlike the fine public buildings constructed prior to the crisis which were built from expertly quarried and carefully worked uniform stone blocks, these were constructed from roughly reworked local materials, re-used from demolished public buildings and mausoleums.

In my own PhD research I link this major change in the nature of the urban landscape to the disappearance during the crisis of the economic surplus that had been such a key feature of the Principate province. One outcome was the ending of the huge *metalla* operations that had provided much of the building stone for the stone built environment, for example the *Classis Britannica*-run ragstone quarries in the upper Medway Valley (Elliott, 2017, 108). In the midst of the crisis, with no wealth available to fund such building projects (even if there had been the political will amidst the turmoil of the ever-changing political leadership in Rome), demand dried up and the *metalla* fell out of use. Then, when the Empire emerged from the crisis as the Dominate Empire, a continued lack of demand in this very different economic landscape ensured they were never to restart.

Another outcome was the changed nature of fortifications in the province post the crisis. For example, the river wall and bastions that were added to the Severan land wall in London in the late 3rd century AD feature heavy use of recycled building material. This included fine sculptured stone depicting Classical scenes which Blagg (1980, 5) argued originated in a monumental arch featuring ornamental screens. Meanwhile, Sheldon (2011, 230) highlights the reuse in one bastion of material from the mausoleum of the province's third procurator, Julius Classicianus. This same pattern is also evident in other wall circuits built around urban centres at this time, itself a sign of changing times, and other fortifications including the later Saxon Shore forts. A prime example here is that at Richborough, with each of its four walls featuring examples of different recycled materials.

In a military context we have two very specific examples of the impact of the 'Crisis of the 3rd Century' in Britain, over and above the change in the nature of the construction techniques used in later fortifications.

Firstly, recent archaeological evidence tracing the impact of the Plague of Cyprian here (and more broadly the crisis in general) shows a dramatic change in the fortunes of the *vicus* civilian settlements of the forts in the north province. As Breeze and Hodgson (2020, 33) explain:

> *The heyday of these extramural settlements appears to have been the 2nd century, continuing into the late 3rd century. Around the 270s, though, several excavations have indicated that these thriving communities came to an abrupt end. At Vindolanda and Housesteads, coin sequences in the extramural settlement stop in this decade, while the excavated areas outside the forts at South Shields, Wallsend, Newcastle, and Burgh-by-Sands along the Wall corridor: at Maryport and Ravenglass on the Cumbrian coast: and other sites in the hinterland of the Wall have failed to produce evidence for occupation continuing after the 3rd century.*

Although this pattern isn't uniform, with for example the extramural settlement at the cavalry fort at Malton (Roman *Derventio Brigantum*) in Yorkshire continuing into the 4th century AD, the picture painted is one of severe economic dislocation. The same also occurs at many sites on the continent, for example with regard to the *canaba* civilian settlement outside the legionary fortress of Oudenburg on the Belgian coast. This was abandoned in the AD 260s. Meanwhile, the same phenomenon is found at the sequence of forts on the middle Danube ranging from Vienna to Osijek, while a specific example at the legionary fortress at Komárom (Roman *Brigetio*) in modern Hungary shows coin, Samian ware and even amphora use disappearing in the mid-3rd century AD (even though the fortress continued in use). It is unclear if the latter evidence, as with the British examples, indicates actual abandonment, or that the use of a local monetary economy switched to one based on bartering due to economic decline.

The second specific example we have of the impact of the 'Crisis of the 3rd Century' on the military establishment in Britain is even more striking. This is the complete disappearance of the *Classis Britannica* regional fleet, which is last mentioned in the funerary inscription of the North African ex-*trierarchus* Saturninus. This was found in Arles in southern France and is firmly dated to between AD 244 and 249, after which the fleet vanishes without a whimper, never to return as a single homogenous force. The implications for the island provinces of Britannia Superior and

Inferior were profound. Indeed, as we will see, the failure to permanently replace the fleet proved a false economy indeed.

A number of theories have been set out to explain why this key regional fleet disappeared when it did. Yet given other such fleets across the Empire also disappear in the later 3rd century AD, for example the *Classis Germanica*, it seems these expensive institutions were simply the victims of the financial pressures of the 'Crisis of the 3rd Century'. Indeed, the only navies known to have survived into the 4th century AD are the two premier Imperial fleets in Italy, these the west coast *Classis Misenensis* and the east coast *Classis Ravennate.* The question here then is not why the *Classis Britannica* disappeared, but when. Some argue one candidate event is in the aftermath of the Severan withdrawal from the far north, though this is clearly too early for the 'Crisis of the 3rd Century' to be a factor. However, a later event is to my mind a far more compelling contender. This is one of the key political events within the crisis as manifest in north-western Europe, namely the advent of the Gallic Empire (called *Imperium Galliarum* by contemporaries) of Cassianus Latinius Postumus. This came into existence amid the renewed Imperial chaos which occurred at the end of the AD 250s at the height of the crisis, initiated in AD 258 by an event far to the east when extensive Gothic raiding severely disrupted Asia Minor. The Goths there had taken advantage of the emperor Valerian's attentions further east in recapturing Antioch-on-the-Orontes from the Sassanid Persians. Then in AD 259, while matters with the Goths were being settled, the Alamanni burst across the Rhine, campaigning as far south as northern Italy before being defeated near Milan by Valerian's son and co-emperor Gallienus. Finally, in AD 260 a calamity occurred when Valerian's campaigning against the Persians faltered at Edessa, his army hamstrung by an outbreak of the Plague of Cyprian. When he tried to secure a peace settlement with the Persian King Shapur 1 he was betrayed and captured during the negotiations. He was never to return to Rome, with some sources pointing to a staggeringly-desperate fate for him, he being used as a footstool by the Persian King and later, after his death, his flayed skin being stuffed and displayed in a Persian temple. From that point onwards Gallienus ruled alone, though he proved incapable of keeping his empire together given the insurmountable external pressures on all fronts. Eventually the eastern frontier was stabilized by the Roman client state of Palmyra, whose King Odenathus pushed the Sassanid Persians out of Syria. However, in the west the troops of the Rhine legions lost faith in Gallienus given his attentions in the east and elevated their military leader Postumus to the purple in AD 260. Thus was born the Gallic Empire.

The territory he carved out included all of the German and Gallic provinces excepting Gallia Narbonensis in the south, and the various provinces of Britain and Spain. It may also have included Raetia to the east, the key province linking the Rhine and Danubian *limes*. Further, the scale of the administration set up by Postumus indicates this wasn't the usual usurpation attempt given he determined to replicate the entire Imperial court at his capital Trier (Roman *Augusta Treverorum*). This included a brand new Senate, two annually elected consuls and his own Praetorian Guard.

Postumus first set about rebuilding the ravaged frontier along the *limes Germanicus* and, given Gallienus' focus on the eastern front, could at this point next have descended on Italy where the emperor lay fatally exposed. However he chose not to, consolidating his position and surviving two attempts by Gallienus to reconquer the northwest in AD 261 and AD 265. Postumus was to outlive the emperor given the latter was assassinated by his senior military leaders in AD 268. Then Postumus himself fell a year later when, after defeating Laelianus (commander of the *legio* XII *Primigenia* at Mainz, Roman *Moguntiacum*, who in turn was attempting to usurp him), his own troops killed him after he refused to give them permission to sack the city. However, at least in the short term, the Gallic Empire survived. A succession of Imperial candidates followed Postumus, though none fared any better. Sequentially, the first was Marcus Aurelius Marius, present at the siege of Mainz and elected there and then by the troops to succeed Postumus after the latter's murder. He lasted just three months before he in turn was killed by Postumus' former Praetorian Prefect Victorinus, the latter then holding the throne until AD 271 when he in turn was killed and replaced by Tetricus I and his son Tetricus II, the latter as the former's Caesar. Both lasted until AD 274 when Gallienus' successor Aurelian defeated them at the Battle of Chalons, bringing the territories of the Gallic Empire back into the Imperial fold.

Set against this swirl of change in political leadership in the north west of the Roman Empire one can see multiple opportunities for the *Classis Britannica* and *Classis Germanica* to find themselves on the wrong side of a power struggle. In the first instance, this could have been with the initial creation of the Gallic Empire by Postumus, who Mason (2003, 148) says made frequent use of the images of war galleys on his coinage and so clearly valued his maritime military capability. Then, the instability caused by the rapid turnover of the Gallic emperors would similarly have provided an opportunity for the regional fleets there to back the wrong horse, as did the final re-conquest by Aurelian. Whatever the truth, it is in this period that the British fleet was finally defeated or disbanded. Given the economic privations of the Empire from that point, it was never to return.

The Pirate King and the Fourth Roman Invasion of Britain

The outcome of the loss of the *Classis Britannica* was soon evident, with control of the North Sea lost given the fleet's key roles had included maintaining open sea control there, and also littoral control along the continental coast as far north as the Rhine Delta (see Chapter 1). By the AD 280s this huge maritime region had become overrun by Germanic pirates operating from the far north of Germany and southern Scandinavia, well beyond the Rhine *limes*. Without fear of challenge or reprisal, these increasingly raided the east coast of Britain and the coast of Gaul, severely disrupting the local economies there which were only just recovering from the 'Crisis of the 3rd Century.' This set the scene for the last Roman maritime campaign of conquest in Britain. This was the clash between two of the great figures of later Romano-British history, the western Caesar Constantius Chlorus (Caesar in the West AD 293–AD 305, Augustus in the West AD 305–AD 306, and father of Constantine I), and Marcus Aurelius Mausaeus Valerius Carausius, dubbed by some the pirate king.

The former found himself in his position of power thanks to the initial round of administrative reforms imposed on the Empire by Diocletian after his accession in AD 284. This included the creation of the tetrarchy with its two *Augusti* senior emperors and two *Caesares* junior emperors, one of each in the west and east. The aim here was to help share the burden of controlling an empire beset on all sides by enemies and which had only just survived collapse during the 'Crisis of the 3rd Century', though in reality Diocletian – the Augustus in the east – still maintained overall control.

However, it was the Augustus in the west, Maximian (originally Caesar there from AD 284 to AD 286, then Augustus AD 286–AD 310), who set in train the improbable rise and fall of Carausius. The background to this tale actually began slightly before the end of the Principate in AD 276 when the Germanic Alamanni burst through the northern *limes* again, penetrating deep into Gaul where they sacked 60 towns. Though the emperor Probus (AD 276–AD 282) restored order, the event destabilized the province of Britannia across the North Sea, with Zosimus saying (1.68.3) the emperor had to send captured Vandals and Burgundians there under the command of a North African *legate* called Victorinus to help put down a revolt, this an early Dominate use of *foederates*. Whatever form this rebellion took, it proved difficult to stamp out, and it wasn't until the later reign of Carus (AD 282–AD 283) that order was finally restored, he taking the title *Britannicus Maximus*.

One outcome of the trouble in Gaul and Britain was a rise in brigandage, with disenfranchised *Bagaudae* peasant insurgents plaguing the countryside, particularly on the Continent. To tackle this Maximian appointed Carausius, a highly successful regional military leader, to head a special task force designed to defeat the brigands. In this he was equally successful. Maximian then turned to him again to defeat the endemic piracy in the North Sea which was peaking at this time. Here Carausius' maritime experience as a young man came to the fore, given he'd grown up on the coast of Belgica Secunda and served as a river pilot before later joining the military.

Carausius established his headquarters in the old *Classis Britannica* headquarters in Boulogne and quickly got to work, in the first instance building a new fleet to tackle the pirates. His campaign was once more a great success, with order soon restored in the North Sea. However, from Maximian's perspective he proved too successful, with the Emperor accusing Carausius of deliberately intercepting the pirates after the raids rather than before so he could pocket the plunder. The unfortunate Carausius was sentenced to death, but was tipped off before the sentence could be carried out. He promptly fled to Britain where in AD 286 he usurped, carving out his North Sea Empire that included north-eastern Gaul and Britain.

Carausius proved a charismatic and popular ruler given his local roots in the region. He also had significant forces at his disposal to maintain him in power, including the three British legions – *legio* II *Augusta* at Caerleon, *legio* XX *Valeria Victrix* at Chester and *legio* VI *Victrix* at York – and the new fleet he had built to defeat the piracy in the North Sea. He was also joined by *legio* XXX *Ulpia Victrix* in Germania Inferior, where it was based at the legionary fortress at Xanten.

Given this position of strength, Carausius now consolidated. In the first instance he established Britain's first official mint in London, with his coins notably superior to those in circulation when he arrived. Clearly with an eye to public relations, on them he styled himself as 'the saviour of Britain' (*Restitutor Britanniae*). Some of his coins also show that he clearly understood the old Severan maxim about keeping the troops happy, they bearing the legend 'Harmony with the Army' (*Concordia Militum*). It is also likely it was Carausius who completed the construction of the later Saxon Shore forts in Britain, for example those at Richborough, Lympne, Pevensey and Portchester (thought to be Roman *Portus Adumi*), he aiming to deter any Roman plans to reconquer the two provinces there.

Maximian was clearly rattled by Carausius' usurpation and planned to move against him as soon as possible. However, first he had to build his own fleet. This was ready for action by AD 289 when it sailed down the Rhine and into the North Sea. However, the expedition proved an epic failure and an uneasy peace was soon agreed, with Carausius following the age-old plan of claiming legitimacy through association by minting coins featuring himself as an equal with Maximian and the eastern Augustus Diocletian.

The latter two clearly didn't recognize this picture of brotherly love and before long the newly-appointed Constantius Chlorus was dispatched westwards with orders to defeat Carausius and return his usurping territories back into the Imperial fold. To do this he made full use of the newly created military command structures instituted by Diocletian, gathering a huge field army comprising many of the legions in the west, and vexillations from others, together with an equal number of auxiliary troops. He also built yet another fleet, knowing ultimately he would have to invade Britain.

Constantius Chlorus proved far more capable than Maximian and by AD 293 had defeated Carausius' Frankish allies around the Rhine estuary, he then recapturing Boulogne. These reverses proved the end for Carausius who was assassinated by Allectus, one of his senior officers, who now took over as the ruler of the remaining territories of the breakaway Empire. Confusion surrounds the actual identity of this far less charismatic leader, with some arguing he was Carausius' procurator, others his senior military commander, and yet others a Frankish mercenary leader given they increasingly appear in his army from this point. Whatever his origins, he only survived three more years before Constantius Chlorus was ready to assault Britain and claim the two British provinces back.

In the Spring of AD 296 the western Caesar mounted a full invasion of Britain, the fourth Roman invasion of Britain after those of Caesar (twice) and Claudius. For his assault he used a clever stratagem, dividing his force into two. In the first instance he sent his own smaller division down the Thames Estuary to pin Allectus in the capital of Britannia Superior along with a significant portion of his army. He then sent the larger part of his force to the Solent on the south coast under the Praetorian

Prefect Asclepiodotus. This slipped past Allectus' fleet in a fog bank and disembarked safely. Heading inland, the army quickly defeated Allectus' land forces, killing the usurper who'd travelled south when word reached him of the invasion there. Constantius Chlorus now moved on London, arriving just in time to save it from being sacked by Allectus' remaining Frankish mercenaries. With Britain finally restored to the Empire, the Caesar made a triumphal entry into London. This event is commemorated in the gold Arras medallion that carries the legend 'Restorer of the Eternal Light' (*Redditor Lucis Aeterna*). This remarkable large coin shows the first ever depiction of London, with Constantius Chlorus on his charger receiving the thanks of the Londoners. Thus was concluded the final Roman maritime invasion of Britain.

Shortly after this time Diocletian enacted the next, far more dramatic phase of his Diocletianic Reformation. This targeted the administrative structure of the Empire, he completely reorganising its political and economic structure into new *dioceses*. These were much larger regional units than the earlier Principate provinces. Each of the bigger units was controlled by a *vicarius* (sometimes called an *exarch* in the Greek-speaking east), a senior official appointed by the emperor who combined the power of the earlier provincial governors and procurators. The *vicarii* were usually based in the most significant city or town in the *diocese*, for example in Britain London, which was also the location of a late Roman active mint using the facilities originally built by Carausius. Meanwhile those appointed to run the new, much smaller provinces within each *diocese* retained the title governor, though now had far less authority within the rigid new administrative structure of the Empire. Diocletian originally created 12 *dioceses*, with that on the main island of Britain being called *Britanniae*. According to the early-4th century AD *Laterculus Veronensis* (Verona List) of units of political control in the later Empire, this now comprised four smaller provinces that were called:

- *Maxima Caesariensis*, broadly the south east of the *diocese* with London its capital (in addition to being the wider *diocene* capital).
- *Britannia Prima*, broadly the south west of the *diocese* with Cirencester its capital. It is not clear if modern Wales was part of this province, or of *Flavia Caesariensis*.
- *Flavia Caesariensis*, thought to comprise the modern Midlands (and possibly Wales), with its capital in Lincoln.

- *Britannia Secunda*, thought to comprise the north of the province, with its capital at York.

A fifth province in the *diocese* called *Valentia* is also later detailed in the late 4th/early 5th century AD *Notitia Dignitatum*, though its existence is problematic. If it did exist, some have speculated it may have comprised the modern Scottish borders, or that it resulted from the division of *Britannia Secunda* into two, this featuring a northern border zone and a southern zone still focused on York. In some translations Ammianus Marcellinus (*The Later Roman Empire*, 28.3.7) also suggests it referenced a new name for the entire *diocese* following *Comes* Theodosius' defeat of the 'Great Conspiracy' in AD 367/368 in the reign of Valentinian I, though there is no further evidence for this. A further theory is that *Valentia* may actually have referenced the renaming of *Maxima Caesariensis* given the *Notitia Dignitatum* indicates its governor was of consular rank, again perhaps in the context of the defeat of the 'Great Conspiracy.'

A further major administrative reform introduced by Diocletian was the addition of substantial extra layers of public administration to support the new *diocene* structure of the Empire. This significantly increased the coercive power of the Roman state to collect taxes after the economic tribulations of the 'Crisis of the 3rd Century', allowing a fully systemized taxation regime to be introduced on all economic production called the *annona militaris*. More often than not, in the provinces much of this was now provided to the State in kind rather than as monetary income, formalising the already existing state of affairs in many areas following the crisis. To facilitate this more flexible system of tax collection Diocletian also instituted his *de pretiss* edict on prices. This came into use in AD 301 as a blunt instrument aimed at reducing the rampant inflation then afflicting the Empire. The list literally set in stone the base price for most of the common goods of the Empire, interestingly including various kinds of British woollen goods.

Diocletian's final administrative reform did have a direct impact on the military establishment in Britain. This was the official separation of the military from the administrative apparatus of the Empire at all levels. At a stroke this freed the military from any form of Senatorial oversight, an event as revolutionary as the Marian reforms of the military at the end of the 2nd century BC. No more would Senators command Roman armies as they progressed along the *cursus honorum*. From this time onwards all senior officers in the military were of the equestrian class, building on a trend initiated earlier by Gallienus (AD 253–AD 268). The armies and fleets of the later Empire were now able to coalesce as required much more quickly, without any administrative oversight excepting that of the *Augusti* and *Caesares*. This was a vital reform needed to deal with the multitude of threats the Empire now faced.

The Rise of Constantine

Constantius Chlorus returned to Britain at some stage in AD 305, this time travelling to the far north despite suffering from an unknown illness. Once there he launched a campaign against the newly emergent Picts who are first mentioned here in contemporary history by the writer Eumenius in AD 297. The name, derived from the Latin *Pictii*, referenced their propensity for body tattoos and painting themselves in woad. The Picts were not a single tribe, but rather a confederation, as with the earlier Maeatae and Caledonians, though on a far larger scale. The Picts almost certainly originated in the northeast of modern Scotland, their cultural footprint gradually spreading as far north as the Orkney Islands and as far south as Fife (and even perhaps the northern reaches of the Scottish Borders). In this they may have been helped by the lowland depopulation event detailed in Chapter 7 following the Severan campaigns there. In this southern zone Pictland came into contact with Roman Britain to the south, and here Roman influence has recently been identified as a factor behind early Pictish scripts and art styles (Noble, Goldberg and Hamilton, 2019, 45).

Pictish armies continued to use the light chariots and skirmishing light cavalry of earlier British armies, but many of their infantry were differentially armed, with a switch to a new shield type the most noticeable difference. Rather than the earlier plank designs these were made of hide stretched across two crossed sticks held together at the juncture. Many are depicted in Pictish artwork, usually carvings on stone monuments, and are shown as small square or round designs. Axes also feature as side arms on the carvings, as do bowmen (unusual in native British armies).

We have no detail of the reasons behind Constantius Chlorus' early 4th century AD campaign in Britain, but it was clearly considered a success given he was using the title *Britannicus Maximus II* by January AD 306. However, it was an event immediately prior to his departure for Britain that far outweighed his subsequent campaign in the far north in importance. This was his summoning of his son Constantine to join him in Britain.

To the point of his departure for Britain Constantius Chlorus had shown himself an adept operator at the top of the Imperial power apparatus. He had to be, given his rival for Imperial favour with Diocletian was much better placed to influence the senior tetrarch. This was Galerius, the Caesar in the east who was based in his capital at Sremska Mitrovica (Roman *Sirmium*) in modern Serbia, there charged with defending the Danube frontier. This meant he was far closer to Diocletian in his tetrarchic capital at Izmit (Roman *Nicodemia*) in modern north-western Turkey than Constantius Chlorus in far off Trier. Galerius was also closer to the western Augustus Maximian in Milan (Roman *Mediolanum*) in northern Italy.

When he set up the tetrarchy Diocletian had planned from the first that he and Maximian would step down and allow a smooth succession to take place. Although before AD 303 there had been a tacit agreement that this would see Constantius Chlorus and Galerius elevated to Augustus in the west and east, with Maximian's son Maxentius promoted to the rank of Caesar in the west and Constantius's son Constantine Caesar in the east (where he was based on the staff of Galerius), in the event this proved not to be the case. Around AD 303 Galerius, sensing an opportunity for advancement to become the senior Augustus after Diocletian's planned resignation, began manoeuvring to ensure that he would be best placed to have authority over Constantius Chlorus after Diocletian's death. This included a clandestine meeting with Maximian to discuss the succession issue to which Constantius Chlorus was either not invited, or the date chosen when they knew he was engaged holding the Rhine frontier. Galerius then went to work on Diocletian, and by the end of AD 304 had convinced the senior tetrarch to appoint Galerius' nominees Maximinus Daia (Galerius' nephew) as the western Caesar and Flavius Valerius Severus (Galerius' old friend) as the eastern Caesar. When as planned Diocletian and Maximian stepped down on the 1st of May AD 305, the various successions played out as planned by Galerius. Constantius Chlorus now found himself dangerously exposed, as did his son serving with Galerius. The latter clearly planned to use the western Augustus' son as political leverage over his father, hence Constantius' requesting his son join him on campaign in Britain. Galerius granted this after a long evening of drinking, with Constantine leaving immediately. Later pro-Constantinian propaganda has him fleeing clandestinely before Galerius could change his mind, using the major military trunk roads linking the east with the west (and their system of *cursus publicus mansio* post-houses along the way) to stay ahead of

Galerius' agents. Constantine arrived in Boulogne just in time to join his father as he crossed to Britain.

This proved a fateful meeting not just in the narrative of British history, but also in the context of the wider Roman world, for after a season campaigning in the far north of the province Constantius Chlorus retired to York where he died on 25 July AD 306. Immediately prior to his death Constantius had recommended his son to the army as his successor, and soon *legio* VI *Victrix* had proclaimed him the Augustus in the west. This was an enormous elevation, and yet Constantine I (as he was now styled) proved to be Roman Britain's most successful usurper by a distance. He was to spend the next 18 years securing his position not just in the west but across the entirety of the Roman world, being sole emperor in the west from AD 312 and the entire Empire from AD 324. Although he is best known for his support for and later adoption of Christianity, in terms of the Roman campaigns of conquest in Britain his major contribution was the fundamental reform he carried out of the Roman military establishment.

Constantine I began this dramatic overhaul of the military after defeating Maxentius, his rival for power in the west, at the Battle of Milvian Bridge in AD 312. One of his first acts was to disband the troublesome Praetorian Guard after it sided with Maxentius against him. He replaced them and the *equites singulares Augusti* Imperial Guard cavalry with new units of mounted guardsmen called the *Scholae Palatinae*. Constantine I also formed a separate unit of guardsmen called the *Protectores* who served as his close personal bodyguard and also provided his staff officers.

Reform of the guard completed, the emperor next turned his attention to the wider military. By this time incursions by Germans and Goths over the Rhine and Danube had become frequent events (they had occupied his father for much of the latter's reign), seriously disrupting the regional economies of the border territories there, while the ever-present threat from Sassanid Persia in the east required a significant commitment from a military establishment frequently beset by civil war. Even taking into account the, by now, common formation of *ad hoc* field armies to tackle crises as they occurred, Constantine I realised total reform was needed. As detailed in Chapter 1, he therefore restructured the entire military establishment into two completely new types of unit. These were *comitatenses* field army troops and *limitanei* border troops. We know the names of many of these units as they are detailed in the *Notitia Dignitatum* list of military units and commands of the later Empire.

Comitatenses translates as troops at the Emperor's immediate disposal. The term was first recorded in AD 325 when three regional field armies were detailed. Two were based in the west, one in Gaul facing the Rhine that deployed troops to Britain as necessary and one in Illyria facing the Danube, and one was based in the east. Their number had increased dramatically by the time of Theodosius I (379 AD–395 AD) who was able to deploy five field armies in the east alone, with more in the west (including a bespoke one in Britain). Mounted troops in the field armies were commanded by a *magister equitum* and foot troops a *magister peditum*, with a *magister militum* in overall command. Sometimes an emperor himself actually commanded a field army, it then being styled a *comitatius praesentalis* (translating as 'field army in the Imperial presence'). *Comitatenses* troops could also be brigaded together into smaller concentrations of troops for specific roles. Again as detailed in Chapter 1, these were commanded by a *Comes* (the origin of the title count) or a *Dux* (the origin of the title duke).

As can be seen in Julian the Apostate's order of Battle at Strasbourg in AD 357 in Chapter 6, the legions and auxilia were by this time virtually identical in composition and equipment. Thus in his front line he fielded the *Moesiaci*, *Pannoniaci, Iovani* and *Herculiani* legions, flanked by elite *auxilia palatina* units (those at Strasbourg were the *Petulantes, Heruli, Cornuti* and *Brachiati*). In his second line he deployed the *Primani* legion, flanked by more *auxilia palatina* troops from the *Celtae, Batavi* and *Regae* units.

Another change in the post-Constantinian reform field armies was a much higher complement of cavalry. This had been a trend in the Roman military since the time of Septimius Severus but was now institutionalised, with mounted troops now making up at least one third of each field army.

One key difference for these *comitatenses* field army troops when compared to their Principate forebears was that they weren't based in permanent legionary fortresses on the frontiers of the Empire. Instead, when not on active service they were billeted among local populations deep within Imperial territory, available there to form the main strike force in a complex system of defence-in-depth. From these new locations regional commanders could then gather troops together as required to counter each new incursion into Imperial territory.

The time to muster these field armies and then use them operationally was provided by the *limitanei*, a totally different fighting force. These troops were located on the frontiers of the Empire in permanent bases, often the old legionary fortresses and forts of the Principate. Here they were based with their families who lived in the associated *canabae* or *vicus* settlements. Their role was to act as a localised policing force in times of peace, and a trip wire when major incursions occurred, buying time for the *comitatenses* field armies to arrive. This was often at great personal cost, with for example the *limitanei* in Gaul being totally destroyed by the raiding Alamanni prior to Julian the Apostate's arrival. One can only guess the fate of their families.

Stepping outside of the chronological narrative for a moment, in late Roman Britain we have insight into the balance between *comitatenses* and *limitanei* troops through the *Notitia Dignitatum*, and also through the archaeological record. Unusually when compared to the rest of the continent, all three legions here appear to have been *limitanei* in nature by this time. The document certainly details *legio* II *Augusta* in existence at the end of the 4th century AD, basing it at the Saxon shore fort at Richborough under the command of the *Comes Litoris Saxonici per Britanniam* (Count of the Saxon Shore). Here one could make the case that *legio* II *Augusta* was a field army unit, based deep in late provincial territory. However, far more likely it was a key component of the *limitanei* border defence force of the south and east coast. The archaeological record backs this up, perhaps also indicating a date by which it had departed Britain. This is in the form of a coin hoard of 875 base coins that included early coins of Honorius (AD 393 to AD 423), the emperor in the west at the time, and Arcadius (AD 395 to AD 408) who was the emperor in the east. This appears to have been the legion's last pay chest, buried after arrival when those transporting it found the legion had already left.

Meanwhile the last reference to *legio* XX *Valeria Victrix* in York is on Carausian coinage dated to the early AD 290s. However, the archaeological record shows the legionary fort there was still occupied in the mid-4th century AD, indicating the legion not only remained there but also by then was a *limitanei* force defending the north west coast against Scots raiding. Given this legion isn't mentioned at all in the *Notitia Dignitatum*, it seems likely that it had been destroyed or disbanded by the end of the century (see below for possible causal events). Finally, *legio* VI *Victrix* is detailed in the *Notitia Dignitatum* under the command of the *Dux Britanniarum*, the commander in charge of the *limitanei* defending the northern frontier.

To the legions one can add a wide variety of other auxilia units, and also units that the *Notitia Dignitatum* calls *numeri*. The latter was earlier in the Roman world a term used to describe irregular units in Roman employ. Here it most likely references the use of *foederate* mercenaries hired to bolster the faltering defences in Britain and elsewhere in the empire. The document details that the *Comes Litoris Saxonici per Britanniam* had an additional eight *limitanei* units, two of which were auxiliary cavalry *alae* and four *numeri*. It should be noted here that although most associate the *Comes* with the Saxon Shore fort network in the south east of England, other late Roman fortifications had already been built at Cardiff (Roman name unknown), Caer Gybi near Holyhead (again, Roman name unknown) and Lancaster on the west coast. These almost certainly also came under his control, as likely did similar fortifications along the continental coast of Gaul. Meanwhile, to maintain the northern frontier the *Dux Britanniarum* had an additional 36 *limitanei* units, with 14 on or around Hadrian's Wall itself and 22 further south (mostly *numeri*) where they joined *legio* VI *Victrix* in and around York. One should note here that, as detailed in Chapter 1, the units in late Roman armies were much smaller than their counterparts earlier in the Empire. In that regard Mattingly (2006, 239) suggests that the total size of the *limitanei* in the service of the *Comes Litoris Saxonici per Britanniam* and the *Dux Britanniarum* was only 12,500 men, with many of them mercenaries rather than regulars.

The *Notitia Dignitatum* also details two further key officials in late Roman Britain, the *vicarius* who as we know administered the *diocese*, and finally a *Comes Britanniarum* who commanded the *comitatenses* field army troops. We have insight here into the seniority of this latter post given its first incumbent was Gratian the Elder, the father of the future emperor Valentinian I (AD 364 to AD 375), himself to play a key role in the narrative of late Roman Britain. The *Notitia Dignitatum* goes on to name the units of the field army, it comprising six mounted units and three foot, giving a total force size of around 6,000 (Mattingly, 2006, 239). There is no archaeological evidence to suggest a force of this size was imposed on any of the major urban centres in Britain as happened on the continent. The field army may therefore have had its own as yet un-located base. For a clue as to where this may have been we can look to Dere Street, the Roman road running north from York. Intriguingly the *Antonine Itinerary* actually shows a branch of Dere Street also heading south from York, 19km onwards to a place called *Delgovicia* (today this location is unknown), and then a further 36km to a location called *Praetorium* (again unknown). This is the name given to the commander's house in a legionary fortress, and might be an intriguing indicator as to the location of the field army base.

Decline and Fall

Back to 4th century AD Britain, in the first instance Constantine I would certainly have taken units of his three British legions and auxiliaries to support his bid for overall control of the western Empire. However, given there is no indication in the written or archaeological record that there was trouble on the northern frontier at this time, these troops soon returned or were replaced. Southern (2013, 306) suggests the emperor may have revisited Britain in AD 307 for an unknown reason, while his contemporary Eusebius of Caesarea details in his panegyric on Constantine I that he may have later campaigned in Britain against an unknown enemy between AD 312 and AD 314 (*de Vita Constanti*, 1.8, 25).

Our primary sources, and indeed the archaeological record, are then silent about events in Britain until the reign of Constantine I's son Constans (AD 337 to AD 350). He'd become emperor along with his brothers Constantine II and Constantius II. After their father's death, he was initially given responsibility for Italy and North Africa, while Constantine II was given responsibility for the west. However, Constans' troops murdered the latter in AD 340 and from that point until his own death in AD 350 Constans ruled the whole western Empire. His first major campaign of the AD 340s was against the Germanic Franks in AD 342 where he successfully expelled an incursion into Gaul. He is then detailed making his famous maritime winter crossing to Britain to deal with some kind of emergency in January or February AD 343. We have little detail of what the issue in the *diocese* was to attract the direct attention of the emperor, but contemporary writers did note how dangerous a voyage this was at that time of year. One retrospective passage in Ammanius Marcellinus briefly alludes to the visit having to do with the *areani*, the frontier scouts based around the northern frontier who performed the same kind of role earlier fulfilled by the *exploratores*. These certainly caused problems in the *diocese* later in the century (see below), and were perhaps colluding with their neighbours north of Hadrian's Wall here. Mattingly (2006, 235) also suggests the crisis might have involved a usurper in the south of Britain. A bronze medallion issued around this time certainly hints at a militaristic reason for Constans travelling to Britain, it showing the emperor in full military uniform astride a war galley threatening the sea with a spear, with military standards adorning the ship's stern. The legend on the medallion reads '*Bononia Oceanen*' which references Boulogne, almost certainly Constans' port of departure for the *diocese*. Whatever the truth, we have no further detail, which seems to indicate matters were settled satisfactorily for the emperor.

Britain next appears in contemporary literature in the context of the usurpation of Magnentius, commander of the *Iovani* and *Herculiani*, those two of the elite *comitatenses* legions in Gaul. By this time the military in the west had grown increasingly dissatisfied with Constans and the western field armies elevated Magnentius, who may have been born in Britain (Kean and Frey, 197), to the western throne at Autun (Roman *Augustodunum*) in eastern Gaul on 18 January 350. This was a key location given it was the site of the numerous State-run *fabricae* manufactories which produced much of the equipment for the western military. The usurpation clearly surprised Constans who was on a hunting expedition near the Pyrenees. Knowing the emperor was separated from any military forces still loyal to him, Magnentius moved quickly and his forces soon cornered Constans near modern Perpignan where he was killed. Soon the *diocese* in Britain and Spain joined Magnentius, later joined by that in Italy, giving him control over the whole western Empire excepting North Africa. However, he wasn't to remain in position for long as the eastern emperor Constantius II, Constantine I's surviving son, quickly moved against him. Magnentius was soon defeated at the Battle of Mursa Major on 28 September AD 351 in modern Croatia, he then retreating to Gaul. He was then defeated again at the Battle of Mons Seleucus in AD 353 in south-eastern Gaul after which he committed suicide.

The major impact of the revolt of Magnentius on Britain actually occurred after the event. This was because Constantius II for some reason decided the *diocese* at the far north-western tip of the Empire deserved special attention to bring it back into the Imperial fold. After hunting down Magnentius' collaborators in Gaul the emperor dispatched a notorious court official called Paulus *Catena* (Paul the Chain) to Britain with similar orders. Notorious across the Empire for his cruelty, his nickname either referenced his ability to weave chains of intrigue around those he was interrogating, or a form of torture whereby the unfortunate victims was weighed down with increasing volumes of chains until they confessed. He specifically targeted the elites of late Roman Britain, to the extent that the *vicarius* Martinus attempted to assassinate him and, failing, then committed suicide rather than face trial. Paulus himself later met a fitting fate, being burned to death by Julian the Apostate after being tried for treason at the Chalcedon tribunal in AD 361.

Julian, the nephew of Constantine I, had been appointed the Caesar in the west by Constantius II in AD 355 and features in the narrative of late Roman Britain twice. In the first instance this was in the context of his campaign against the invading Alamanni and Franks in Gaul that began in AD 355 and culminated with his decisive victory at the Battle of Strasbourg in AD 357. Here, he struggled to feed his army given much of Gaul had been lost to the Germanic invaders. He therefore turned to Britain, effectively a redoubt to the west comparatively free of predatory Germans, building a new fleet in AD 356 to transport the grain. The Greek sophist and rhetorician Libanius provides a detailed commentary on why this was necessary, saying (*Oratio*, 18.82-3):

> *In the past, grain was shipped from Britain and up the Rhine. But after the barbarians took control they did not let it pass. Most of the ships, dragged onto dry land long before, had rotted. A few did still sail, but these unloaded their cargo in coastal ports, so it was necessary for the grain to be transferred on wagons instead of river, which was very expensive. (Julian) thought that there would be problems if he was not able to restore the traditional means of grain-shipment, so he quickly built more ships than before, and put his mind to how the river could take receipt of wheat…*

The fleet Julian built here was enormous, he taking 10 months to construct 400 new vessels to add to the 200 still seaworthy he had inherited in Gaul, giving him a total of 600 ships. Zosimus, who says the total was actually 800, adds they were built along the Rhine with timber felled in local forests (*New History*, 3.5.2).

However, Julian's reliance on Britain to keep his army on its successful march in Gaul may have come at a price. Even though not detailed by the primary sources, it is likely he also withdrew some troops from there to support him in Gaul given the desperate state he'd found it in. This left the western and northern defences undermanned, and unsurprisingly the Scots in Ireland and the Picts in the far north pounced on the opportunity, this event perhaps the context for the disappearance of *legio* VI *Victrix* in York. Ammianus Marcellinus provides useful detail here, saying that in AD 360 (*The Later Roman Empire*, 20.1.1):

> *The savage tribes of Scots and Picts had broken the terms of the treaty and were conducting raids into Britain, laying waste those areas close to the frontiers. Fear permeated the provinces* [of the diocese], *exhausted already by all of the disasters of previous years. Julian was over-wintering in Paris and already had enough warriors of his*

> *own: he was loath to cross the sea to help* [as had Constans earlier] *as that would leave Gaul without a ruler, and the Alamanni were again threatening war.*

A key point to note here is that some translators view the reference to the Scots as actually to the Attacotti, a fierce warrior tribe who frequently fought with the Scots and Picts. Of Scots descent themselves, they are frequently mentioned by Ammianus Marcellinus and others, more so later in the century (see below). The Attacotti were particularly noted for their ferocious charge when trying to break an enemy battle line. The Romans were so impressed with them that they recruited them *en masse* into bespoke auxilia units, with four units detailed in the *Notitia Dignitatum*. These were most likely *auxilia palatina* units.

Back to the narrative, instead of risking himself Julian decided to send Flavius Lupicinus, his *magister equitum* master of horse in Gaul, to Britain to shore up the western and northern defences and to deal with the incursions there. He arrived in the depth of winter after another dangerous out-of-season maritime crossing, landing at the Imperial Gateway at Richborough. He was accompanied by a small but highly experienced force from the Gallic field army. This included the *Heruli* and *Batavi auxilia palatina* units, and vexillations from the *Moesiaci* legion. The primary sources say these were lightly armed, perhaps indicating that they travelled without a baggage train and were more akin to a flying column designed to fire-fight the western and northern insurrections.

Lupicinus led his troops along Watling Street in northern Kent to the *diocene* capital of London where he used chests full of silver coinage to pay the military units already in Britain, and no doubt the loyal suppliers of grain for Julian's army in Gaul. This indicates these payments were in arrears, again indicating the scale of the crisis in the west and north. Matters settled in London, Lupicinus then set out for the west and north to tackle the problems there, no doubt commandeering the surviving field army units on the way. We have no detail about whether he was successful or not, though from a historiography perspective this isn't a surprise given Ammianus Marcellinus wasn't a fan and so would certainly be reticent about giving any praise. For example he describes Lupicinus as a (*The Later Roman Empire*, 20.1.2):

> *...warlike man and skilled in military affairs, but apt to boast and talk in the style of a tragic hero. It was long a matter of debate whether his greed predominated over his cruelty or the reverse.*

Whether triumphant or not, Lupicinus didn't stay in Britain long enough to enjoy the fruits of his labour. This was because dramatic events in the east set in train a sequence of events that would transform Imperial succession both there and in the west. This began when the Sassanid Persian king Shapur II decided to take advantage of Rome's western focus by launching a lightning offensive against the Roman east. Constantius II, caught off guard, called for reinforcements from across the Empire to tackle the new threat. This included reaching out to Julian, by now based in Paris (Roman *Lutetia*), to request the *Heruli* and *Batavi* units now in Britain join him in the east.

When word of this reached Julian's troops in Gaul they reacted with anger given their loyalty to the Caesar and proclaimed him a full Augustus. This was a direct challenge to Constantius II and put Julian in a dilemma as he knew Lupicinus was loyal to the Constantinian dynasty and would view him as a usurper. Ammianus Marcellinus provides more detail here, saying (*The Later Roman Empire*, 20.9.9):

> *Lupicinus was an arrogant man with ideas above his station, and there were concerns that if he heard the news from across the Channel he might stage a coup. So an official was dispatched to Boulogne to keep close watch and stop anyone from crossing the channel. As a result Lupicinus returned before he could learn what had happened and was unable to cause any unrest.*

It seems that here the shrewd Julian allowed Lupicinus to complete his mission in Britain, and then promptly arrested him when he arrived back in Boulogne. However, Lupicinus wasn't out of Imperial favour for long, with his career back on track after Julian's untimely death fighting the Parthians in AD 363. Lupicinus ultimately rose to the consulship in Rome in AD 367.

Julian's legacy in Britain after Lupicinus' campaign should have been continued open ocean control of the North Sea, and of the littoral zone around the British coastline, given the huge navy he'd gathered while in Gaul. However, once more the cost of keeping a fleet-in-being proved too much, and it was soon disbanded. Britain again quickly paid the price, with raiding from Germanic pirates soon on the rise once more. Then, in AD 376 a major event occurred so dramatic in scale Marcellinus Ammianus styled it the *'barbarica conspiratio'*. We know it today as the

'Great Conspiracy.' Here, it appears the *limitanei* along Hadrian's Wall, and perhaps some units even further south, rebelled. This allowed Picts from two tribes in the far north, called the Dicalydones and the Verturiones, to raid deep into the *diocese*. They also bypassed any garrison units remaining loyal to Rome by using maritime transport to land warriors south of the frontier. This may have been as far south as the Humber Estuary given the series of late Roman signal stations protecting the fertile East Riding of Yorkshire at Huntcliff, Goldsborough, Ravenscar, Scarborough and Filey that may have been in existence by then. However, what made this deep incursion so much more dangerous than earlier ones was the fact that the Picts seem to have coordinated their offensive with others who had designs of Romano-British plunder. Ammanius Marcellinus provides great detail here, saying the Picts were joined by Germanic pirates, Scots from Ireland, and Attecotti warriors from southwest Scotland (*The Later Roman Empire*, 27.8.5). Quite how these very diverse protagonists coordinated their combined offensive is problematic. However, it was initially highly successful, overwhelming the Roman military establishment in Britain. It is worth considering how widespread the devastation in Britain was here. Given the Picts were raiding both across the northern frontier and down the east coast, much of *Britannia Secunda* was vulnerable to attack. Similarly, with the Scots and Attecotti attacking in the northwest, this province was open to attack there too. Scots raiding also impacted *Britannia Prima* in the South West, while Germanic raiding put the entire east coast under threat, ranging from *Britannia Secunda* through *Flavia Caesariensis* and down to *Maxima Caesariensis*, with even the *diocene* capital London at risk.

Though the *limitanei* and field army did put up initial resistance, the Roman troops were soon scattered. We hear nothing of the *Dux Britanniarum* after the revolt of his *limitanei*, and it seems likely he remained with *legio* VI *Victrix* behind the impressive late Roman defences in the legionary fortress in York. The Multangular Tower visible there today next to the Yorkshire Museum shows just how sophisticated these defences had become by the late Roman period. A further issue he faced was the seeming betrayal of the *areani* scouts beyond Hadrian's Wall who, instead of giving advance warning of the initial Pictish offensive, instead helped them. In this they were perhaps only following the example of the rebelling northern *limitanei*. Meanwhile the primary sources say that a commander named Nectaridus, who they describe as the *Comes Maritime Tractus*, was killed fighting the invaders somewhere in the diocese.

This was almost certainly the *Comes Litoris Saxonici per Britanniam*, leading his own *limitanei*. Meanwhile the *Comes Britanniarum,* a man named Fullofaudes, was ambushed while leading the field army and presumably also killed given we hear nothing more of him. The whole *diocese* was now open to devastation, with the various groups of invaders free to pillage at will, and with any remaining *comitatenses* and *limitanei* staying safe behind the various fort and town defences across the *diocese*.

The emperor in the west by this time was Valentinian I who was fortunately in northern Gaul campaigning against the Alemanni. Hearing the news from Britain, he quickly marched his field army troops towards the Gallic coast. He then dispatched his *comes domesticorum* Severus, who commanded his *Protectores* close bodyguards and staff, to Britain to investigate. This was a senior figure indeed, showing how serious things had become in the *diocese*. However, for some reason he performed unsatisfactorily and was soon recalled, to be replaced by the *magister equitum* Iovinus who had more military experience. He quickly assessed the situation, realised the scale of the crisis and reported back to the emperor that urgent reinforcements were needed. However he too was recalled, perhaps because Valentinian I had fallen ill, and the emperor now turned to a senior military figure who was to become one of the great military leaders of the later Empire. This was Flavius Julius Theodosius (often called Theodosius the Elder), a soldier of Spanish birth whose second son became the emperor Theodosius the Great (and indeed accompanied him in this campaign). Granted the title *Comes Rei Militaris per Britanniarum* by Valentinian I, he crossed to Britain late in the year with a small force comprising four *comitatenses* field army units, numbering around 2,000 men in total. The scene was now set for the last major Roman campaign of conquest, or rather re-conquest, in Britain.

On arrival in Richborough Theodosius immediately headed for London, but on the way had to contend with marauding bands of insurgents in the vicinity of the *diocene* capital. This shows how desperate the situation in Britain had become. What is not clear is whether these were Germanic invaders, or *Bagaudae* insurrectionists. If the latter, they were most likely former Roman troops who'd fled the colours in the face of overwhelming odds. Theodosius soon caught up with them given they were weighed down with plunder, cattle and prisoners. However, instead of butchering them on the spot the *Comes* actually offered them immunity, recruiting any former soldiers back into his force. This speaks volumes regarding the anarchy he was clearly facing in Britain. He then arrived in London in triumph, welcomed as a saviour by those citizens still sheltering behind its strong walls.

Theodosius' first task was to set in place a new *diocene* government which Moorhead and Stuttard (2012, 214) describe as impressive given the nature of the task at hand. At its centre he appointed an official called Civilis as the new *vicarius*, who Ammianus Marcellinus describes as '*a man of fiery temper but uncompromising integrity*' (*The Later Roman Empire*, 28.8.7). In short, just the man for the job. The *Comes* then turned to the military in Britain, appointing a *legate* on his own staff called Dulcitius as the new *Dux Britanniarum* to restore the northern frontier, with the former incumbent by this time either dead or removed from office. Here the archaeological record is instructive, providing detail of Dulcitius' campaign in the north as he set about his difficult task. In particular, a significant number of Valentinian I coins have been found at Corbridge and Piercebridge, showing Dere Street used as he headed to the northern frontier to challenge the Picts. Similarly, coins of the same issue have been found at South Shields, showing the military supply base there was being used once more to support the offensive. It is here we find the *numerous barcariorum Tigrisiensum* detachment of Tigris boatmen operating on the River Tyne later detailed in the *Notitia Dignitatum*, perhaps an auxiliary unit supporting Dulcitius' reconquest operations. Meanwhile, we can also track Dulcitius' offensive against the Scots and Attecotti in the northwest and northern Wales, once more through coin finds of Valentinian I. These have been found at Caernarvon (Roman *Segontium*), Maryport on the Cumbrian coast, and Carlisle.

Theodosius campaigned well into AD 368, using a series of lightning strikes to expel any remaining marauders from the *diocese*, gathering more troops as he did so. The primary sources say he led his troops in person, with Ammianus Marcellinus saying (*The Later Roman Empire*, 28.3.2):

> *He scattered and put to flight various tribes, whose impatience to attack anything Roman was inflamed by the belief that they could act with impunity.*

The primary sources also say that the *Comes* had to deal with an insurrection at the same time, led by a man of high birth called Valentinus who had been exiled to Britain for an unspecified crime. It is interesting in itself that the place chosen as a punishment for Valentinus was Britain, now more than ever the wild west of Empire. Moorhead and Stuttard (2012,

215) say he tried to weave together an alliance of fellow exiles (again telling) and disaffected troops, aiming to launch a coup against the *Comes*. However, Theodosius got wind of it, had Valentinus and the ringleaders arrested and sent them to Dulcitius for execution. The Latin chroniclers go further here, saying that Valentinus was actually at the heart of the 'Great Conspiracy', but we have no further evidence for this.

Order restored, Theodosius now set about rebuilding the *diocese*, putting right any damage to the built environment and restoring the frontier fortifications. Regarding the latter, the entire *diocese* was given over to the labour, this indicated by a series of remarkable contemporary inscriptions on Hadrian's Wall. These show gangs of labourers rather than the military were being used, and from far afield too. Those mentioned include representatives from the Durotriges *civitates* in the southwest, the Catuvellauni in the south and the Brigantes in the north. Some of the most significant reconstruction work was carried out in the forts along the wall, including at Birdoswald (where a new civilian settlement appears in its interior, indicating the troops there had remained loyal), Housesteads, Halton Chesters and Rudchester. Meanwhile, rebuilding also occurred at Vindolanda on the Stanegate Road just to the south of the wall. Fortification rebuilding was also carried out around the coastline of the *diocese*, for example at Caernarvon and Caer Gyb in northwest Wales and at the naval base at Bitterne on the Solent. Massive new fortifications were also built around some of the key small towns in Britain which provided a local administrative function, for example those gathering the *annona militaris*. Examples include Alcester (Roman *Alauna*) in Warwickshire and *Cuneteo* on the River Kennett in Wiltshire. Moorhead and Stuttard (2012, 226) describe this overall process as a bid to build a ring of defences around the rich agricultural farmland in the south, so important in still supplying the armies on the Rhine with grain, and also to protect the means by which it was administered. Theodosius also appointed a new *Comes Litoris Saxonici per Britanniam* (given most of the coastal forts were still in operation) and *Comes Britanniarum*, and did his best to bring the military establishment in Britain up to strength once more. However, this didn't include the *areani* who he disbanded at a stroke given their earlier treachery. A Roman presence north of Hadrian's Wall did continue, given the finding of large quantities of Valentinian I bronze coins at Kelso in Roxburghshire. Coins of this type are most often associated with military pay rather than the more valuable gold and silver issues used to reward or bribe local tribal leaders.

Matters satisfactorily resolved, Theodosius returned to Valentinian I's court in late AD 368 in triumph, with Ammianus Marcellinus saying (*The Later Roman Empire*, 28.3.8):

> *After his excellent management of these affairs and others like them, Theodosius was recalled to court…So great was his popularity that a large crowd escorted him to the Channel, which he crossed with a smooth voyage. He was welcomed at the Imperial headquarters with rejoicing and congratulations, and promoted to the rank of magister equitum in place of Jovinus, who was considered lax.*

However, Theodosius was never a man to rest on his laurels and spent his remaining 18 years on campaign against the Alamanni, Sarmatians and latterly Mauretanian rebels in North Africa. While there in AD 375 he received word that his champion Valentinian I had died, an event that led directly to his demise given he had a very different relationship with the latter's brother and successor in the east, Valens. According to the Latin chroniclers Theodosius was soon arrested and put to death in early AD 376 in Carthage, he being baptised shortly beforehand. While modern commentators suggest this was in the context of factional in-fighting in the Imperial court, one contemporary narrative had it that Valens had been told in a prophecy that he would be succeeded by a man whose name featured 'Theod' as the first two syllables. Thus, Theodosius was dispatched at the first opportunity. However, if this improbable tale is true, Valens killed the wrong Theodosius. Soon Valens himself suffered one of the most humiliating deaths of any Roman emperor when he and his army were annihilated at the epoch-defining Battle of Adrianople in AD 378. At that point Valens' successor Gratian (now taking control of the east as well as the west, where he had previously been Augustus) summoned the younger Theodosius out of premature retirement following the family's fall from grace under Valens. He was given command of the Roman armies in the east and was soon the Augustus there, going on to become one of the greatest of Roman emperors. Theodosius I was also the last emperor to die with Britain still part of the Roman Empire.

Back to AD 378, *Comes* Theodosius' left a strong legacy in Britain, with a stable military and civilian leadership providing a degree of security not seen for generations. However, this was to last only another 13 years before trouble once more broke out along the northern frontier. There, in AD 382 a Romano-British military leader called Magnus Maximus appears in action for the first time. Maximus was born on the Spanish estates owned by Theodosius the Elder and grew up with the younger Theodosius, now the emperor. Southern (2013, 340) says he may actually have been a relative, and he certainly accompanied the expedition to Britain in AD 367. He is another of the great figures of Romano-British history given he appears as a central character in later narratives detailing the transition from Roman to post-Roman Britain. A prime example is in the 6th century AD monk and historian Gildas' *De Excidio et Conquestu Britanniae* (On the Ruin and Conquest of Britain). He also features in a number of early Welsh genealogies which give him the role of founding father in some of the key dynasties of several medieval Welsh kingdoms, including Gwent and Powys. His fame was such that even today some suggest it was his exploits that are the foundation of the King Arthur myth.

We don't know which of the three military leadership posts Maximus held at the time, though given the trouble in AD 382 was in the north it seems likely he was either the *Dux Britanniarum* commanding the *limitanei* there, or the *Comes Britanniarum* leading the *comitatenses* troops in the field army. Here again the Romans found themselves in danger of being overwhelmed, and reinforcements from the continent were called for. Illustrating the rapidly changing nature of the late Roman army, these turned out to be a unit of Alamanni *foederates* called the *numerus Alamannorum* who arrived to fight under their own king, Fraomarius (Moorhead and Stuttard, 2012, 230). The campaign was a success, with Maximus apparently taking the title '*Britannicus Maximus*' and celebrating a great victory.

However, all was not well. Maximus had ambitions of his own, enhanced when he viewed his childhood friend Theodosius I prospering as the eastern Augustus. In the west Gratian was becoming increasingly unpopular, especially after he took to wearing Gothic costume. This went down particularly badly with the army after their losses in the shattering defeat at Adrianople. The emperor was especially unpopular in Britain, almost certainly in the context of the demise of Theodosius the Elder at Gratian's bidding. Then, when the latter lavished recently recruited Alan *foederates* with gifts, the field army in Britain revolted and declared Maximus the new Augustus in the west. He became one of the more successful British usurpers, eventually defeating Gratian who was later killed, and then carving out an Empire in the west that included Britain, Gaul, Spain and North Africa, with his imperial capital at Trier. However, crucially he failed to occupy Italy after the intervention of Theodosius I, and in AD 384 settled for being recognised the Augustus in the west, with the 12-year-old Valentinian II co-emperor in Italy.

Maximus was a shrewd man and knew he needed the support of the elites and military in the west to remain in power. For example, before he had left Britain for the continent he'd reopened the mint in London and ordered a new issue of gold and silver coins struck so that he could secure the loyalty of his followers. With his coffers full, he also paid off the confederacies and tribes in the far north and west with a view to securing the borders there while he was away. However, after four years in power he finally overplayed his hand and marched into Italy with a view to becoming sole ruler in the west. This was the pretext Theodosius I needed to act once and for all, he mobilising a huge field army which he marched westwards to intercept Maximus. The two former friends met in battle at Aquileia in north-eastern Italy, with Theodosius I the victor. Maximus was captured and pleaded for his life but, stripped of his royal clothing, was condemned to death out of hand. Soon a messenger was heading northwest to Trier with orders to eliminate Maximus' line, with a Frankish general promptly killing his son. Such was the price of failure in a Roman civil war.

However, even in death, Maximus left a toxic legacy in Britain. When he initially departed the *diocese* in his bid for glory in AD 383 he'd taken most of the field army troops with him, and even perhaps units of *limitanei*. Though he himself may have returned to Britain in his four years in power given gold coins were again struck in the London mint (an act only carried out when an emperor was close by) it seems most of these troops didn't. Indeed later tradition has him granting them lands on the Armorica Peninsula, whether they had family back home or not. Meanwhile, the *Notitia Dignitatum* details troops from Caernarvon now stationed in the western Balkans.

With the Roman military establishment in Britain at its bare minimum, the *diocese* was again vulnerable and soon the Picts, Attecotti and Scots were on the march south and east again, particularly after the death of Maximus. Further, some of the Scots arriving in Wales also started to settle, with small communities appearing on the Lleyn and Gower peninsulas in Wales from this time. Matters came to a head in AD 398, three years after Theodosius I's death, when there appears to have been one last Roman expedition to save the *diocese*. Of the event Gildas later wrote (*De Excidio et Conquestu Britanniae*, 16–17):

When all at once, like starved and ravening wolves that leap with hungry jaws into the sheepfold when the shepherd is away, the old enemy burst across the frontier. They slaughtered everything (and) again the Britons sent ambassadors to Rome...The Romans, moved as much as men can be by such accounts of horror, swiftly sent their cavalry by land and their sailors by sea. Like eagles, they plunged the talons of their sword-points into the shoulders of their enemies.

By this time the leading figure in the Roman west was Flavius Stilicho, the western *magister militum* military leader entrusted as guardian to the 14-year-old Honorius, the new emperor in the west after the death of his father. Whether Stilicho himself led this final expedition to Britain we do not know, but he certainly took credit for it. For example, the contemporary panegyric poet Claudian says (*Works*, *De Consulatu Stilichonis*, 261ff):

Then, wrapped in the skin of a Caledonian beast, her cheeks tattooed, her sky-blue garments like the waves of Oceanus falling round her feet, Britannia spoke: 'My neighbours would have killed me, but Stilicho protected me – for the Scot roused all Ireland against me and the sea foamed under their hostile oars. Now, thanks to Stilicho, I need not fear the Scottic javelin nor tremble at the Pict, nor scour suspiciously each wind along the coast for the approaching Saxon.

These two primary references are remarkable given the evocative level of detail they provide. First, they show that once more the *diocese* was facing a threat on multiple fronts, which again required an intervention similar in scale to that of *Comes* Theodosius in AD 367. Gildas' mention of what were almost certainly field army cavalry units being sent to the *diocese* also shows that flying columns were again used to track down and destroy the invaders, while both sources show how control of the open ocean continued to be a problem for Roman Britain in the absence of a standing fleet. Claudian's final mention of Saxon raiders is also illustrative of the perils of living along the east coast littoral in the *diocese*, with its river systems penetrating deep inland. Already, those residents there who could leave were doing so, to settle in the west of Britain or in Gaul (for example in Armorica once more). Soon it was the Germans themselves who would be settling in the *diocese*, occupying the increasingly abandoned east coast. The scene was now set for the desperate end game of Roman Britain.

Conclusion

The campaigns of conquest in Britain left a dramatic legacy that still impacts the islands here to this very day, and in many ways. In my conclusion, I first look at this legacy in terms of the urban and transport network in modern Britain, much of it a direct result of the conquest campaigns. I then detail how today's political settlement in the main islands of Britain is also the result of the Roman campaigns of conquest. Finally, I consider the effects of the final campaigns of conquest in Britain, which I argue led directly to what I term 'Britain's First Brexit', an event which again impacts society here today. It is in this final discussion that I detail the story of Roman Britain's demise.

Looking first to the urban landscape in Britain today, in Chapters 4, 5 and 6 I set out the overly-long and painful Roman campaigns of conquest in Britain, from the time of Claudius' AD 43 invasion through to Agricola's Mons Graupius campaign in AD 83. This covered a period of 40 years in which the Romans slowly, painfully expanded the initial territory of the province in the southeast up to the Solway Firth - Tyne line, and for a short time even further north into the farthest reaches of modern Scotland. This process was very different to the Roman experience conquering territories elsewhere in the Empire, these usually far swifter, with the conquered land then more quickly incorporated into the Roman world. For example, Julius Caesar took only eight years to conquer the far larger territory of Gaul, which soon became a key economic and cultural part of Roman-controlled territory. Further, the Roman conquest of Britain wasn't a single event, but a series of separate campaigns under a wide variety of governors, some more successful than others. This meant a number of stop lines were set out as newly conquered territory was consolidated. A key example would be the 'Fosse Way Frontier' of the later AD 40s as Plautius halted his advances in the South West and Midlands before departing back to Rome. This slow, grinding process of conquest, with frequent halts, had a very specific impact then and now, given the need to continually build fortresses and forts to secure newly-won territory. Each had its own *canaba* or *vicus*, and many went on to become Roman towns in their own right. Examples proliferate across the landscape of modern Britain, given they survived the end of Roman Britain to become much of today's city and town urban landscape. Think of Exeter, Cardiff, Gloucester, Chester, Manchester, Leicester, Lincoln, York, Lancaster, Newcastle and Carlisle. The clue here is also in the name, with the Latin *castres* (military camp) giving us the *ster* (or a close derivative) at the end of many of these names. The same is true of the rural landscape of modern Britain where many smaller settlements also had their origins as Roman forts.

This system of fortresses and forts, designed to put the stamp of Rome across the growing province, was matched by a series of military trunk roads built to support the conquest campaigns and later secure the province. To this day they broadly, for much of their length, form the backbone of the pre-motorway A road network in Britain. As Bishop details (2014, 41):

> *Since most of the major roads in* [Roman] *Britain…had their origins in the military campaigns of the conquest period, it is not unreasonable to suggest that the various components of the network can be dated to the aftermath of the earliest military activity in each area.*

Examples are found across the territory of the province, including Watling Street (the A2 and A5), Ermine Street (the A1), Dere Street (the A1 and A68) and the Fosse Way (the A46/ A249).

Next, looking at the political settlement of the modern British Isles, the Roman campaigns of conquest also played a key role in setting in place the political geography that still exists today. In the first instance, after Agricola's brief consideration of an Irish campaign in AD 81, the Romans never again cast their gaze across the Irish Sea with a view to conquest. Therefore Ireland never became part of the Roman Imperial project, and from that time onwards went in its own direction. Indeed, the Scots later played a key role in the failure of the Roman *diocese* in Britain. Second, and equally important, the Romans never conquered the far north of the main island of Britain, despite two enormous attempts to do so under Agricola in the later 1st century AD and Septimius Severus in the early 3rd century AD. This meant the region now called Scotland was also a place of difference, and from that time the northern frontier a place of friction between the far north and the south. It also had serious implications for Roman Britain, given it meant a far larger military presence was needed than would otherwise have been the case to maintain this northern frontier. In earlier research I estimate this was around 12 per cent of the entire Roman military establishment in what was only 4 per cent of its geographic area (Elliott, 2016, 64). Further, it meant that the entire regional economy in the north and west was bent on maintaining this presence, making the experience of *Romanitas* very different for those living there when compared to the more affluent south and east.

Finally turning to 'Britain's First Brexit', a lively debate continues to this day about the nature of the ending of Roman Britain. Some argue it was a dramatic, brutal event, while others see it much more a process of gradual change. As can be seen in Chapter 8, while there was clearly a decline in the fortunes of Roman Britain, especially after the demise of the regional fleet in the mid-3rd century AD and the increasingly common removal of troops by usurpers, time and again the Romans propped up their presence here. Indeed, this led to the later campaigns of conquest (or reconquest), including those of Constantius Chlorus and *Comes* Theodosius. Even at the very end of the 4th century AD Stilicho was still willing to commit field army cavalry units and naval forces to defeat another major incursion into the *diocese*. Yet, while these campaigns in isolation were seemingly successful, as a collective attempt to keep Britain in the Empire over time they ultimately failed, given Britain eventually did leave the Empire, and catastrophically. I am therefore firmly in the dramatic and brutal decline camp, interpreting the archaeological and other data as indicating Britain dropped cataclysmically out of the Roman Empire in the first decade or two of the 5th century AD.

The key implication of this is the very different way Britain left the Empire compared with the same, later experience on the continent. Starting with the continent, the Western Roman Empire officially ended in AD 476 with the forced abdication of the last western emperor, Romulus Augustulus. The protagonist of his demise was a Roman general of Germanic descent called Odoacer. The latter was then declared the king in Italy by his Heruli, Rugian and Sciri warriors. By that time much of the western empire had long fallen out of Roman rule, and as the 6th century AD began the political settlement in western Europe was beginning to resemble the familiar pattern of the early Middle Ages. Think the Franks and Burgundians in modern Germany and France, the Visigoths in Spain, and the Ostrogoths in Italy and the north-western Balkans.

In these areas the assimilation of the Roman political, economic and social establishments into the new regimes was by no means easy or devoid of serious dislocation. However, this tended to be at the very top of society, with the pre-existing ways of life below continuing as before. As Scarre explains (1995a, 135):

The transition from Roman province to Germanic kingdom did not mark an abrupt break with the past. In many areas the existing provincial aristocracy continued to hold land and power, to write and worship as before only now as vassals of Germanic (or Gothic) elites.

This transition was eased by the fact that the incomers already knew the ways of the Romans. As set out in Chapter 1, Germans and Goths had long served in the Roman military, and at the very highest level too. Stilicho himself was a Vandal, the later *magister militum* Ricimer a Suevi. Further, large numbers had been living within the borders of the Empire for many years, while other new incomers only had to travel a short distance across the Rhine or Danube where they had been based for generations.

We can see in the clearest terms the legacy of this comparatively benign handover of power in continental Europe today. Think Romance languages, Catholic Church, legal systems with their origins in Roman law codes, and thriving agricultural economies only supplemented by large-scale industry in the past 200 years. In many ways modern Europe is Roman Europe.

However, the transition from Roman to post-Roman in Britain was far different, and darker in every way. Picking up the chronological narrative from the end of Chapter 8, while Stilicho's emergency deployment of troops to the *diocese* in AD 398 did stabilise the frontiers once more, they soon returned to the continent. Further, there was no subsequent attempt to bring the complement of *limitanei*, let alone *comitatenses*, back up to strength as had been the case with *Comes* Theodosius' campaign in AD 367/ 368. To make matters worse, by the early 5th century Rome found itself facing a new existential threat in the west. This was Alaric and his Visigoths, who invaded Italy in AD 401. Soon the *magister militum* was casting around the western *diocese* for reinforcements, his eyes alighting on far off Britain. In that regard, we know that at least one unit from the *diocese* fought in the Roman victory over Alaric at Pollentia near modern Turin in AD 402, this detailed by Claudian who says that among the Roman army was (*Works, De Bello Gothico*, 416):

A legion that had been stationed among the far-off Britons, which had reined in the fierce Scot and had scanned the strange patterns tattooed on the dying Picts.

This was most likely *legio* II *Augusta*, so recently detailed in the *Notitia Dignitatum* based at Richborough, where its final, unused pay chest was found. With troops being increasingly stripped away, and Imperial attention purely focused on the threat in Italy, Roman Britain was entering its final crisis.

Back on the continent, by AD 406 the predations of Alaric and his Visigoths in Italy had been joined by persistent infringements over the northern *limes* into Gaul by Germanic Vandals and Suebi, and Iranian Alans (the latter long settled north of the Rhine). This had unintended consequences in Britain, with Zosimus saying (*New History*, 6.3.1):

> *The Vandals joined forces with the Suebi and Alans and, sweeping across these lands, they ravaged the Transalpine tribes. So widespread was the slaughter they carried out that even the Roman army in Britain (such as it was) was afraid: indeed such was its fear that the barbarians might attack, that it was forced to appoint the usurper emperors, Marcus and Gratian.*

We know very little about these men except they were clearly a failure in the eyes of the remaining military in Roman Britain. Each was, in turn, executed. Then, on New Year's Eve AD 406, an event occurred that had dramatic implications for the whole western Empire. This was when, in the midst of a severe winter, the Rhine froze solid, allowing vast numbers of Germanic tribesmen and Alans into Gaul. With the *limitanei* quickly overrun, and the local field armies no doubt fighting with Stilicho in Italy, the region was devastated and civic order collapsed. This left Roman Britain dangerously disconnected from the rest of Imperial territory in the west and quickly a new usurper was appointed. This was a man called Constantine III, of whom we know little regarding his early life except his sons were called Constans and Julian. If nothing else this was a man with a keen eye for recent Roman history. The only real direct insight we have here is from the Latin chronicler Orosius who says Constantine III (*Seven Books of History Against the Pagans*, 7.40.4):

> *...was elected from the lowest ranks of the military, simply because his name seemed propitious, and not because of any bravery he might have had.*

This bleak description seems most unlikely given the usurper's subsequent initial success in carving out his own territory in the west, with the emperor there, Honorius, forced to acknowledge him as a co-Augustus in AD 409. It is worth noting that Orosius was a church historian and perhaps here he unwittingly gives us insight into Constantine III's political strategy, the new usurper harking in his rhetoric back to the great days of Roman Britain, just as Carausius had once done. The fact his younger son was called Julian after the apostate emperor also clearly shows he had no evident love of the church. Constantine III also had the full support of the military both in Britain and Gaul given their initial support, and he soon defeated the marauding Germans and restored the northern *limes* along the Rhine. Then, having seen off a number of attempts by Honorius to remove him from power, he consolidated his position and set up an Imperial capital in Arles. As with Magnus Maximus before him, it was only when he overplayed his hand against Honorius that Constantine III fell, he finally being captured and beheaded by the emperor's general Constantius (later briefly Constantius III) in August or September AD 411.

Back in Britain, Constantine III's usurpation in AD 407 set in train a series of events that finally brought down Roman Britain. It was he who removed any final *comitatenses* field army troops when he made his play for power on the continent, and most likely the better *limitanei* too. This left only the few remaining *limitanei* border troops to defend the entire *diocese*. The inevitable followed, with Britain swamped by Germanic, Pictish and Scots raiders in AD 408/ 409. Moorhead and Stuttard (2012, 238) describe '*…the fast disintegration of the last vestiges of security and order…*' at this time. By AD 409/ 410 the Romano-British elites had had enough of not getting any return from Rome for their taxes and unceremoniously expelled the Roman tax collectors, (whether these reported to Constantine III, Honorius, or both, dependent on the timing). Zosimus provides detail here, saying (*New History*, 6.5.3):

> *The barbarians caused such suffering among the inhabitants of Britain…that they revolted from the Roman Empire. They no longer recognized Roman law, but reverted to their native customs. So the Britons armed themselves and took many risks to ensure their own safety and keep their towns free from barbarian attacks.*

The event described here is 'Britain's First Brexit', with the Romano-British elites choosing to go their own way. Unsurprisingly things didn't end well. After more intense raiding, the elites in Britain changed their mind and asked for help from Rome once more. We know this through the controversial Rescript of Honorius, an official response to an appeal detailed by Zosimus (*New History*, 4.35). In the rescript the emperor tells the British *civitates* (regions) '*…to look to their own defences*', indicating the rescript is a response to an appeal for help, (a not surprising response from the emperor given Britain's recent support for Constantine III). The controversy comes about because some argue the geographic reference in the document is to Bruttium in Italy, not Britain. If it was Britain, then Zosimus' earlier quote illustrates what the '*…many risks to ensure their own safety…*' actually were. When it became clear to the Romano-British elites that help really wasn't going to come from the continent they hired their own *foederate* mercenaries, these Germans in the east and Scots in the west. Interestingly, around this time the archaeological record shows a new phenomenon emerging for the first time. This was the slow re-emergence of pre-Roman tribal identities as the horizons of those living in the former Romano-British *civitates* began to narrow. In Chapter 8 I recorded how the various gangs of labourers recruited from around the *diocese* to help rebuild the northern frontier after the successful campaigns of *Comes* Theodosius recorded their presence by referencing the *civitates* region they came from in inscriptions. The examples I detailed included the Durotriges, Catuvellauni and Brigantes. Now, as the new *foederates* arrived, they were not only deployed on the outer borders of the former *diocese* to give protection against the predations of the Scots, Attecotti, Picts and Germans. We know this because many of the earliest German cemeteries in Britain are not around the western and northern frontier or around the coast, but inland along the borders between the various *civitates*. Clearly the elites across Britain were not just looking externally for potential aggressors, but at their neighbours too.

The next major event we have detail of is the visit of St Germanus, Bishop of Auxerre, on a religious mission to Britain in AD 429. His brief was to stamp out the preaching of one Agricola, a disciple of Pelagius. The latter was a religious heretic excommunicated by the Pope in AD 416 and denounced by Honorius himself in AD 418. Germanus, a former provincial governor and lawyer, reported that parts of the former *diocese* were still clinging desperately to the last vestiges of *Romanitas*, this particularly the case in the southwest. One report also styles him a former *dux*, and his last alleged action in Britain before returning to the continent gives this credence. This has him leading a force of post-Roman Britons to the rescue of fellow soldiers surrounded by a predating force comprising Picts and Germans. Though the main account suggests religious intervention, with the enemy fleeing after the repeated chants of Alleluia by the Britons, reading between the lines it seems St Germanus here led a successful ambush.

Things continued to decline in Britain, with coin use ending around AD 430. By this time the population was in rapid decline, heading back to the 2 million of the LIA. A final, desperate attempt to maintain any official contact with the Western Empire occurred in AD 446 when the British elites again reached out to the continent. This time it was in the form of a letter to a Roman general in Gaul called Agitius, usually identified as the *magister militum* Flavius Aetius. He was the future vanquisher of Attila the Hun, and had been the most powerful man in the western Empire since at least AD 433 (Southern, 2013, 356). The letter, usually referred to as the 'Groans of the Britons', is detailed by Gildas. He paints a harrowing picture, having the Britons say (*De Excidio Britanniae,* 20):

> *The barbarians drive us into the sea, the sea drives us back to the barbarians, between these two forms of death we are either slaughtered or drowned.*

The *magister militum's* reply was predictably no, given he was already hard pressed in Gaul. This marks the final end of Britain as any shadow part of the Roman Empire, which itself collapsed in the west in AD 476 as detailed above.

With the chronology of the end of Roman Britain set in place, we can now look at why its experience of departure from the empire was so different to that on the continent that it remains a place of difference to this day in the eyes of many. Britannia had already been differential within the empire due to the lengthy campaigns of conquest, inability to conquer the far north and subsequent huge military presence (at least until late in the Dominate phase of empire). This was now locked in place for posterity for two reasons:

- As set out in Chapter 8 and here, from the later decades of the 4th century AD much of the east of the province had become increasingly depopulated as the elites and middle classes who could afford to leave chose to do so, given the never-ending Germanic raiding. In recently published research Hingley is instructive here. Using the *diocene* capital London as his example, he says (2018, 248):

> *There is currently little to indicate that life continued inside the walled area after the first decade of the 5th century AD.*

Matters were made worse after the 'First Brexit' with the hiring of the *foederates* detailed above to replace the non-existent soldiery. Over the long term many proved very unreliable, often rebelling. Meanwhile, of the Romans who left Britain, as detailed many fled to Armorica where the refugees soon gave the region a new name: Brittany.

- The Germans coming to Britain, first as raiders and later settlers, were not from regions immediately north of the Rhine and Danube, but from the far north of Germany: Saxony, Frisia, Jutland and southern Scandinavia. They had not had close contact with the Roman Empire as had the Franks and Goths to their south. Therefore, they did not know the ways of the Romans, and on arriving shunned many aspects of Roman culture, particularly the built environment which they totally avoided. Indeed, when they began to settle in London they totally avoided the Roman walled town and built their own trading emporium called *Lundenwic* on the northern banks of the Thames, around 1.5km to the west. Today this is the area known as Aldwych, this name derived directly from this early German settlement given it means old *wich*, or old port.

Thus when the Germans arrived in Britain, there was little left in the east of Roman society for them to take over, and even if there was, they didn't know how to in a way that would preserve what had existed before. The result was no continuation of the use of Latin as a language – note I am writing now in English, a German language. There was no adherence to Roman law codes, with our Common Law here based on laws of Germanic origin. Finally, there was also a differential experience regarding Christianity. With Britain now fully cut off from the Catholic centre in the Mediterranean, the church in the islands of Britain evolved along its own path. This caused much confusion and consternation when Augustine arrived here in AD 597 with orders to spread the faith of the Rome-based Catholic church. Over the next 200 years this new German culture then gradually, unstoppably scoured its way east to west across the main island of Britain, finally establishing the long-lasting political entities of Northumbria, East Anglia, Mercia and Wessex.

Above I have set out why I think the Roman campaigns of conquest in Britain, or later the long-term failure of the late campaigns of reconquest (even if those of *Comes* Theodosius and Stilicho were initially successful), helped create the Britain of today. Whether through the built environment across the breadth of modern England and Wales, its road networks, or the political settlement of the main islands of Britain, the world of Rome is still with us to this day. This is perhaps no better illustrated in the age in which we live than by *'Britain's First Brexit'*, an event so traumatic that its consequences still shape Britain's relationship with its European neighbours.

Timeline of Roman Britain

Below I outline a timeline of key events in the history of Roman Britain to provide a framework for this study of the Roman campaigns of conquest here. To provide context I include key events in the wider history of the Roman Republic and Empire where relevant.

Date	Event
509 BC	*Overthrow of Tarquin the Proud, Roman Republic begins.*
113 BC	*Beginning of the Cimbrian War.*
107 BC	*Marius elected Consul for the first time.*
100 BC	*Gaius Julius Caesar born.*
88 BC	*Sulla's First Civil War.*
86 BC	*Marius dies.*
83 BC	*Sulla's Second Civil War.*
82 BC	*Sulla becomes dictator, Caesar flees to Asia to join the military.*
78 BC	*Sulla dies, Caesar returns to Rome.*
75 BC	*Caesar captured by Cilician pirates while travelling to Rhodes.*
73 BC	*Caesar, appointed as one of the 15 pontiffs serving the Pontifex Maximus, returns to Rome.*
63 BC	*Caesar elected Pontifex Maximus.*
62 BC	*Caesar is a praetor, then proconsul in Hispania Ulterior.*
60 BC	*First Triumvirate.*
59 BC	*Caesar is consul.*
58 BC	*Beginning of Caesar's Gallic Wars. He campaigns against the Helvetii and Suebi.*
57 BC	*Caesar campaigns against the Belgae.*
56 BC	*Conference of Lucca, campaign against the Veneti, Battle of Morbihan.*

55 BC	*Massacre of the Usipetes and Tencteri, Caesar's first incursion to Britain.*
54 BC	*Caesar's second incursion to Britain.*
53 BC	*Rebellion of the Eburones and Nervii tribes in Gaul. Death of Crassus at the Battle of Carrhae against the Parthians.*
52 BC	*Gallic revolt under Vercingetorix, siege of Alesia. End of the Gallic Wars.*
49 BC	*Caesar crosses the Rubicon river with legio XIII. Spanish campaign against the Optimates.*
48 BC	*Battle of Pharsalus, death of Pompey in Egypt.*
47 BC	*Alexandrian War, Caesar campaigns against Pharnaces II.*
46 BC	*Battle of Thapsus, quadruple triumph in Rome.*
45 BC	*Battle of Munda.*
44 BC	*Caesar appointed dictator for life, assassinated on the Ides of March.*
42 BC	*Battle of Philippi*
31 BC	*Battle of Actium*
27 BC	*Roman conquest of northern Spain begins. Octavian becomes Augustus. Beginning of the Principate Empire.*
AD 9	*Varus' three legions, together with nine auxiliary units, destroyed in Teutoburg Forest, Germany, by the Cherusci tribe and others led by Arminius.*
AD 40	*Caligula's planned invasion of Britain aborted.*
AD 43	*The third, and successful, Roman invasion of Britain under the emperor Claudius, with the legionaries, auxilia and naval milites commanded by Aulus Plautius. Province of Britannia established.*
AD 44	*The future emperor Vespasian successfully campaigns in the south west of Britain, leading legio II Augusta.*
AD 47/48	*Vespasian successfully concludes his campaign to conquer the south west of Britain, returning to Rome with Plautius. The new governor Publius Ostorius Scapula subdues the first revolt by the Iceni tribe in the north of East Anglia, and campaigns in Wales and the north.*

AD 49	*A coloniae for veterans founded at Colchester, with legio XX Valeria Victrix moving to Gloucester. Ostorius campaigns in Wales.*
AD 50	*Construction begins of first forum in the newly-founded city of London.*
AD 51	*The leader of the British resistance to Roman rule, Caratacus, is captured by the Romans after being handed over by the Brigantian Queen, Cartimandua.*
AD 52	*The Silures tribe in southern Wales is pacified by Governor Didius Gallus.*
AD 54	*Claudius dies, Nero becomes the emperor.*
AD 57	*Quintus Veranius Nepos becomes the governor in Britain, dying in office. Rome intervenes in favour of Queen Cartimandua in a dispute over the leadership of the Brigantes.*
AD 58	*Gaius Suetonius Paulinus becomes the Governor.*
AD 59/60	*The initial subjugation of the Druids in the far west, and the initial invasion of Anglesey by Paulinus. This campaign is cut short by the Boudiccan revolt.*
AD 60/61	*The Boudiccan revolt takes place, featuring the destruction of Colchester, St Albans and London. The revolt is defeated by Paulinus, followed by the death of Boudicca.*
AD 61/63	*Publius Petronius Turpilianus becomes the governor, followed by Marcus Trebellius Maximus.*
AD 66	*First 'Great' Jewish Revolt.*
AD 68	*Nero is overthrown, with Galba becoming the emperor.*
AD 69	*The Year of Four Emperors. Vespasian is the ultimate victor and becomes emperor. In Britain Cartimandua, Queen of the Brigantes and ally of Rome, is overthrown by former husband Venutius. Marcus Vettius Bolanus is the new governor.*
AD 70	*The Classis Britannica regional navy in Britain is named for the first time in the context of the Batavian Revolt of Civilis on the River Rhine.*
	Fall of Jerusalem to Titus.
AD 71	*Vespasian orders the new British governor Quintus Petilius Cerialis to campaign in the north of Britain. The Brigantes are defeated, with Venutius captured and killed.*

AD 74	*Sextus Julius Frontinus is appointed as the new governor in Britain. Further campaigning in Wales follows, and Chester is founded.*
AD 77	*Gnaeus Julius Agricola becomes the new governor in Britain. Wales and western Britain are finally conquered.*
AD 78	*Agricola consolidates Roman control of Brigantian territory, and then begins planning his campaign in the far north of the islands of Britain.*
AD 79	*Agricola begins his campaign to subdue the whole of the north of Britain, including Scotland. Vespasian dies and is replaced by his son Titus.*
AD 80	*Agricola continues his campaigning in Scotland.*
AD 81	*The death of Titus who is succeeded by his younger brother Domitian.*
AD 82	*Agricola continues his campaigning in Scotland.*
AD 83	*Agricola brings the combined Caledonian tribes to battle at Mons Graupius in the Grampians, south of the Moray Firth (possibly even further north). After his victory the Classis Britannica circumnavigates northern Scotland. The conquest of Britain is declared 'complete', with construction then beginning of a monumental arch at Richborough in modern Kent to commemorate the event.*
AD 87	*Roman troops are withdrawn from the far north of Britain because of pressures elsewhere in the Empire. The legionary fortress of Inchtuthill in Tayside is abandoned.*
AD 90	*Lincoln becomes a colonia settlement.*
AD 96	*Domitian is assassinated, this event bringing to an end the Flavian dynasty. He is succeeded by Nerva. Gloucester becomes a colonia settlement.*
AD 98	*The death of Nerva, who is succeeded by Trajan. In Britain, Publius Metilius Nepos is the new governor, followed by Titus Avidius Quietus.*
AD 100	*Trajan orders the full withdrawal of Roman troops from Scotland, and then establishes a new frontier along the Solway Firth - Tyne line. All of the defences north of this line are abandoned by AD 105.*

AD 101	*Beginning of Trajan's first Dacian campaign.*
AD 103	*Lucius Neratius Marcellus is the new governor.*
AD 105	*Beginning of Trajan's second Dacian campaign.*
AD 115	*Beginning of Trajan's campaign against Parthia. Beginning of the Second Jewish Revolt. Marcus Atilius Bradua is the new governor in Britain.*
AD 117	*The death of Trajan, he being succeeded by Hadrian. This coincides with major disturbances in the north of the province of Britannia.*
AD 122	*The emperor Hadrian visits Britain, initiating the construction of Hadrian's Wall on the Solway Firth - Tyne line. Aulus Platorius Nepos is the new governor, arriving with the emperor and being tasked with the wall's construction.*
AD 132	*Beginning of the Third 'bar Kokhba' Jewish Revolt.*
AD 138	*The death of Hadrian, he being succeeded by Antoninus Pius. Quintus Lollius Urbicus is the new governor in Britain.*
AD 142	*Military engagements north of Hadrian's Wall continue under Quintus Lollius Urbicus, on the orders of Antoninus Pius, in an attempt to subdue the tribes of northern Britain and southern Scotland, the latter region being conquered again. Construction then begins of the Antonine Wall along the Clyde - Forth line as a new northern frontier.*
AD 145	*Gnaeus Papirus Aelianus is the new governor in Britain.*
AD 155	*Central St Albans is destroyed by a major fire.*
AD 157	*Gnaeus Julius Verus is the new governor in Britain.*
AD 161	*The emperor Antoninus Pius dies, and is succeeded by Marcus Aurelius and Lucius Verus. Beginning of the Roman-Parthian War.*
AD 162	*Marcus Statius Priscuss is the new governor of Britain, followed by Sextus Calpurnius Agricola. The Antonine Wall is evacuated, with the northern border once again moving south to the line of Hadrian's Wall.*
AD 166	*Beginning of the Marcomannic Wars.*
AD 169	*Death of Lucius Verus. More trouble in northern Britain.*
AD 174	*Caerellius is the new governor in Britain*

AD 175	*5,500 Sarmatian cavalry are sent to Britain, perhaps because of a military emergency.*
AD 178	*Ulpius Marcellus is the new governor in Britain.*
AD 180	*Marcus Aurelius dies, being replaced by Commodus.*
AD 182	*The tribes either side of Hadrian's Wall start raiding along and across the border, with Roman troops responding with counter-raids. Towns far to the south of the wall begin constructing the first earth-and-timber defence circuits, indicating that tribal raiding penetrated far into the province.*
AD 184	*Commodus receives his seventh acclamation as Imperator, taking the title Britannicus indicating some kind of military victory in the province. Revolt of the Roman legions in Britain.*
AD 185	*Some 1,500 picked troops from Britain travel to Rome with a petition for the emperor Commodus. They ask that he dismisses the Praetorian Prefect Perennis. The new governor in Britain is the future emperor Publius Helvius Pertinax who subdues the legions, surviving an assassination attempt in the process.*
AD 191/192	*Decimus Clodius Albinus becomes the new governor in Britain.*
AD 193	*The 'Year of the Five Emperors', with Septimius Severus emerging as the ultimate victor.*
AD 196	*British governor Albinus usurps, invades Gaul and is proclaimed emperor by the legions from Britain and Spain.*
AD 197	*Albinus is defeated by Severus at the closely fought Battle of Lugdunum (modern Lyons) and is killed. Planning begins to divide the province of Britain into two, Britannia Superior and Britannia Inferior. Virius Lupus is the new governor in Britain.*
AD 197/198	*Severus sends military commissioners to Britain aiming to quickly suppress the remaining supporters of Albinus. Roman troops rebuild parts of Hadrian's Wall (some of which may have actually been destroyed) and other parts of the northern defences that had been damaged by an increase in tribal raiding after Albinus had travelled to Gaul with his troops. Construction also starts at this time of the land walls of London. Severus begins his reforms of the military, while he himself campaigns in Parthia for two years.*

AD 202	*Severus campaigns in North Africa. Gaius Valerius Pudens is the new governor in Britain.*
AD 205	*Lucius Alfenus Senecio is the new governor in Britain.*
AD 207	*News arrives in Rome from Britain (perhaps the letter from Senecio detailed by Herodian) asking Severus for urgent assistance in the form of the emperor himself or more troops. He responds with both.*
AD 208	*Severus arrives in Britain with the Imperial household and a huge army, he planning a major campaign against the Maeatae and Caledonian tribal confederations north of Hadrian's Wall.*
AD 209	*The first Severan campaign in Scotland begins.*
AD 210	*The second Severan campaign in Scotland begins, led by Caracalla as the emperor is too ill to actively participate. Genocide ordered by Severus.*
AD 211	*Severus dies at York, with his sons Caracalla and Geta becoming joint emperors. The campaign in the north of Britain is suspended with the brothers returning to Rome. Caracalla murders Geta. Britain is later officially divided into two provinces, Britannia Superior and Britannia Inferior.*
AD 216	*Marcus Antonius Gordianus is the new governor of Britannia Inferior.*
AD 222	*Tiberius Julius Pollienus Auspex is the new governor of Britannia Superior.*
AD 223	*Claudius Xenophon is the new governor of Britannia Inferior.*
AD 224	*Ardashir I of Persia defeats his Parthian overlords over a two-year period, bringing the Sassanid Persian Empire into being. Rome now has a fully symmetrical threat on her eastern border.*
AD 225	*Maximus is the new governor of Britannia Inferior.*
AD 226	*Calvisius Rufus becomes the new governor of Britannia Inferior, being followed by Valerius Crescens and then by Claudius Appelinus.*
AD 235	*Assassination of Severus Alexander, ending the Severan dynasty beginning the 'Crisis of the 3rd Century'. Maximinus Thrax becomes emperor.*
AD 237	*Tuccianus becomes the new governor of Britannia Inferior.*

AD 238	*Marcus Martiannius Pulcher becomes the new governor of Britannia Superior. Maecilius Fuscus becomes the new governor of Britannia Inferior, quickly followed by Egnatius Lucilianus.*
AD 242	*Nonius Philippus becomes the new governor of Britannia Inferior.*
AD 244	*Aemilianus becomes the new governor of Britannia Inferior.*
AD 249	*The last potential mention of the Classis Britannica regional fleet, on epigraphy in Arles commemorating Saturninus, ex-Captain in the British Fleet.*
AD 250	*Scots raiding takes place along the west coast, with Germanic raiding along the east coast.*
AD 253	*Desticius Juba becomes the new governor of Britannia Superior.*
AD 260	*The 'Gallic Empire' is declared by Postumus, this splitting Britain, Gaul and Spain away from the Empire for 14 years.*
AD 262	*Octavius Sabinus becomes the new governor of Britannia Inferior.*
AD 268	*Postumus is murdered by his own troops.*
AD 274	*The emperor Aurelian defeats the 'Gallic Empire', with Britain, Gaul and Spain then re-joining the Empire.*
AD 277	*Vandals and Burgundian mercenaries are settled in Britain, with Victorinus defeating a British usurpation.*
AD 284	*Diocletian becomes the emperor, initiating the Diocletianic reforms of the military. The end of the 'Crisis of the 3rd Century' and beginning of the Dominate phase of Empire.*
AD 286	*The usurpation of Carausius, splitting Britain and northern Gaul away from the Empire.*
AD 293	*The western caesar Constantius Chlorus recaptures northern Gaul from Carausius who is then assassinated by Allectus, the latter then taking over control from his former master in Britain.*
AD 296	*The fourth Roman invasion of Britain, with Constantius Chlorus invading to defeat Allectus, the western caesar then returning the two provinces to the Empire. Around this time Britain is declared a diocese as part of the Diocletianic Reformation, with the four provinces of Maxima Caesariensis, Britannia Prima, Flavia Caesariensis and Britannia Secunda.*

AD 297	*The first use of the term Pict to describe the confederation of tribes in northern Scotland.*
AD 305/306	*Constantius Chlorus campaigns in the north of Britain, then dies in York in AD 306. His son Constantine is proclaimed emperor by the legionaries of legio VI Victrix.*
AD 312	*Constantine becomes the sole emperor in the west after winning the Battle of the Milvian Bridge against Maxentius, with his military reforms beginning around this time.*
AD 314	*Constantine and Licinius agree to end the persecution of Christians, while three British bishops attend the Council of Bishops at Arles.*
AD 324	*Constantine becomes the sole emperor of the whole Empire.*
AD 325	*The first mention of* comitatenses *field army troops.*
AD 337	*Constantine prepares for war with Sassanid Persia but falls ill in Nicomedia and dies.*
AD 343	*The emperor Constans makes a surprise winter crossing of the English Channel to Britain following the defeat of his brother Constantine II three years earlier, possibly in the context of a military emergency in the north of the diocese or a usurpation attempt.*
AD 350	*The military leader Magnentius (possibly born in Britain) usurps power in Gaul, with the provinces in Britain and Spain quickly supporting him, and ultimately the whole of the Western Empire.*
AD 351	*Magnentius is defeated by the eastern emperor Constantius II at the Battle of Mursa Major, he then retreats to Gaul. Magnentius is defeated again at the Battle of Mons Seleucus, after which he commits suicide. Constantius II sends Paul 'the Chain' to Britain to purge the aristocracy after the revolt of Magnentius. The vicarius of the diocese, Martinus, commits suicide rather than face trial.*
AD 356	*The emperor Julian builds a new fleet of 600 to 800 ships to transport grain from Britain to feed his Rhine army.*
AD 357	*The Battle of Strasbourg, where Julian defeats the Alamanni.*
AD 358	*Alypius becomes the new vicarius of the diocese.*
AD 359	*British bishops attend the Council of Rimini.*

AD 360	*Julian sends his magister equitum Lupicinus to Britain to suppress incursions by the Scots and Picts.*
AD 367	*Civilis becomes the new vicarius of the diocese. The 'Great Conspiracy' of Picts, Attecotti, Scots and Germanic raiders attacks Britain, overwhelming the frontier defences. Comes Theodosius arrives in Britain to suppress the revolt and restore order, with Magnus Maximus serving under him. The northern frontier is then rebuilt yet again.*
AD 378	*The Battle of Adrianople takes place where the eastern armies of the emperor Valens are defeated by the Gothic army of Fritigern. This is a defeat the Empire struggles to recover from.*
AD 383	*Magnus Maximus (now the British military commander, and possibly the vicarius of the diocese) campaigns against Pictish and Scots raiders. He is proclaimed the emperor by his troops, then invades Gaul which declares its support for him, as does Spain.*
AD 387	*Magnus Maximus invades Italy.*
AD 388	*Magnus Maximus is defeated and executed by Theodosius 1, emperor in the East.*
AD 391	*Theodosius 1 bans pagan worship, although the practice still continues in Britain.*
AD 395	*Chrysanthus becomes the new vicarius of the diocese.*
AD 398	*The magister militum Stilicho sends field army troops to Britain to suppress further incursions in the west and north.*
AD 401	*Stilicho withdraws many troops from Britain to help defend Italy against the Goths, with Britain left dangerously exposed to further attack. Victorinus becomes the new vicarius.*
AD 405	*Heavy Scots raiding on the south-western coast of Britain occurs, this being a possible date for the capture of St Patrick.*
AD 406/407	*Vandals, Burgundians, Alans, Franks and Suevi overrun the limes Germanicus near Mainz and then invade Gaul. In swift succession the military in Britain declare Marcus, then Gratian and finally Constantine III to be the emperor. The latter crosses to Gaul with the remaining comitatenses field army troops from Britain, setting up his capital at Arles. The diocese now only has the remaining limitanei troops to defend its borders.*

AD 409/ 410	*The British aristocracy throw out their Roman administrators, with the diocese cut adrift from the remaining parts of the Western Empire. The western emperor Honorius allegedly tells the Britons to 'look to their own defences'.*
AD 411	*Constantine III is captured and executed on the orders of Honorius.*
AD 429	*St Germanus visits Britain to debate with the Pelagian Christians there. Further conflict takes place with Scots and Pictish raiders.*
AD 430	*The effective end of coin use in Britain.*
AD 446	*The Britons appeal to Aetius by letter in 'the groans of the Britons' request for military assistance, but no troops are available to help at this time.*
AD 451	*The magister militum in the west, Flavius Aetius, defeats Attila the Hun at the Battle of the Catalaunian Plains.*
AD 476	*The last western emperor, Romulus Augustulus, is deposed by his magister militum Flavius Odaocer. The end of the Roman Empire in the west.*

List of References and Bibliography

Ancient Sources

Ammianus Marcellinus, *The Later Roman Empire*. 1986. Hamilton, W., London: Penguin.

Apuleius, *The Golden Ass*. 2008. Walsh, P.G., Oxford: Oxford World Classics.

Marcus Aurelius, *Meditations*. 1964. Staniforth, M., London: Penguin.

Julius Caesar, *The Conquest of Gaul*. 1951. Handford, S.A., London: Penguin.

Marcus Cato, *De Agri Cultura*. 1934. Ash, H.B. and Hooper, W.D., Harvard: Loeb Classical Library.

Cassius Dio, *Roman History*. 1925. Cary, E., Harvard: Loeb Classical Library.

Claudian, *Works*. 1989. Platnauer, M., Harvard: Loeb Classical Library.

Diodorus Siculus, *Library of History*. 1939. Oldfather, C.H., Harvard: Loeb Classical Library.

Eusebius, *Ecclesiastical History: Complete and Unabridged*. 2011. Crusé, C.F., Seaside, Oregon: Merchant Books.

Eusebius, *de Vita Constanti*. 2011. Crusé, C.F., Seaside, Oregon: Merchant Books.

Flavius Eutropius, *Historiae Romanae Breviarium*. 1993. Bird, H.W., Liverpool: Liverpool University Press.

Sextus Julius Frontinus, *Strategemata*. 1969, Bennett, C.E., Portsmouth, New Hampshire: Heinemann.

Quintus Horatius Flaccus (Horace), *The Complete 'Odes' and 'Epodes'*. 2008. West, D., Oxford: Oxford Paperbacks.

Gaius, *Institutiones*. 1946. De Zulueta, F., Oxford: Oxford University Press.

Gildas, *De Excidio et Conquestu Britanniae*. 2010. Williams, H. A., Moscow: Dodo Press.

Herodian, *History of the Roman Empire*. 1989. Whittaker, C. R., Harvard: Loeb Classical Library.

Historia Augusta. 1921, Maggie, D., Harvard, Loeb Classical Library.

Homer, *The Iliad*. 1950. Rieu, E.V., London: Penguin.

Justinian, *The Digest of Justinian*. 1997. Watson, A., Philadelphia: University of Pennsylvania.

Libanius, *The Julianic Orations*. 1989. Norman, A. F., Harvard: Loeb Classical Library.

Livy, *The History of Rome*. 1989. Foster, B. O., Cambridge, MA: Harvard University Press/Loeb Classical Library.

Paulus Orosius, *Seven Books of History Against the Pagans*. 1936. Woodworth, R. I., New York: Columbia University.

Pausanias, *Guide Greece: Central Greece*. 1979. Levi, P., London: Penguin.

Pliny the Elder, *Natural History*. 1940. Rackham, H., Harvard: Harvard University Press.

Pliny the Younger, *Epistularum Libri Decem*. 1963, Mynors, R.A.B., Oxford: Oxford Classical Texts - Clarendon Press.

Plutarch. *Lives of the Noble Greeks and Romans.* 2013. Clough, A. H., Oxford: Benediction Classics.

Polybius, *The Rise of the Roman Empire*. 1979, Scott-Kilvert, I., London: Penguin.

Quintilian, *Institutes of Oratory*. 2015, Selby Watson, J., Scotts Valley, California: Create Space Independent Publishing Platform.

Statius, *Silvae*. 2004, Nagle, B.R., Bloomington: Indiana University Press.

Strabo, *The Geography*. 2014, Roler, D.W., Cambridge: Cambridge University Press.

Suetonius, *The Twelve Caesars*. 1957. Graves, R., London: Penguin.

Cornelius Tacitus, *The Agricola*. 1970, Mattingly, H., London: Penguin.

Cornelius Tacitus, *The Annals.* 2003, Grant, M., London: Penguin.

Cornelius Tacitus, *The Histories*. 2008, Fyfe, W. H., Oxford: Oxford Paperbacks.

Albius Tibullus, *Catullus. Tibullus. Pervigilium Veneris.* 1989. Cornish, F. W., Postgate, J. P. and Mackail, J. W., Harvard: Loeb Classical Library.

Aurelius Victor, *De Caesaribus*. 1994. Bird, H.W., Liverpool: Liverpool University Press.

Zosimus, *New History*. 1982. Ridley, R.T., Leiden: Brill.

Modern Sources

Allen, S. 2001. *Celtic Warrior 300 BC–AD 100.* Oxford: Osprey Publishing.

Avery, A. 2007. *The Story of York*. Pickering: Blackthorn Press.

Barker, P. 1981. *The Armies and Enemies of Imperial Rome*. Cambridge: Wargames Research Group.

de la Bédoyère, G. 2017. *Praetorian: The Rise and Fall of Rome's Imperial Bodyguard*. New Haven: Yale University Press.

de la Bédoyère, G. 2017. 'The Emperors' Fatal Servants'. *History Today*. March 2017 Issue, 58–62.

Bentley, P. 1984. 'A Recently Identified Valley in the City'. *London Archaeologist*, V.5 Number 1, 13–16.

Bidwell, P. 2007. *Roman Forts in Britain*. Stroud: Tempus.

Bidwell, P. 2012. 'The Roman Fort at Bainbridge, Wensleydale: Excavations by B. R. Hartley on the *principia* and a summary account of other excavations and surveys. *Britannia*. Vol.43, 45–113.

Birley, A. R. 1981. *The Fasti of Roman Britain*. Oxford: Clarendon Press.

Birley, A. R. 1999. *Septimius Severus: The African Emperor.* London: Routledge.

Birley, A. R. 2005. *The Roman Government of Britain*. Oxford: Oxford University Press.

Birley, A. R. 2007. 'The Frontier Zone in Britain: Hadrian to Caracalla'. in: de Blois, L. and Lo Cascio, E. eds. *The Impact of the Roman Army (200 BC-AD476)*. Leiden: Brill. 355–370.

Bishop, M.C. 2014. *The Secret History of the Roman Roads of Britain*. Barnsley: Pen & Sword.

Bishop, M.C. 2016. *The Gladius*. Oxford: Osprey Publishing Ltd.

Blagg, T. 1980. 'The Sculptured Stones'. in: Dyson, T. ed. *The Roman Riverside Wall and Monumental Arch in London – Special Paper No 3*. London: London and Middlesex Archaeological Society, 125–193.

Breeze, D. J. 2000. *Roman Scotland*. London: Batsford Ltd/Historic Scotland.

Breeze, D. J. and Dobson, B. 2000. *Hadrian's Wall*. London: Penguin.

Breeze, D. J. and Hodgson. 2020. 'Plague on Hadrian's Wall?' *Current Archaeology*, Issue 365, V.30, 28–35.

Brodribb, G. 1979. 'A Survey of Tile at the Roman Bath House at Beauport Park, Battle, East Sussex'. *Britannia*, V.10, 139–156.

Burgess, R. W. 1993. 'Principes cum Tyrannis: Two Studies on the Kaisergeschichte and Its Tradition'. *The Classical Quarterly*. V.43, 491–500.

Campbell, D. B. 2011. 'The Fate of the Ninth'. *Ancient Warfare*, V. IV.5, 48–53.

Campbell, D. B. 2018. *The Fate of the Ninth*. Glasgow. Bocca dela Verita Publishing.

Connolly, P. 1988. *Greece and Rome at War.* London: Macdonald & Co (Publishers) Ltd.

Cornell, T. J. 1993. 'The End of Roman Imperial Expansion'. in: Rich, J. and Shipley, G. eds. *War and Society in the Roman World.* London: Routledge, 139–170.

Cornell, T. J. and Matthews, J. 2006. *Atlas of the Roman World.* Oxford: Phaidon Press Ltd.

Cotton, J. 1996: 'A miniature chalk head from the Thames at Battersea and the "Cult of the Head" in Roman London', in Bird, J. Hassall, M. and Sheldon, H. *Interpreting Roman London: Papers in Memory of Hugh Chapman*, 85–96.

Cowan, R. 2003a. *Roman Legionary, 58 BC–AD 69.* Oxford: Osprey Publishing.

Cowan, R. 2003b. *Imperial Roman Legionary, AD 161–284.* Oxford: Osprey Publishing.

Cowan, R. 2007. *Roman Battle Tactics 109 BC–AD 313.* Oxford: Osprey Publishing.

Cunliffe, B. 1988. *Greeks, Romans and Barbarians. Spheres of Interaction.* London: Batsford Ltd.

Cunliffe, B. 2008. *Europe Between the Oceans.* New Haven: Yale University Press.

Cunliffe, B. 2013. *Britain Begins.* Oxford: Oxford University Press.

D'Amato, R. and Sumner, G. 2009. *Arms and Armour of the Imperial Roman Soldier.* Barnsley: Frontline Books.

D'Amato, R. 2009. *Imperial Roman Naval Forces 31BC–AD500.* Oxford: Osprey Publishing.

D'Amato, R. 2016. *Roman Army Units in the Western Provinces (1)* . Oxford: Osprey Publishing.

D'Amato, R. 2018. *Roman Heavy Cavalry (1)* . Oxford: Osprey Publishing.

Davies, M. 2009. 'The Evidence of Settlement at Plaxtol in the Late Iron Age and Romano-British Periods'. *Archaeologia Cantiana*, V.129, 257–278.

Elliott, P. 2014. *Legions in Crisis.* Stroud: Fonthill Media Ltd.

Elliott, S. 2016. *Sea Eagles of Empire: The Classis Britannica and the Battles for Britain.* Stroud: The History Press.

Elliott, S. 2017. *Empire State: How the Roman Military Built an Empire.* Oxford: Oxbow Books.

Elliott, S. 2018a. *Septimius Severus in Scotland: The Northern Campaigns of the First Hammer of the Scots.* Barnsley: Greenhill Books.

Elliott, S. 2018b. *Roman Legionaries*. Oxford: Casemate Publishers.

Elliott, S. 2019. *Julius Caesar: Rome's Greatest Warlord*. Oxford: Casemate Publishers.

Elliott, 2020. 'Clash of the Titans: The Battle of Lugdunum, AD 197'. *Ancient Warfare*, XIII-3, 27–35.

Erdkamp, P. ed. 2013. *The Cambridge Companion to Ancient Rome*. Cambridge. Cambridge University Press.

Fields, Nic. 2006. 'Headhunters of the Roman Army'. *Minerva*. November/December, 9–12.

Frere, S. 1974. *Britannia: A History of Roman Britain* (3rd edn). London: Routledge.

Frere, S. 2000. 'M. Maenius Agrippa, the Expeditio Britannica and Maryport'. *Britannia*. V.31, 23 - 28.

Gaffney, V. Fitch, S. and Smith, D. *Europe's Lost World: The Rediscovery of Doggerland*. York: Council for British Archaeology.

Garrison, E. G. 1998. *History of Engineering and Technology: Artful Methods*. Boca Raton, Florida: CRC Press.

Geoffrey of Monmouth, *The History of the Kings of Britain. An Edition and Translation of De gestis Britonum (Historia regum Britanniae*, trans. N. Wright, (2007), Woodbridge.

Goldsworthy, A. 2000. *Roman Warfare*. London: Cassell.

Goldsworthy, A. 2003. *The Complete Roman Army*. London: Thames and Hudson.

Goldsworthy, A. 2006. *Caesar*. London: Weidenfeld & Nicholson.

Goldsworthy, A. 2014. *Augustus*. London: Weidenfeld & Nicholson.

Graafstaal, E. 2018. 'What Happened in the Summer of AD 122. Hadrian on the British Frontier–Archaeology, Epigraphy and Historical Agency'. *Britannia*. V.48, 76 - 111.

Grainge, G. 2005. *The Roman Invasions of Britain*. Stroud, Tempus.

Haywood, J. 2009. *The Historical Atlas of the Celtic World*. London: Thames & Hudson.

Heather, P. 2013. *The Restoration of Rome*. London: Macmillan.

Hingley, R. 1982. 'Roman Britain: The structure of Roman imperialism and the consequences of imperialism on the development of a peripheral province'. in: Miles, D. ed. *The Romano-British Countryside: Studies in Rural Settlement and Economy*. Oxford: BAR/Archaeological and Historical Associates Ltd, 17–52.

Hingley, R. 2005. *Globalizing Roman Culture – Unity, Diversity and Empire*. London: Routledge.

Hingley, R. 2018. *Londinium: A Biography*. London: Bloomsbury Academic.
Hodgson, N. 2014. 'The British Expeditions of Septimius Severus'. *Britannia*, V.45, 31–51.
Holder, P. 2003. 'Auxiliary Deployment in the Reign of Hadrian', in: J.J. Wilkes (ed.): *Documenting the Roman Army. Essays in honour of Margaret Roxan*, Bulletin of the Institute of Classical Studies Supplements. London, 101–146.
Holland, T. 2019. *Dominion*. London: Little, Brown.
Hornblower, S. and Spawforth, A. 1996. *The Oxford Classical Dictionary*. Oxford: Oxford University Press.
James, S. 2011. *Rome and the Sword*. London: Thames and Hudson.
Jones, B. and Mattingly, D. 1990. *An Atlas of Roman Britain*. Oxford: Oxbow Books.
Kamm, A. 2011. *The Last Frontier: The Roman Invasions of Scotland*. Glasgow: Tempus.
Kaye, S. 2015. 'The Roman Invasion of Britain AD, 43. Riverine, Wading and Tidal Studies Place Limits on the Location of the Two Day River Battle and Beachhead'. *Archaeologia Cantiana*, V.136, 227–240.
Kean, R. M. and Frey, O. 2005. *The Complete Chronicle of the Emperors of Rome*. Ludlow: Thalamus Publishing.
Keppie, L. 1984. *The Making of the Roman Army, from Republic to Empire*. London: Batsford.
Keppie, L. 2000. 'The Fate of the Ninth Legion: a problem for the Eastern Provinces?' in: Keppie, L. ed. *Legions and Veterans: Roman Army Papers 1971–2000*. Stuttgart: Franz Steiner Verlag Wiesbaden GmbH, 247.
Keppie, L. 2015. *The Legacy of Rome: Scotland's Roman Remains*. Edinburgh: Berlin.
Kiley, K. F. 2012. *The Uniforms of the Roman World*. Wigston: Lorenz Books.
Knüsel, C.J., and Carr, G.C. 1995: 'On the significance of the crania from the river Thames and its tributaries'. *Antiquity* 69, 162–9.
Kolb, A. 2001. 'The Cursus Publicus'. in: Adams, C. and Laurence, R. eds. *Travel and Geography in the Roman Empire*. London: Routledge, 95–106.
Kulikowski, M. 2016. *Imperial Triumph: The Roman World From Hadrian to Constantine*. London: Profile Books.
Lambert, M. 2010. *Christians and Pagans*. New Haven: Yale University Press.
Le Bohec, Y. 2000. *The Imperial Roman Army*. London: Routledge.

McWhirr, A. and Viner, D. 1978. 'The Production and Distribution of Tiles in Roman Britain with Particular Reference to the Cirencester Region'. *Britannia*, V.9, 359–377.

Marsh, G., and West, B. 1981: 'Skullduggery in Roman London', *Transactions of the London and Middlesex Archaeological Society* 32, 86–102.

Mason, D.J.P. (2003). *Roman Britain and the Roman Navy.* Stroud: The History Press.

Mattingly, D. 2006. *An Imperial Possession, Britain in the Roman Empire.* London: Penguin.

Mattingly, D. 2011. *Imperialism, Power and Identity – Experiencing the Roman Empire.* Princeton: Princeton University Press.

Matyszak, P. 2009. *Roman Conquests: Macedonia and Greece.* Barnsley: Pen & Sword.

Merrifield, R. 1965. *The Roman City of London.* London, Ernest Benn.

Millett, M. 1990. *The Romanization of Britain.* Cambridge: Cambridge University Press.

Millett, M. 1995. *Roman Britain.* London: Batsford.

Milne, G. & Richardson, B. 1985. 'Ships and Barges. 96–102'. in: Milne, G. (ed.) *The Port of Roman London.* London: B T Batsford.

Moffat, B. 2000. 'A Marvellous Plant: The Place of the Heath Pea in Scottish Botanical Tradition'. *Folio.* Issue 1. 13–15.

Moody, G. (2008). *The Isle of Thanet. From Prehistory to the Norman Conquest.* Stroud: Tempus.

Moorhead, S. and Stuttard, D. 2012. *The Romans Who Shaped Britain.* London: Thames and Hudson.

Myers, S. D. 2016. *The River Walbrook and Roman London.* PhD thesis, Unpublished: University of Reading.

Noble, G., Golderg, M and Hamilton, D. 'Pictish Symbols: Inscribing Identity Beyond the Fringe of Empire'. *British Archaeology.* July/August 2019. 45.

Oleson, J. P. 2009. *The Oxford Handbook of Engineering and Technology in the Classical World.* Oxford: Oxford University Press.

Oman, C. 1938. *England Before the Norman Conquest.* London: Methuen.

Oosthuizen, S. 2019. *The Emergence of the English.* Leeds: ARC Humanities Press.

Ottaway, P. 2013. *Roman Yorkshire.* Pickering: Blackthorn Press.

Parfitt, K. (2013). 'Folkestone During the Roman Period'. in: Coulson, I. ed. *Folkestone to 1500, A Town Unearthed.* Canterbury: Canterbury Archaeological Trust, pp. 31–54.

Parker, A. 2019. *The Archaeology of Roman York*. Stroud: Amberley Books.

Parker, P. 2009. *The Empire Stops Here.* London: Jonathan Cape.

Pausche, D. 2009. 'Unreliable Narration in the Historia Augusta'. *Britannia* V. 8. 115–135.

Perring, D, 2017. 'London's Hadrianic War'. *Britannia*, V.41, 127–147.

Pitassi, M. 2012. *The Roman Navy.* Barnsley: Seaforth.

Pollard, N. and Berry, J. 2012. *The Complete Roman Legions.* London: Thames & Hudson.

Potter, D. 2009. *Rome in the Ancient World: From Romulus to Justinian.* London: Thames & Hudson.

Potter, T. W, and Jackson, R. P. J. 1982. 'The Roman Site of Stonea, Cambs'. *Antiquity*, V.217, 110–120.

Rankov, B. 2009. 'A Secret of Empire (imperii Arcanum): an unacknowledged factor in Roman imperial expansion'. in: Hanson, W. S. ed. *The Army and Frontiers of Rome: Papers offered to David J. Breeze on the occasion of his sixty-fifth birthday and his retirement from Historic Scotland.* Portsmouth, Rhode Island: Journal of Roman Archaeology Supplementary Series, no. 74, 163–172.

Redfern, R. and Bonney, H. 2014. 'Headhunting and amphitheatre combat in Roman London, England: new evidence from the Walbrook valley', *Journal of Archaeological Science*, No 43. 214–26.

Reid, R. 2016. 'Bullets, Ballistas and Burnswark: A Roman Assault on a Hillfort in Scotland'. *Current Archaeology*, Issue 316, V.27, 20–26.

Robertson, A. S. (1980) 'The Bridges on the Severan Coins of AD 208 and 209'. in: Hanson, W. S. and Keppie, L. J. F. (eds), *Roman Frontier Studies*. Oxford: BAR/Archaeological and Historical Associates, 131–140.

Rodgerds, N. and Dodge, H. 2009. *The History and Conquests of Ancient Rome*. London: Hermes House.

Ross, S. and Ross, C. 2020. 'Recent Roman Discoveries During the A1 Upgrade in North Yorkshire'. *Current Archaeology*. Issue 359, V.30, 18–22.

Rowsome, P. 2008. 'Mapping Roman London: Identifying its Urban Patterns and Interpreting Their Meaning'. in: Clark, J. Cotton, J. Hall, J. Sherris, R. Swain, H. (eds) *Londinium and beyond. Essays on Roman London and its Hinterland for Harvey Sheldon*, Council for British Archaeology Research Report, vol. 156, pp. 25–32, York.

Russell, M. 2011. 'What Happened to Britain's Lost Roman Legion?' *BBC History Magazine*, May issue. 40–45.

Salway, P. 1981. *Roman Britain*. Oxford: Oxford University Press.

Scarre, C. 1995a. *The Penguin Historical Atlas of Ancient Rome.* London: Penguin.

Scarre, C. 1995b. *Chronicle of the Roman Emperors.* London: Thames and Hudson.

Sheldon, H. 2010. 'Enclosing Londinium'. *London and Middlesex Archaeological Society Transactions.* V.61, 227–235.

Southern, P. 2013. *Roman Britain.* Stroud: Amberley Publishing.

Southern, P. 2016. *Hadrian's Wall: Everyday Life on a Roman Frontier.* Stroud: Amberley Publishing.

Starr, C. G. 1941. *The Roman Imperial Navy 31BC–AD 324.* New York: Cornell University Press.

Strong, D.E. (1968). 'The Monument'. in: Cunliffe, B. ed. *5th Report on the Excavations on the Roman Fort at Richborough, Kent.* Oxford: Oxford University Press, 40–73.

Todd, M. 1981. *Roman Britain 55 BC–AD 400. The Province Beyond the Ocean.* Glasgow: Fontana Press.

Tomlin, R. S. O. 2016. *Roman London's First Voices.* London: Museum of London Archaeology.

Wallace-Hadrill, A. ed. 1989. *Patronage in the Ancient World.* Routledge: London.

Watson, G. R. 1969. *The Roman Soldier: Aspects of Greek and Roman Life.* Ithaca, New York: Cornell University Press.

Weber, W. 1907. *Untersuchungen zur Geschichte des Kaisers Hadrianus.* Leipzig: B.G. Teubner.

Wheeler, R.E.M. 1928: *London: Volume 3, Roman London,* Royal Commission on Historical Monuments of England, London.

Whitby, M. 2002. *Rome at War AD 293–696.* Oxford: Osprey Publishing.

Wilkes, J.J. 2005. 'Provinces and Frontiers'. in: Bowman. A. K., Garnsey, P. and Cameron, A. eds. *The Cambridge Ancient History Vol. XII, The Crisis of Empire, AD 193–337.* Cambridge: Cambridge University Press, 212–268.

Windrow, M. and McBride, A. 1996. *Imperial Rome at War.* Hong Kong: Concord Publications.

Wolff, C. 2015. 'Units: Principate'. in: le Bohec, Y. ed. *The Encyclopedia of the Roman Army Vol. 3.* Hoboken, New Jersey: Wiley and Blackwell. 1037–1049.

Index